PENGUIN HANDBOOKS

MOTOR YACHTING AND BOATING

Peter Stuart-Heaton was born in Yorkshire in 1919, and was educated at Charterhouse. After a varied career which included working as a Clerk in the House of Lords, he has settled to a routine of publishing, book distribution, and writing and illustrating books. He has written many books on ships, the sea and sailing. His only grouse in life is that the summer is too short!

His published works include: *Sailing* (1949); *Cruising* (1952); *A History of Yachting* (1955); *The Yachtsman's Vade Mecum* (1961); *Boatcraft* (1963); *Songs Under Sail* (1963); *The Sea Gets Bluer* (1965); *The Sea Gets Greyer* (1966); *So They Want to Learn Sailing* (1966); *Peter Heaton on Sailing* (1967); *Boat* (1969); *Cruising: Sail and Power* (1970); *Make Sail* (1972); *A History of Yachting in Pictures* (1973).

PETER HEATON

Motor Yachting and Boating

PENGUIN BOOKS

Penguin Books Ltd, Harmondsworth, Middlesex, England
Penguin Books Australia Ltd, Ringwood, Victoria, Australia
Penguin Books Canada Ltd, 41 Steelcase Road West, Markham, Ontario, Canada
Penguin Books (N.Z.) Ltd,
182–190 Wairau Road, Auckland 10, New Zealand

—

First published by Pelham Books Ltd 1973
Published with revisions in Penguin Books 1976

—

—

Made and printed in Great Britain
by Richard Clay (The Chaucer Press), Ltd,
Bungay, Suffolk
Set in Linotype Times

To WUG

Contents

List of Photographic Plates

1. Shetland Speedwell
2. Shetland 610
3. Shetland 2+2
4. Marina Blue Fin with Mercury outboard
5. Marina Blue Fin turning
6. Marina Sports G.T. Mark 2 with Evinrude outboard
7. Marina Blue Fin – showing underwater hull form
8. Marina 610 Safari
9. Marina 16ft cruiser
10. Avenger 16
11. Avenger 16 planing
12. Avenger 21
13. Coronet 24ft cruiser, from above
14. Bertram 38 ft sports fisherman
15. Moonraker 36, showing cabin interior
16. Moonraker 36, showing saloon interior
17. Twin three-bladed screws
18. View of propellers and rudder in dry dock
19. Large diesel yacht entering a small harbour, needing skill and experience
20. Start of the Paris 'Six Heures' race
21. James Beard's Cougar powered by an Evinrude engine

List of Drawings

Acknowledgements

I wish most gratefully to acknowledge the assistance received from the following:

The Royal Yachting Association, Victoria Way, Woking, Surrey for permission to reproduce from their current books of *Rules and Regulations* governing British Powerboat Racing. The Inland Waterways Association, 114 Regent's Park Road, London N.W.1 for permission to quote from their current literature.

I would also like to thank the following who generously allowed me to reproduce their photographs, drawings and plans, and who contributed a great deal of useful information. They are, in order of appearance – Shetland Boats, Bury St Edmunds, Suffolk; Marina Boats, Tything Road, Kinwarton, Alcester; J. G. Meakes Ltd, the Boat Centre, Marlow, Buckinghamshire; Christopher Tremlett, Topsham, Devonshire; Avenger Boat Company, Shuttleworth Road, Elms Industrial Estate, Bedford; Dell Quay Marine Ltd, Dell Quay, Chichester, Sussex; East Kent Marine, Victory Gate Wharf, Sandwich, Kent; Knox-Johnston Marine Ltd, Satchell Lane, Hamble, Hampshire; Fairey Marine Ltd, Hamble, Hampshire and Brian Manby of 30 St Thomas Street, Lymington, Hampshire (who took the wonderful photos of the Fairey Boats). Also: Hurley Marine, Valley Road, Plympton, Devonshire; Cheverton Work-boats of Cowes, Isle of Wight; Newbridge Boats, New Zealand Works, Church Street, Bridport, Dorset; Frederick C. Mitchell and Sons, Parkstone, Poole, Dorset; J.C.L. Marine Ltd, Brundall, Norwich; Dagless Ltd, Brigstock Road, Wisbech, Cambridgeshire; Lancer Marine Ltd, Broadlands Boat Yard, Oulton Broad, Lowestoft, Suffolk; James & Caddy Ltd, Weymouth, Dorset; Solent Yachts Ltd, Warsash, Hampshire; WaterMota Ltd, Newton Abbot, Devonshire; Stuart Turner Ltd, Henley-on-Thames, Oxfordshire; Volvo Penta, c/o Bolinders Company, 150 King's Cross Road, London W.C.1; Gardner Engines, Barton Hall Works, Patricroft, Eccles,

ACKNOWLEDGEMENTS

Lancashire; Lister Blackstone Mirrlees Marine Ltd, Dursley, Gloucestershire; Mercedes-Benz (Great Britain) Ltd, Great West Road, Brentford, Middlesex; Perkins Ltd, Peterborough; South Western Marine Factors Ltd, 43 Pottery Road, Parkstone, Dorset; and E. P. Barrus Ltd, 12–16 Brunel Road, London W.3, agents in Britain for Johnson Outboard Engines, who supplied the magnificent cut-away drawing of an outboard. Also Messrs Foto Call of 3 Fleet Lane, London E.C.4 for the excellent photographs of racing boats (plates 20 and 21).

Introduction

ALL forms of the powerboat disease are highly contagious! A friend takes you for maybe just a short spin and suddenly you know that you, yourself, must have a boat. It is as simple as that. You-must-have-a-boat!

But the chances are that you don't know enough of the many and varied forms powerboating can take to be certain which is the best for you, best for your pocket, your time, where you live, your family, etc. So in this book I have attempted to tell you about the basic forms of motor yachting and boating and to introduce you to a selection of typical craft. There are sections on pilotage and navigation, on powerboat racing, and on cruising the inland waterways. Of course, the engine, the heart of our boat, receives full attention in one chapter. There is a section on ship-handling both from the point of view of the motor cruiser and of the fast sports runabout.

Of course, you can get along perfectly well with 'left' and 'right' in place of 'port' and 'starboard'. To many people, nautical phrases and terms go ill with a boat whose wheel and instrument panel far closer resemble that of a car than a ship. Who is to say they are wrong? Nevertheless for the purpose of teaching boat-handling and seamanship, I have used the time-honoured language of seamen, of mercantile fleets, of navies and of many, many boating folk. It is no more snobbish or old-fashioned than is the traditional jargon of motor-racing, of golf, or of cricket and football.

There is such a difference between long distance cruising, sports-boating and powerboat racing, for example, that a book which included references to them all might seem only to appeal to each reader according to the space devoted to his or her favourite. But until you have learned even a little, you cannot really know which is for you; furthermore, one's tastes often change and broaden with experience. It is very possible over the years to enjoy coastal motor-

17

cruising, long distance motor-cruising, sailing dinghy racing, class racing, ocean racing, sports boating and fishing. I know this, because I have done it, and continue to do so. Once the boat bug has you, it doesn't let go!

By comparison with other sections devoted to boating, I have only touched on the subject of powerboat racing. But I have told you where to find it. You can't learn to race from a book. It is a fast-growing sport and among the hundreds who practise it, you will surely find plenty to advise and guide you. There are some excellent journals on the international market which cater for the racing man. As I have already written, this is primarily a book to help the beginner in motor boating. But you will find plenty of people in all forms of the sport ready and willing to give you free of their knowledge. The sea has a great freemasonry and boating friends remain good friends for life. Powerboating is truly a wonderful sport. May this book help to start you off!

CHAPTER 1

What Sort of Boat?

'Each to his choice, and I rejoice'
RUDYARD KIPLING

ANYONE who wants to become a motor boat owner can, given certain requisites like a little cash, quite easily do so. If they know exactly what they want it is just a matter of searching, but if they don't, then the choice is bewildering indeed! However, certain basic factors can help us bring this choice within comprehensible limits. One obvious factor is the amount of money we have to spend. Another is where we are going to use our boat; for example, pottering about in inland waterways, sea-angling or hopping from port to port. Exploring the canals and inland waterways necessitates a different boat from that which will be required to win powerboat races or by those who plan to make extensive cruises in a boat able to look after herself in most weathers.

It is quite possible that the reader has no very clear idea of what sort of boat he or she would really like to buy. Frequently the sea bug is caught from a passage or short trip made in a friend's boat, quite probably in idyllic weather conditions. The craft in which such a passage might be made could well be totally unsuitable for the newly infected sea-fever sufferers; either far beyond their means or totally unsuitable for the waters in which they themselves would be sailing. All they know is at the time that they have caught the 'bug' and that they want a boat of their own.

A lot of worry and distress can be avoided if a sensible choice is made at the start and so I propose to set out the various types of boat available from the smallest to the reasonably large in a chapter through which the reader can browse and so approach the delightful task of choosing his boat with some knowledge of the different types available and their varying merits. I have not put in prices and I have a very good reason for this. Due to inflation, a book accurate at the time of going to print will be hopelessly outdated before it has been on the bookstalls for six months!

Dinghies

The smallest boat which can support a power unit is a dinghy. This is an open boat, ranging from about $7\frac{1}{2}$ ft to say 15 ft in length. A dinghy may be propelled by oars, by sail, or by outboard motor. When an outboard motor is clamped to the dinghy's stern producing a small craft suitable for day cruising on inland waters in sheltered conditions, you have the smallest and simplest version of a power-boat.

Dinghies up to about 11 or 12 ft can easily be transported on the roof of a motor car and by this means their operational range is enormously increased. Larger dinghies may be trailed behind a car. The larger dinghies may also be fitted with an inboard engine – a $1\frac{1}{2}$ h.p. two-stroke engine being perfectly suitable for this purpose. Such dinghies, of say 15 ft in length, can provide the minimum requirements of a cruising boat since a tent can be rigged over the boat or alternatively a tent can be carried aboard for setting up ashore later. If this is your intention the outboard motor is preferable to the inboard because of the space occupied in the hull by the latter.

Runabouts and sportsboats

Moving on in terms of sophistication from the dinghy, we find a wide group of open motor boats called runabouts and sportsboats. A runabout may be powered by either outboard or inboard engine and steered by means of a wheel whereas the dinghy is steered either by its outboard engine tiller or in the case of the inboard engine by tiller as well. So we come to the smallest type of genuine motor boat, for the distinguishing mark of the motor-cruiser or the motor-racer is wheel steering. When we come to look later in this chapter at examples of the types of boat which I am listing here we will find a number of mouth-watering little vessels which come under the heading of runabout or sportsboat.

Motor-cruisers

We now come to the smallest of the largest group, which is to say, the motor-cruisers. Broadly speaking, a motor-cruiser is a power vessel with a permanent fixed shelter and accommodation on board for one or more persons to sleep and generally live aboard, if only for a short while. There is a huge demand for small motor boats of this type. Demand creates supply and there is a vast range of small cruisers from 15 to 21 ft, providing accommodation for two people. Purely from the point of view of accommodation it is perfectly possible to find cruisers able to accommodate four or even six people but the gain in size is not necessarily a gain in operational range. Such a vessel though large may not necessarily be seaworthy. It is possible to find craft which are not for the open sea, although eminently suitable for inland waterways, that is to say, rivers and canals.

To summarize then, the prospective owner today has the choice of an open boat or a cabin boat. There are numerous types and sizes of open boat. As we have seen, it may be powered either by outboard or inboard engine. Then we have the small runabout suitable for relatively sheltered water. There is also the larger open or half-deck boat suitable for fishing or picnic parties or simply messing about in. When we come to cabin craft, we find again many sizes and types. As these increase in size so does their range of operation and so does comfort aboard.

Racing boats

But it may well be that the reader is one of those who relish the element of competition; these are the people who look to racing craft for their fun. Once again the same basic principles will determine our choice of craft. Locality – whether we will be doing our racing on small water areas like reservoirs or in estuaries, or in the open sea, or a combination of these. The amount of money we have available is obviously going to govern our decision in choice of boat, and once again this choice is wide; ranging from the small hydroplanes and sportsboats to offshore racing craft like those which compete annually in the classic international offshore powerboat races. In between these extremes are the host of fast, seaworthy vessels capable of offering both comfortable cruising and a creditable performance in their class in an offshore race.

*

If you become infected with the boating bug while making a casual trip in a friend's boat, and if that friend is both knowledgeable and experienced then there can be no substitute for the direct and personal advice which he or she can give you. Such friends however are not always immediately forthcoming and this is where a book can help. I would ask the reader, therefore, to treat the author as this friend substitute, and examine with me a wide range of available craft.

In order that we can understand properly what we are looking for when we examine these craft it will be necessary (and I apologise in advance to those who already possess this knowledge) to learn certain basic things about ships. These basic things are a few but important general terms by which various parts of a ship are known and some basic facts about design, especially in relation to speed and seaworthiness. We then go on to consider the various materials of which a boat may be built and we study types and methods of construction. In Chapter 2 we study the heart of our prospective boat, her engine. We examine various types, how they work and how their power is converted into our boat's forward movement through the water. Then armed with our knowledge, we begin in Chapter 3, our examination of a selection of different types of powerboat; a task which will well reward us for the work done in the previous chapters. As the initiated well know, the search for a boat can be almost as much fun as handling her.

Nautical terms

As I have already written the use of the proper nautical terms for parts of a boat and for boating matters is neither old-fashioned nor snobbish. They are simply the right terms and we use similar languages to speak of cars, motor-cycles and airplanes. There are of course exceptions: for example, although a professional sailor speaks of any vessel as 'she' or 'her', those to whom 'it' is preferable will doubtless use that pronoun. But I confess I have never heard a boat called 'he', even when bearing a masculine name.

The main body of any ship or vessel is called the *hull*. We see in figure 1 the parts of the hull. The hull is divided into three parts – *fore-part*, *midship-part* and *after-part*. The extreme end of the forepart is the *stem* and the extreme end of the after-part is the *stern*. A person standing in the hull is facing *forward* when facing the *stem* and facing *aft* when facing the stern. Anything moving in the direction of the stem is moving *forward* and in the direction of the stern is moving *aft* and the line joining the centre of the stem to the centre

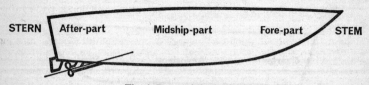

STERN   After-part   Midship-part   Fore-part   STEM

Fig. 1 Parts of the hull (1)

of the stern running lengthwise in the ship is known as the *fore-and-aft centre line*. Figure 2 illustrates this. This fore-and-aft centre line also divides the ship into two halves. A person facing the bow and standing in the centre of the ship will have the *starboard* on the right-hand and the *port* side on the left. Figure 3 shows the surfaces of a hull. The sides of the hull are termed as *starboard* or *port side* and they meet at the *keel* which runs along the bottom of the ship. The curved fore-part is called the *bow*, either port or starboard and the curved after-part is called the *quarter*, port or starboard; the centre part is called amidships. Any continuous horizontal surface

AFT ◄---------

FORE-AND-AFT CENTRE LINE

---------► FORWARD

Fig. 2 Parts of the hull (2)

is known as a *deck*. Look now at figure 4 for various hull terms. The greatest width of the hull is the *beam*; the depth of the keel below the waterline is the *draught*. From the deck (or the upper deck if more than one in a very large vessel) to any point along the hull along the waterline is known as the *freeboard*. The curve of the surface of a deck is known as the *camber*. The *bilge* is the almost flat part of the bottom of the hull both inside and outside and the fins designed to decrease a ship's rolling and give stability normally located at the turn of the bilge are known as *bilge-keels*. When a boat's sides curve outwards above the waterline they have *flair*; when they slope or curve inwards above the waterline they have

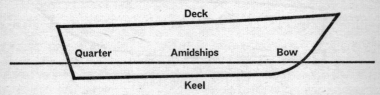

Fig. 3 Surfaces of the hull

tumble home. The degree of rise of the vessel's bottom above the base-line measured at the full breadth of the turn of the bilge, is known as the *dead-rise*.

Tonnage measurements

Lloyd's Register of Yachts shows amongst other things, the registered net and gross tonnage and the Thames Measurement tonnage of each yacht. Net tonnage actually represents the earning capacity of a merchant ship being a measure of that part of her which can be used for carrying either cargo or passengers. In the case of a yacht, provided that that yacht is a registered British ship, the net tonnage, which is normally carved on or fixed to her main beam or some suitable central place, is the measurement employed when assessing harbour dues, port dues, canal tolls etc. The gross tonnage is the measurement of the total internal volume of the vessel reckoned in tons of cubic capacity.

The Thames Measurement tonnage is a formula for measuring yachts based on the length on deck and on extreme breadth. It was originally concerned exclusively with sailing yachts. The racing yachtsmen of the early nineteenth century, looking for some yardstick to measure their craft for purposes of handicapping in races, had adopted an old builder's measurement system which dated from 1770. People building new yachts at this time could cheat this rule

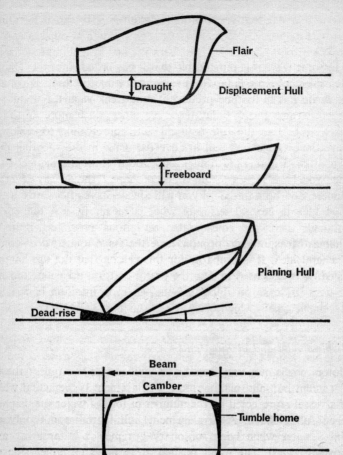

Fig. 4 Parts of the hull (3)

and different clubs varied the way in which the rule was applied in order to prevent this cheating. Chief among them was the Royal Thames Yacht Club and in their modification in 1855 they hit upon a formula which has persisted to this day. The formula is as follows:

$$\frac{(\text{Length} - \text{Beam}) \times \text{Beam} \times \frac{1}{2} \text{Beam}}{94}$$

In some ways it is remarkable that it has lasted since the Thames Measurement Rule is far from satisfactory and, indeed, by penalizing beam has in its time produced some freak yachts. For the purposes of yacht racing today there are other much more up-to-date descriptions like the International Off-shore Rating for example. Nevertheless, one sees still in advertisements in the yachting press terms like '5 tonner', '7 tonner' etc. The truth of the matter is that once you have seen a 6 tonner; or perhaps I should say several 6 tonners, and been on board you will always have afterwards, a very good idea in general terms of what is meant by a 6 tonner and although there are considerable variations possible within the Thames Measurement formula, nevertheless '6 tonner' does convey a general idea. It is probably for this reason that the use has persisted. It is also used to describe motor craft on occasion, and may be used to do so provided that the vessel in question is of a displacement type – which brings us to our next definition.

Displacement and planing hulls

Motor vessels may very broadly be divided into two types: the displacement hull and planing hull. Displacement is the actual weight of a vessel represented by the number of tons of water she displaces when fully loaded. A displacement hull therefore not only displaces water when lying stationary but pushes water away as it moves forward. The water pushed away flows on either side and beneath the hull. As a displacement hull increases its speed through the water, it makes waves first in the form of waves at bow and stern and then, as speed still increases, a wave crest will appear near the bow and a second wave crest further aft. This wave-making effect is very important. As the speed-to-length ratio increases, so increases the length of the wave. We shall be going into this effect more closely later. For the present it will be obvious that the underwater shape of a displacement hull is something to which the naval architect gives very close attention.

The other type of hull, the planing hull, displaces water also when lying stationary but when moving the design of the vessel is such that the bows rise and the boat planes over the surface of the water rather than cutting through it as in the case of the displacement hull. We have now come to a significant point in our definitions, for these two types of hull represent the principal division in power craft. The less of a hull there is in contact with the water, the less surface friction, the less wave-making and the greater speed. We can therefore postulate two extreme types; the deep, beamy, comfortable, seaworthy motor fishing vessel type of craft and the small hydroplane with its large outboard engine stuck up behind, skimming across the water at some sixty miles an hour and barely touching the surface. Between these two extremes there are, as we shall see, many variations. With any displacement hull speed is closely related to water-line length or rather the distance between the bow wave and the stern wave. This limits the speed of the displacement vessel. The speed of waves is related to the distance between the crests and has been placed at 1·34 times the square root of the length between crests. Now if we wish to go faster than this limit we have to leave the stern wave behind and climb up on to our bow wave. In order to do this our boat must be light, the hull must be the right shape and we must have plenty of power to drive us.

So we have seen that speed is related to weight and to power and to some extent to length. The less displacement with the same power the more speed. Now clearly most people will want, as is only human, the best of both worlds; a vessel which has reasonable space on board with reasonable domestic comfort and at the same time is capable of fairly high speeds. To see how far or not this can be achieved let us consider a little further this question of hull design.

Hull forms

Broadly speaking, the bottom of a powerboat hull is rounded or V-shaped. The effect of rounded sections, especially forward, is to produce an easy-riding hull. In order to cut through the water such a vessel will have a sharp bow with fine lines forward. If these are too fine a vessel of this type will dive into the waves and such a boat is very wet at sea. The V-bottomed, planing type hull is not wet, it is surprisingly dry but it bumps and pounds in rough weather.

Between the extreme round and extreme V-bottoms are two main compromises. The inverted ox-yoke section is one. This has the good riding qualities of the round bottom and also some of the desirable qualities of lift and dryness of the V-bottom. There is however a tendency with the ox-yoke type to pound. A better compromise and one which has found favour with offshore powerboat racing craft, is the type which has a chine for the after-body which moves forward into a round sectioned fore-body. We have seen earlier in our definitions what is meant by dead-rise. In the modern designs pioneered by the American designer Raymond Hunt, the deep V of an almost constant 25 per cent dead-rise is most noticeable. This constant rise of floor makes a very comfortable boat; it is particularly suitable for a boat that is going to be driven hard in the open sea. As I have said many, if not most, people will want to have a boat designed with a speed-to-length ratio that falls somewhere between the pure displacement hull and the pure planing hull; in fact a semi-planing hull that can cruise at fast speeds without causing discomfort to those on board or structural damage to itself.

Seaworthiness and stability

So far we have been talking about speed but there is another important factor which the designer has to consider, namely, seaworthiness. In this connection we come to the important question of stability. In designing a boat a naval architect must take into consideration two natural laws, gravity and buoyancy. Gravity is the force drawing everything towards the centre of the earth and is in consequence a downward force. Buoyancy is the force of water lifting any solid body placed into it, an upward force. The force of buoyancy as we have already seen equals the volume of the vessel or the weight of the water displaced by that vessel. For a boat to float in a correct state of rest in the water, the central point of these two forces, gravity and buoyancy, must lie in the same straight line, the one being directly over the other. Look now at figure 5. The force of the water pressure acting upwards, that is to say the buoyancy, is shown by the arrows. (B) represents the centre of this buoyancy, the centre point of this upward force. The centre point of the downward acting force, gravity, is shown by (G). For the boat to float upright, the two points must be in the centre line of the ship. Now if the designer has made a mistake and the shape of the vessel is such that the centre of buoyancy does not come under the centre of gravity then the boat will tip one way or the other and will not have stability. If these two centres of forces are not in a straight line in her upright position, then our boat will list over until the centre

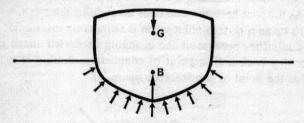

Fig. 5 Stabilizing forces in a hull (1)

of the upward force (buoyancy) is directly in line with the centre of gravity. She will list over until this state is reached and will then remain stationary and so we have a boat with a permanent list.

Figure 6 shows us (B) representing the centre of buoyancy in the heeled position. You see here a boat heeled over let us say by the force of either wind or waves or a combination of the two.

We see in the illustration how as the boat heels over, so the centre

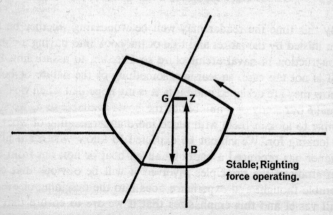

Stable; Righting force operating.

Fig. 6 Stabilizing forces in a hull (2)

of buoyancy moves out from under the centre of gravity. I have marked it by two vertical lines and the letters (G) (Z) represent the horizontal distance between these two lines. This line G Z represents a righting force. It is not the complete righting force, which is partly a product of G Z and partly of displacement. The naval architect will find G Z for a number of angles of heel and he will plot one against the other, producing a curve of what are known as righting levers. As the boat heels more so does the righting lever G Z increase in length up to a certain point when it reaches its maximum. After this it diminishes because of the changing immersed shape of the hull, moving back until a point of complete instability is reached, known as the point of capsize. (See figure 7.)

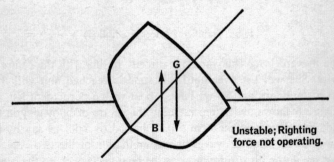

Fig. 7 Stabilizing forces in a hull (3)

By this time the reader may well be wondering whether he has been misled by the jacket and title of the book into buying a course of instruction in naval architecture so I hasten to assure him that such is not the case. In learning something of the nature of boats, of how they are designed and built, it is my hope that when we come to make our study of a number of the boats available to us we shall be able to look at them with much more understanding of what we are looking for. We cannot be expected to know whether a given designer has produced a badly balanced boat or not, but from this brief study of the principles involved it will be obvious that considerable thought and experience goes into the designing of even a small vessel and this emphasizes that if we are to ensure that we get a well-designed and properly balanced boat we must, so to speak, look at the name on the label. An experienced and reputable naval architect is our insurance against a bad boat.

Construction

But our boat must not only be properly designed, she must be well built. A boat unlike a house has to be built in such a way as to withstand certain special stresses. These stresses are known as 'hogging' and 'sagging'. Hogging is when the boat is supported by a wave amidships. Sagging is when the ends of the boat are supported by waves. The sides, the deck and the bottom of a boat can be thought of as forming a box-girder that must be able to take these strains. The principal part of a boat's structure is her outer skin. Although to the landsman it may appear that the function of the outer skin is to keep out the sea, in practice it has another important function in that it forms the sides of our box-girder and provides longitudinal stiffness. Stiffness is also provided by the keel, by the stringers and other longitudinal members such as the sides of a deck house or the cockpit coaming. The frames and deck beams, which may be thought of as the ribs of a human being, are the transverse members of our box-section girder.

Wood construction

Let us consider wood construction first since this is the traditional material for boat-building. Although other materials are fashionable nowadays yet wood-building has many advantages. Wood is a natural material; it has withstood the test of time. It is resilient and can stand sudden shocks. It is relatively easy to work with either hand or machine-tools and can be easily fastened and glued. In relation to its weight it is strong. Even when a hull has been built it is easy to carry out alterations and modifications as the result of experience. Properly looked after it is extremely durable and, finally, it is extremely attractive in appearance. The fact that so many fibre-glass boats have wood trimming is not just to please traditionalists; it is because wood looks good.

But are there disadvantages? Yes, there are a few; for example, by comparison with a fibre-glass boat, wooden boats cost more. A wooden boat is vulnerable to dry-rot and to worm. There are fewer and fewer skilled shipwrights capable of working in wood as the years go by and this again tends to put up the price of wooden boats. By comparison with a fibre-glass boat, a wooden boat needs more maintenance. Not everybody wants to spend the early part of

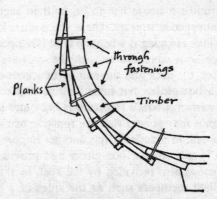

Fig 8 Clinker construction

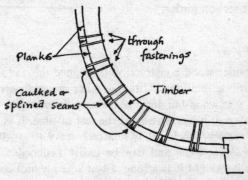

Fig. 9 Carvel construction

the season scraping and varnishing and rubbing-down and painting, or alternatively paying a yard to do this. Nevertheless there is much to be said for wooden construction; there are a variety of methods.

Traditional methods are the clinker and carvel. Figure 8 shows clinker building; figure 9 shows carvel building. It will be seen that the difference consists in the fact that clinker planking overlaps the one below it while carvel planking meets to give a smooth surface. The 'vees' left in the outer surface are filled either by caulking or splining with wood. A carvel built boat is easier to maintain than clinker but the vees between the planks must be properly caulked. A more costly method than caulking is by using splines. With this method caulking is inserted first and then the thin wedge wooden sections are glued and driven into the seam over the caulking. After they have set they are planed down resulting in a beautiful smooth outer skin.

Another more complicated method of building is that of using multiple wood skins. There are three basic forms: double diagonal, diagonal inner skin and fore-and-aft outer skin, and both skins fore-and-aft but over-lapping. Figure 10 illustrates the double diagonal

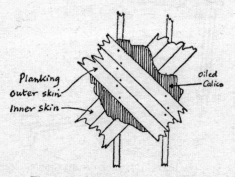

Fig. 10 Multiple wood construction

method. This method of construction has the merit of great strength, but it has however one definite disadvantage. If a leak should develop and water enters the outer planking and lodges between the planks, rot can eventually develop which, as can be easily imagined, may not be discovered until much damage has been done. It will be clear too that because of the nature of this method of construction the repair of say a hole in the ship's side can be a costly business. Because of its complications this type of construction costs more than carvel or clinker. A second-hand boat built in this fashion should be surveyed with great care but having given that caution

I would emphasize that a multiple skin boat if well looked after and maintained, will give many, many years good service.

Marine-plywood and moulded hulls

Many small boats nowadays are built in marine-plywood. Look at figure 11. This shows hard-chine construction in plywood. This method of building is so easy that it is a boon to the amateur builder. Plywood is available in large sheets. It can be used for other parts of a boat as well as for the hull; for example decking, bulkheads, coachroof and all kinds of fittings below decks.

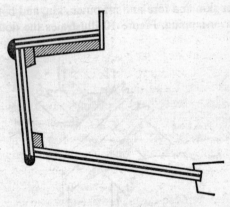

Fig. 11 Plywood construction

Another popular method of construction is that of moulded hulls. This can be in two forms, cold and hot. Cold moulding makes use of glue that sets at normal temperatures and it is the glue which gives the hull its strength. The method is as follows. Layers of timber about three millimetres thick are tacked on to the mould, making use of a trigger tacker to force small staples through the wood and so hold it in position. As the second layer of timber is started, each staple must be removed as the second layer is tacked over the first; then another layer is added and so on, until the required thickness is reached – a thickness normally governed by Lloyds' rules for planking.

Hot moulding has certain advantages but requires so much outlay of capital to provide the necessary equipment that it is really only suitable for production-line building such as employed by Fairey Marine Ltd who have for a long time been producing an excellent range of hot-moulded hulls. With this method, a 'male' mould of timber is used. This is moulded to the interior shape of the hull and is fastened down to a flat metal plate which in turn is mounted on a trolley. With the production-line method, once the line is set up planks are drawn on by operators, passed through a glueing machine and tacked down into place. As with the cold-moulded method, as layer after layer is added the staples are removed. The stem, transom, keel and hog are assembled with the hull and become an integral part of the whole. When the hull is completed a curing-bag is secured over the laid-up shell and sealed down. The bag is then evacuated and the hull is ready for the oven. In the oven steam is applied at a temperature of 100° centigrade and a pressure of 50 lb. per sq. inch for half an hour. The hull then has a cooling period after which it is ready for further work.

This method of construction has distinct advantages. It is strong, it is proof against worm and rot, it has very low water absorption, it has low specific gravity. Furthermore with production-line methods costs can be kept down and maintenance costs are virtually as low as those of hulls built in fibre-glass reinforced plastic. Generally speaking, the rounded hull form is superior to the chine form and so a moulded hull has this advantage over the marine-ply chine hull which we discussed earlier. It is obviously a more complicated business for the amateur builder to tackle but the hull may be bought for completion at home; often a very satisfactory procedure and one which reduces costs by about a third of the price of the finished boat.

Aluminium construction

The twelve metre yachts, in which the races for the America's Cup are now sailed, may by an amendment of the rules be built in future in aluminium. Ever since the first race back in the middle of the nineteenth century when the schooner *America* outsailed a British fleet of yachts in a race round the Isle of Wight, the initiative in the

America's Cup races has been with the Americans and at the time of writing this they still hold the trophy. The initiative to build these craft in aluminium came from the Americans and it is a fact that building in aluminium has never been popular in Europe by contrast with the U.S.A. A number of reasons can be suggested for this, ranging from the rapidly expanding use of glass reinforced plastic construction (which is less expensive than aluminium) to the fact that it would seem that aluminium has never really appealed to the conservatively minded European yachtsman. Of course building in aluminium demands special skills and building techniques. Undoubtedly a reason which appeals to Olin Stevens and other America's Cup designers is the combination of lightness and strength which an aluminium hull possesses.

Glass reinforced plastics

But undoubtedly the most widely used method of construction, and one which is expanding all the time is that of glass reinforced plastics. The abbreviation G.R.P. has now become generally accepted to describe this method. The method consists of combining polyester resins with fibre-glass, a method which produces one of the strongest materials known to man. An even stronger hull may be built by using epoxy resins; these however are more expensive than the polyesters.

The advantages of G.R.P. construction are many. It is completely resistant to worm. It is as we have already seen enormously strong. Shapes and fittings which would be costly in other materials can be moulded in, thus offering great scope to the designer. It is resistant to paraffin, petrol, diesel oil, engine oil and other chemicals which may be carried aboard a boat. Finally, but most important, maintenance is greatly reduced. Of course, plastics are a relative novelty and we do not know how long a fibre-glass boat will last compared with wood or steel. It is known, however, that this material becomes harder and more brittle as it gets older and this may in time prove to be a considerable disadvantage; but only time will tell. Glass reinforced plastic is combined of very strong glass fibres bonded together with a relatively low-strength resin. These glass fibres can be distributed in the form of a woven cloth, or as a mat of chopped fibres, or as continuous strands, or a combination of these.

As we have already seen G.R.P. construction has great advantages for the naval architect. With wooden construction all sorts of different shaped and sized pieces of wood, the stem, frames, floors, beams, planks, keel etc. have to be fitted together and fastened; they must fit exactly and the fastenings must be very secure. By contrast, fibreglass boats can be built of only two pieces, the hull and the deck. Epoxy resins and polyesters are syrup-like liquids which can be cured into hard solids. We have already seen that epoxy resins have higher physical properties than polyesters; in addition epoxy resins shrink much less than polyesters during cure. It is sometimes thought that G.R.P. boats can go for season after season without being painted. This is not the case. As with any other hull kept afloat the bottom will collect barnacles and weed unless painted regularly with anti-fouling paint. The topsides become dirty during the season since fibre-glass collects dirt. A G.R.P. boat may indeed last two or three seasons without painting but in time scratches and other blemishes will collect and the only way to give the hull the clean and gleaming appearance so dear to the heart of all proud boat-owners is to paint it.

Steel construction

We now come to steel construction. The Dutch are the leading nation in building small boats in welded steel. I say welded steel because riveted construction has been virtually superseded today by welding. Quite small boats, launches and yachts for example, can be built in welded steel and this form of construction has a number of advantages. One lies in the fact that tanks can be welded in as an integral part of the hull, the shell plating of the boat forming one side of the tank and floors or bulkheads the other sides. Construction is simple and relatively easy and a steel boat has great strength, but there are two main disadvantages. One is weight; this is particularly apparent when compared with G.R.P. or aluminium. The other disadvantage is rusting. Spraying with hot zinc and sandblasting before painting reduce rusting and some high-strength steels rust less than others; nevertheless, the tendency to rust is a real disadvantage. This problem of rusting with steel is very much related to size. With a large yacht this weakness can be combated by allowing extra thickness in the plates so permitting gradual wastage and yet giving a serviceable life that can be predicted. A large motor yacht can be plated. With vessels of say 75 ft and over in length, steel construction is holding its own against G.R.P. One point that should be mentioned is that one frequently notices with steel yachts, rust 'weep' marks spoiling the appearance of an otherwise immaculate vessel and there is little doubt that for an all-season-round smart appearance steel yachts require pretty continuous maintenance.

CHAPTER 2

The Engine, the Transmission and the Propeller

JUST as a sailing boat in a good Force 4 breeze will make little progress if her sails are set wrongly, so a power yacht may have the right fuel but the wrong engine. The engine is the heart of the boat. Miraculous strides have been made in transplanting hearts to save and prolong life but few surgeons would consider replacing the heart of a lion with the heart of a field mouse. Even so one sees from time to time around the coasts examples of inadequate power in boats which are almost as ludicrous.

And while it may be impossible to plant the heart of a lion into the body of a field mouse one also sees small vessels powered by ludicrously large engines in the hope of obtaining greater speed through the water. This question of power/weight ratio is important and we shall discuss it presently. Let us look first of all then at broad questions of suitability of power unit to vessel.

For a dinghy sportsboat, or small cruiser, up to say, 24 ft overall, an outboard engine or in some cases two outboard engines is perfectly satisfactory. There are many people however who would prefer an inboard engine and there is also now a large and growing number of supporters of the inboard/outboard engine or 'outdrive'. Let us examine the principal arguments for and against these three types of motor.

Outboard and inboard engines

The outboard motor has no need for rudder or stern gear. It is relatively cheap to buy. There are few maintenance costs. Fuel consumption is low. Outboards tilt up and the boats can be beached without any risk of damage to the propeller. Fire risk on board is reduced with an outboard. The main arguments against the outboard centre round reliability but this nowadays carries little weight.

That once familiar sight of the sweating figure trying vainly to start his recalcitrant outboard engine as the tide takes him steadily towards danger is seldom seen today. The modern outboard is a reliable engine. Furthermore as racing enthusiasts know all too well, the outboard not only starts but keeps going; witness their performance in the recent Round Britain Race and others, and by the same token, as we shall see later, they come nowadays in large sizes.

So what is there to be said for the inboard engine? We are speaking at the moment of course of relatively small vessels. Nobody has yet built an outboard which will power a 2,000 ton converted frigate! A big advantage is protection from the weather; the inboard engine is far easier to make adjustments to while under way. The outboard engine is exposed to the elements; it can even be swamped in rough weather. Making a minor repair under way can be a major undertaking. The inboard engine is quieter, and that is an understatement! The inboard has a greater gearing range and handling the boat under all circumstances is easier. It has been said that the inboard engine smells more than the outboard, especially in the case of a petrol engine, but of this I am personally not convinced.

In general terms the inboard engine is advantageous for cruising boats, boats liable to make offshore passages taking the weather as it comes. The outboard is suitable for dinghies and small craft which are often beached, for runabouts and small vessels which make short journeys in sheltered water. But these are very broad distinctions. As we have seen, the modern big powerful outboard can be used in pairs or in threes to drive some of the most powerful offshore racing boats. We shall see examples of powerful outboards as we progress through this book. But what of the I/O – Inboard/Outboard or outdrive engine? This is a relative newcomer.

Outdrive engines

In 1959 Jim Wynne brought out, in cooperation with Volvo Penta of Sweden, the first outdrive. In point of fact outdrives had been in use commercially for a number of years but the 1959 Volvo Penta was the first successful outdrive suitable for use in a small boat. As can be gathered from its name, with an outdrive, the engine is inside the hull and the screw is outside the hull. The engine power is transmitted through two 90 degree angles. We shall be examining some outdrives later. A big advantage by comparison with the outboard engine is that an outdrive has a fuel consumption more like the conventional inboard engine. Furthermore, since the engine is inboard it can be serviced or repaired afloat. It can be built more strongly since there is no necessity to compress a lot of parts, moving and stationary, into the small space at the top of an outboard engine. But it also has an advantage over the inboard engine in that although it is more robust than the outboard it is still very much more compact than the average inboard engine. It is sighted right aft, frequently in fact, bolted to the transom itself. In consequence, by comparison with its inboard sister the outdrive engine takes up very little space in the hull.

The outdrive engine contains a reverse-stroke reduction gearbox, bevel drives and propeller shaft, and steering swivel. All are lubricated by an internal pressurized system. The propeller unit can be tilted to clear weed or obstructions. In short, the outboard unit provides an economical four-stroke engine which is fully protected from the weather, which is easily accessible and which takes up little space right in the after part of the boat.

But whether we elect to have an inboard or an outboard or an inboard/outboard engine in our boat the function we shall be asking it to perform is precisely the same. Let us examine that function in some detail, from the engine itself through the transmission to the propeller. Marine engines broadly speaking can be divided into two types: petrol engines using spark ignition and diesel engines using compression ignition. These may further be divided into two-stroke and four-stroke engines.

Two-stroke and four-stroke engines

The two-stroke petrol engine has a very simple operating cycle. Figure 12 illustrates the two-stroke cycle. A petrol and oil mixture is used. As the mixture vapour passes through the engine the oil lubricates the surfaces. While this simplicity makes for cheapness there is a disadvantage in that having oil mixed with the petrol results in some loss of power.

The upward stroke, by creating a partial vacuum in the crank case, sucks in the petrol and air mixture from the carburettor by means of the suction port. The piston has been compressing in the upward stroke, the mixture above it. At the top of this stroke the mixture is ignited with a spark from the sparking plug.

The explosion of the mixture causes the downward stroke, and as the piston moves down it first uncovers the exhaust port which releases the burnt gases and at the same time, or a fraction of a second after, it uncovers the transfer port. The downward movement of the piston has been compressing new mixture in the crank

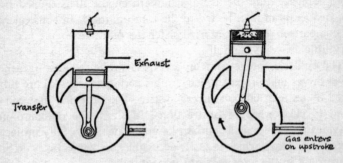

Fig. 12 Cycle of the two-stroke engine

case and this is forced through the transfer passage, deflected by the shape on the top of the piston, so that it scavenges what remains of the burnt gases, and fills the cylinder-head with new explosive mixture waiting for the next upward stroke.

The spark which the sparking plug provides is produced by simple magneto ignition. A flywheel magnet and a stationary coil combine to generate high voltage which, led to the sparking plug, arcs across the gap between its points causing the spark which ignites the vapour mixture in the cylinder head.

Two-stroke engines are used for small single and twin cylinder inboard engines. Outboard engines making use of the two-stroke cycle may have one, two, three or up to six cylinders. Look now at figure 13 which shows the cycle of the four-stroke engine. Reading from left to right, we have: induction, compression, ignition, exhaust. What is happening can be easily seen from the drawing and needs little explanation. A mixture of air and petrol is sucked in on the downward stroke of the piston and enters by means of the

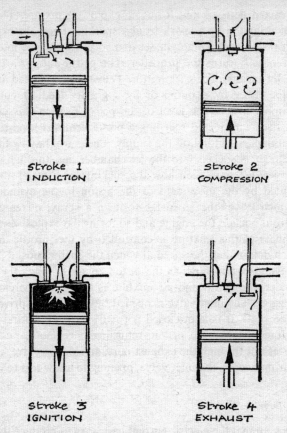

Fig. 13 Cycle of the four-stroke engine

valve port shown on the left of the sparking plug. In the compression stroke the piston, rising up in the cylinder, compresses the mixture which is held in the cylinder head by the two valves closing the two ports as can be seen. At the top of the stroke, both valve ports still closed, the spark plug ignites the mixture. Finally, in the exhaust stroke, the piston rising again drives the burnt gases out through the now uncovered exhaust port, shown on the right of the spark plug.

Now both the two- and the four-stroke engine have, as can be seen, certain points in common. They both make use of the principle of transforming heat from fuel into movement. Petroleum spirit is mixed with air and forms an explosive mixture. This mixture is then ignited by a spark from a sparking plug; the explosion forcing a piston through a cylinder and so providing the movement which eventually turns the propeller. The petrol and air are mixed together by means of a carburettor. Petrol is introduced into the carburettor either by a pump or by a gravity feed. It enters the float chamber and as the level of the petrol rises in this chamber the float rises with it and reaching a pre-determined level shuts off the petrol inlet so cutting off the supply. The petrol having filled the float chamber is sucked into the jet chamber and through a small hole, the jet. We have seen how the sucking force which does this is generated by the movement of the piston in the cylinder. The petrol which leaves the jet in the form of a spray, mixes with air sucked from outside the engine and so forms the explosive mixture. The richness of this mixture is controlled by the throttle and it is this which determines the speed at which the engine runs.

We have also seen how, as the piston comes to reach the end of the cylinder, the petrol and air mixture is cut off by the closing of an inlet valve. The inlet valve is opened by a cam-shaft driven from the engine shaft. It is kept closed normally by being spring-loaded. On the fourth stroke the piston, returning once more, pushes the burnt gases out through the exhaust port; an exhaust valve, working in similar manner to the inlet valve, opening to allow this to happen.

Simple electrics

We have seen that the electric current necessary to produce the spark which jumps across the gap in the sparking plug is generated by a dynamo. This is usually driven by the engine at a pressure of 12 to 6 volts. The electric current which jumps across the gap of the sparking plug is at a pressure of several thousand volts. The points of the sparking plug are a 20,000th of an inch apart and situated right in the centre of the explosive mixture when at its moment of highest compression.

The low tension current of 12 or 6 volts must be transformed into a high tension current of several thousand volts and this is done by passing it through a piece of equipment known as a coil. The coil consists of insulated wire, long lengths of it wound round and round. From the outlet terminal of this coil the high tension current is led to a distributor. In the distributor is a rotating contact arm known as the rotor-arm. As the piston nears the end of its stroke this rotor-arm is making contact with a metal stud and from this stud a cable runs to one of the sparking plugs. The purpose of the distributor is exactly that. It distributes the high tension ignition current to each sparking plug in turn so that the spark fires just before the piston reaches the top of the compression stroke. By firing a split second or two before the piston reaches the top of the stroke, the explosion of the petrol and air vapour, which is not instantaneous, will have built up to its fullest pressure at the moment when the piston is right at the top of the stroke. The spark in fact comes slightly in advance of the fully extended piston position and this is known as 'advanced ignition'.

It is possible to manipulate the degree of the advance of the ignition and the most effective position varies both with the type of fuel used and with the make of engine. We have seen that some degree of advance is desirable. If ignition is too advanced for one reason or another and the explosion occurs too far before the piston has reached the top of its stroke, then you get 'knocking' or 'pinking'. The remedy for this is obvious; lessen the advance, in fact 'retard' the ignition. An engine may knock for other reasons however. It may well be that a simple remedy is to use fuel of a better grade. Alternatively knocking may be caused by pre-ignition through carbon in the combustion chamber. In this case small particles of carbon which have accumulated in the combustion chamber can become sufficiently hot to fire the vapour mixture before the spark and so you get pre-ignition and knocking.

Cooling systems

The whole question of overheating is obviously very important. One definition of an engine is that it converts heat from fuel into movement. It will be clear that such an engine would become literally red-hot unless some efficient system had been devised for cooling it. Generally speaking, marine engines are cooled by water, by taking in, in fact, some of the water in which the ship is floating. Such an engine in consequence cannot be run for long if the boat is hauled out of water. The water inlet for inboard-engine boats will be found well below the waterline. At the inlet point there should be first an efficient strainer to prevent particles of grass etc. getting into the engine cooling system and also a sea-cock. It is an important matter of principle, incidentally, that any hole in a ship's hull below the waterline should have a sea-cock and the prudent skipper makes certain at intervals that these cocks can be turned off and are not allowed to stick.

A mechanical pump draws the water directly into the cylinder block. Where price is of great importance this is undoubtedly the cheapest method. It has however, certain disadvantages. The water drawn in is contaminated with salt, mud, small particles of weed, perhaps chemicals, silt etc. Over a period of time these will accumulate both blocking pipes, and corroding the cylinder block. Water drawn through the hull from the sea or river will be cold. It may well be very cold and can result in the engine temperature being below that recommended by the manufacturers.

The alternative method is one more like that of a car; that is to say, it makes use of a closed fresh water system. This closed fresh water system is cooled with 'raw' water in a heat exchanger. The raw water is also used for cooling the exhaust system. This system has distinct advantages. The cooling of fresh water can be controlled and the correct temperature for the operation of the engine fixed.

Obviously this system costs more. It requires a header tank and the heat-exchanger mentioned. It also requires two pumps, one for circulating the fresh water and the other for pumping the outside water through the heat-exchanger and the exhaust system.

There are also obtainable air-cooled marine engines; and quite a wide range of them too, from small two-stroke units to large engines of over 80 bhp. With the small units, a flow of air over a system of fins on the cylinder head will be sufficient, but in the case of larger engines fans must be used to blow air in larger volume. Air-cooled engines have the merit of simplicity. They do not need any holes and sea-cocks below the water-line – a good point in their favour. Since no water pipes, pumps, heat-exchangers, etc., are required, the engine can be simpler in design. An air-cooled engine warms up quickly in cold weather and there is in consequence less corrosion.

But are there disadvantages? It must be admitted that there are. One of these is that air-cooled engines are noisier than water-cooled engines. There is often a space factor too, since an air-cooled engine tends to be longer than a water-cooled engine to allow the necessary space for the finning on the cylinder heads; space having to be allowed between each cylinder to permit a sufficient volume of air to pass. As we have already seen, overheating is a serious matter and the supply of a sufficient quantity of cooling air involves careful planning and design not only to ensure an adequate volume of cold air but, and this is important, the exhausting of the hot air, having done its job.

Oil lubrication system

So far we have discussed the prevention of an engine overheating by cooling it with sea water or river water drawn in through the ship's bottom, by making use of a closed fresh water system and heat-exchanger, and by using air cooling. This is all right as far as it goes but it will be clear that it is dealing with the outside of the engine in so far that the working surfaces would become red-hot and seize up were there not some system of lubricating to prevent this internal overheating. For this we use oil, a very thin film, only about 1,000th of an inch thick, but this is sufficient to keep an engine running sweetly and without it the engine would soon seize up.

From this it will be obvious that oil is of paramount importance. It must flow freely the moment the engine is started up when in fact it is cold, but it must also flow freely when the engine is hot after continuous running.

We have seen earlier that two-stroke engines are lubricated by having oil mixed with the petrol. The four-stroke engine is lubricated by a continuous circulation of oil through its working parts. Oil, kept in the sump, is circulated by a pump, which, located near the bottom of the sump, is driven by the engine.

When an engine is cold, oil will be circulating at quite a high pressure but after the engine has run for a moment or two this settles down to on the average about 40 lb. per sq. inch. Most engines are fitted with a pressure gauge to indicate this oil pressure. Having

47

been pumped to the bearing surfaces under pressure, the oil then drains back to the sump. As any motorist will know, all oils become in time contaminated with corrosive particles. Corrosion in this manner is still a serious enemy of the marine engine. Much is done however by a proper filtration system which will prevent harmful particles from circulating in the engine. The filter can be situated in the main oil supply receiving the oil from the pump before it arrives at the lubrication points of the engine. Alternatively, oil filters can be fitted in a separate circuit through which some of the oil from the sump can be diverted. The first system is the most commonly found.

The diesel engine

So far we have been discussing petrol engines. The fast-revving petrol engine is always in demand, especially where powerboat racing is concerned. But there are those who favour a relative absence of electrics in a ship and for them the diesel engine, which fires by compression only and needs no electrically generated spark, has much to recommend it. Many yachtsmen who have practical knowledge gained from thousands of miles of serious cruising, lay emphasis on one thing in an engine – reliability. To many, the diesel is synonymous with reliability.

The diesel is a true compression ignition engine as opposed to a spark ignition engine. The principle of it is that air sufficiently compressed will generate enough heat of itself to ignite fuel oil. No carburettor is required and nothing is drawn into the cylinder but air, on the induction stroke, this air being compressed by a piston to a high degree. At the instant of greatest compression, fuel oil is injected into the cylinder head. The compressed, heated air ignites the fuel and the resultant power and exhaust strokes are the same as those of the four-stroke petrol engine. Since the diesel works on the principle of self-ignition, no sparking plugs are needed. Instead of the sparking plug, a precision apparatus called a fuel-injector is used. Although Diesel, the inventor, never extended the diesel system to two-stroke engines, there is now a range of two-stroke marine diesel engines such as those produced by Foden.

Before leaving this subject a word on paraffin engines. These work on the same principle as a petrol engine. A paraffin vapourizer is used. The carburettor jet is somewhat larger and compression is reduced so as to avoid pre-ignition. To start the engine, petrol is used and then switched over to a vapourizing oil fuel when the vapourizer has become hot. The vapourizer becomes hot through the heat of the engine.

A marine engine is specially designed for the job it has to do. With a displacement hull a steady drive is required rather than acceleration. We shall be discussing later the special requirements of racing craft. It will be clear that when we come to choose our boat we must see that the type of engine which is installed is suitable for the boat. Of course any reputable boat-builder will have paid as much attention to the suitability of the engine for a particular craft as he does to the design of the hull of that craft; and it would be bordering on the presumptuous for us to question the suitability of the power units in boats designed and/or built by people who have been in the business for many years. But it is my intention in these preliminary chapters of this book, to give the newcomer some basic knowledge of the subject in most of its aspects, without I hope becoming too technical, so that he or she can not only approach the subject with more confidence but may even manage to avoid some early, and perhaps costly, blunders.

Speed : length ratio

It will be clear that it is both uneconomical and impracticable to install a large inboard engine in a small runabout designed to take an outboard. By contrast however, one or more outboards may be fitted to a boat very successfully and at considerably less cost than one or more inboards. With a displacement-type hull, provided that she is fitted with an engine of adequate horsepower, any increase in horsepower will result in very little extra speed through the water. The planing hull on the other hand, can make use profitably of very large horsepowers in proportion to size. The square root of the waterline length is the economical and easily attained speed of a displacement hull. To go above this speed she has to be driven hard, all the extra speed being costly in the way of extra fuel. At low speeds a vessel is slowed almost entirely by friction but as she moves faster and starts to make her own waves this wave-making retards her speed. To force her beyond the economical speed requires considerable power. We see therefore that speed is closely linked to the length of the hull, the formula being:

$$\frac{\text{speed in knots}}{\text{square root of the waterline length in feet}}$$

or put another way: $\dfrac{V}{\sqrt{L}}$ this we call the speed : length ratio.

To find the right power for a given vessel might appear to be a simpler business than in practice it is. It can be argued that all that is necessary is to estimate the effective horsepower to drive a hull at its proposed cruising speed; the effective cruising speed being more than the economical cruising speed but perfectly within the capabilities of the engine. For example a 25 ft cabin cruiser with a 10 h.p. petrol engine giving 1,000 r.p.m. will drive that vessel at 5 knots economical speed but up to $7\frac{1}{2}$ knots or 8 knots will be well within its powers. But in fact the designer needs to have a great deal of knowledge in order to determine the power needed for a given vessel. For example, he must consider not only the resistance of the hull, that is to say friction, but wave-making and the important question of air resistance; and also the propulsive efficiency of the transmission.

Reduction gear

To revert for a moment to our 25 ft motor cruiser with the 10 h.p. engine. We could use this 10 h.p. engine to drive a larger craft but in this case instead of driving direct to the propeller we must make use of a reduction gear. The normal ratio of such a reduction gear is two to one. If we extend our 25 ft cruiser to 30 ft, running our engine at 1,500 r.p.m. would give us the same speed, making use of a reduction gear, as we had with our 25 ft cruiser, that is to say about $7\frac{1}{2}$ to 8 knots.

The power of the engine is transmitted into a forward (or astern) movement of the boat through the water by means of the propeller shaft terminating in the propeller or 'screw'. We have seen that the reduction gear has the function of reducing the high revolutions per minute of the engine to permit the propeller to work efficiently. It is fair to say that reduction gear is necessary in all but high speed craft.

There is also another function of the marine gear-box in that it provides the means of disengaging the engine from the propeller so that the boat can remain stationary although the engine is still running. The gear-box may also be used to reverse the direction of rotation of the shaft so that the vessel can move astern. The gear-box is an important part of our boat's equipment. Marine gear-boxes are either hydraulically or mechanically operated.

Propeller shafts and propeller blades

We have seen how the engine converts heat from fuel into movement in the form of a rotating crankshaft. We have seen too, how the speed of the crankshaft is controlled by the throttle which in turn controls the richness of the mixture. The speed of the propeller shaft may be controlled by a reduction gear and the gear-box controls the actual movement of the shaft, reversing the propeller when it is desired to move astern, and allowing the propeller to remain stationary when this is required.

A screw-propeller operates somewhat like a wood screw. As the screw is turned, it advances further into the wood. Engines run 'forward' with a right-handed or left-handed drive and the boat will turn more easily in the direction of the rotation of this drive, that is to say, of the propeller. If a boat has twin engines, they should be what is known as 'handed'. This means that one engine should turn with a right-handed rotation and the other should have a left-handed rotation; the rotation being away from the centre-line of the boat. The tail shaft and the propeller shaft are coupled with a gland filled with grease. This gland must be kept packed tight but not too tight.

There are four main factors governing a propeller; the diameter, the blade area, the number of blades and the pitch. In addition there is 'hand' which we have already discussed and which is determined by the rotation of the shaft. The diameter of a propeller is the diameter of the circle made by the tips of the blades. The number of blades varies on cruising boats; three blades being commonly found. The area of the blades is exactly what it sounds like. The 'pitch' is the depth of the screw. Going back to our analogy of a wood screw, this means that every time the propeller revolves once it advances a distance equal to its pitch. If there were no slip an 18 inch pitch screw-propeller would drive a vessel forward 18 ins. with one revolution.

To measure the diameter you measure from the centre to the outer tip of the propeller and multiply by two. Most propellers are three-bladed and it is difficult to measure directly across two blades and get a true measurement, although it is possible to do this in a four-bladed propeller. In designing a propeller, the pitch and the diameter and the total area of all the blades of the propeller must be carefully considered to develop the best combination of these three factors; the most important relation being that of pitch to diameter.

Although the wood screw analogy is useful for understanding the meaning of pitch, in practice, a propeller is not cutting through a solid mass and the water causes the propeller to slip. The inevitable result of this is that a certain amount of the propulsive force is lost This varies considerably, depending upon the shape of the under-water body, the type of boat, the revolutions of the propeller etc. One of the reasons for the use of reduction gear is to restrict the speed at which the propeller turns, so increasing the revolutions of the engine, which results in a gain in power. Some boats are fitted with reversing propellers. With these the blades are not fixed but can have their pitch varied. The blades which are moved by a rod inside the propeller boss, can easily be moved into all degrees of pitch, including right round into reverse. It will be clear that the person driving a boat can put on whatever pitch he wishes so that when driving against or before the wind the variable pitch propeller can give more control over both engine and vessel. Some variable pitch propellers are controlled hydraulically.

To keep the pitch of our propeller blades as true as possible it is important that the propeller shaft itself should be as level as possible. The propeller shaft coming out of the hull projects downwards at an angle to give the propeller itself room to work in clear water beneath the hull. It is important that this angle should not be too steep. The steeper it is then the greater the variation you have in propeller pitch. With a two-bladed propeller the descending blade increases its pitch while the rising blade decreases its pitch by the amount which the propeller shaft is inclined. Any variation in pitch in other words as a result of marked inclination of the shaft occurs twice in each revolution of the shaft.

Supposing that the inclination of the shaft is 15° (a fairly common inclination), when a powerboat gathers speed she lifts her bow and this can quite well be up to 15°. This means that the shaft at speed is at an angle of 30° to the level line and 30° have been added to the pitch on each blade as it descends and 30° of pitch has been taken off each blade as it rises. The pitch of propellers, the angling of propeller shafts and the subject of propeller deficiency in general is a complicated subject. But once again if your boat has been designed and built by reputable people who know their job you need have no fears.

Rudders and steering gear

Let us now consider the question of rudder and steering gear. In the case of the outboard engine it is the propeller itself which changes direction and consequently changes the direction of the thrust. With an inboard engine with a propeller shaft in a fixed position carried by a strut, change of direction is effected by a rudder.

A rudder may be balanced or not. With a balanced rudder, the rudder blade extends both fore-and-aft of the stock; the forward part being about one third of the immersed area of the rudder. A very efficient form of rudder is one which is faired into the propeller strut. In such a case the propeller strut is abaft the propeller instead of in front of it so that the propeller is working in unbroken water as only its shaft is disturbing the water ahead of it.

The rudder is moved by its stock which in turn is moved by either a tiller or a quadrant. The tiller, with the exception of the steer-board of the Viking ships, is the simplest method of steering a boat. It is simply a shaft which projects forward at right angles to the stock. Move it over to port and the rudder blade moves over to starboard and the boat if going ahead will turn to starboard; and vice-versa. With a quadrant we have an arm, to either end of which may be attached cables which are led to the steering wheel. In a simple mechanical quadrant steering device, several turns of the cable are passed over a hub turned by the steering wheel. If the steering wheel is turned round to starboard the ship will turn to starboard; in other words although putting a tiller over to starboard has the effect of turning a boat going ahead to port, moving the wheel in quadrant steering to starboard will have the effect of turning the boat to starboard when going ahead. Instead of using a quadrant the steering cable can be connected to a tiller, a perfectly sensible and workable arrangement for a small cruiser.

Larger vessels sometimes make use of chain instead of wire rope and there are a number of sophisticated mechanical rudder control devices on the market including several which are power-assisted. Of course the larger the craft the heavier the gear and the more likely is a hydraulic steering system going to be needed. One thing is very important and that is that whatever form of steering is used, it should be easy to get at; to hide the cable firmly away, perhaps for aesthetic reasons, is the height of folly. Broken steering gear must be able to be got at and mended quickly, and in this context a boat should have an emergency tiller, the simplest form being a metal bar rising up from the squared rudder head, bending forward and having sufficient length of arm to give control over the boat under all conditions.

We have now examined some basic types of craft, have looked at some commonly found types of engines and our examination has taken us from the crankshaft through the gears down the propeller shaft to the screw itself. We have had a brief look at the question of pitch and we have examined the rudder and some commonly found types of steering gear. With, I hope, some knowledge gained we can now start looking at some boats.

CHAPTER 3

A Selection of Boats

'Conception, my boy ... is what makes the difference in all art.'
DANTE GABRIEL ROSSETTI

SHETLAND

FROM Shetland Boats Ltd of Stanton, Bury St Edmunds, Suffolk, in England, come some attractive small cruisers and day-boats to the designs of naval architect Colin Mudie. When I say small boats I mean that the Shetland range is from a little over 15 ft (4·686 m.) to a little over 20 ft (6·172 m.) in length.

Scorpion

The smallest of the range is the Scorpion. This is a 15 ft 6 ins. by 6 ft 4 ins. triple G.R.P. hull very suitable for inland waterway fun. Into this the designer has cleverly packed a cabin with two single berths convertible to a double, and a headroom of 4 ft 9 ins. (1·478 m.) and has managed to do so without making the vessel look ungainly. Exact measurements are as follows: length 15 ft 6 ins. (4·686 m.); beam 6 ft 4 ins. (1·930 m.); weight approximately 750 lb. (340 kg.).

But this little boat is by no means restricted to canals and inland waterways, she is perfectly suitable for estuary cruising. And she is no slouch, using an outboard motor for propulsive power, she can reach speeds up to 29 m.p.h. with a 40 h.p. outboard.

17 ft 7½ ins. (5·372 m.) is a popular length in the Shetland range, for in this we have the Sheltie and the Shetland 535 and also the Shetland Suntrip.

Sheltie

The simplest of these is the Sheltie. Her other dimensions are: beam 6 ft 7½ ins. (2·018 m.) and her approximate weight is 750 lb.

(340 kg.). Propulsion is by outboard motor, the hull being suitable for any long-shaft outboard up to 40 h.p. Speeds vary accordingly; for example, a 10-h.p. engine gives approximately 10 m.p.h. while a 50-h.p. engine gives approximately 30 m.p.h. The Sheltie is basically an open boat suitable for a club launch, for fishing and for camping or for just pottering about. The small cuddy in the fo'c'sle has a headroom of 4 ft (1·219 m.).

Shetland 535

This boat is a proper little cruiser, having two 6 ft 9 ins. berths in the fore-cabin. To port is a toilet and to starboard a cooker. Dimensions are virtually the same as the Sheltie. Headroom in the cabin at its maximum is 4 ft 5 ins. (1·346 m.) Any long-shaft outboard motor can be used up to about 40 h.p.

Suntrip

This boat in the Shetland range of the same dimensions and very similar to the 535 has one essential difference: the cabin space is much reduced, the cooker and toilet having been removed to enlarge the cockpit. The boat still has two berths, but that is all. On the other hand, there is 40 sq. ft of cockpit with ample and well-designed seat accommodation.

Shetland Speedwell, Shetland 610 and Shetland 2 + 2

With these three boats the length has increased to 20 ft 3 ins. (6·172 m.). In the case of the 610 and the 2+2 beam is 8 ft (2·438m.); with the Speedwell beam is 6 ft 10 ins. (2·083 m.). So with the Speedwell the beam is narrower, and she is indeed designed for navigating inland waterways. This boat has two single berths in the cabin and a dinette table which can convert into a large double berth. She has a sink and galley to port and a toilet to starboard. There are two optional folding berths in the cockpit. Any suitable long-shaft outboard may be used. You can go up to 65 h.p., which gives a speed of approximately 27 m.p.h. Plate 1 shows the Speedwell.

With the Shetland 610 we come into not only more room below

but faster speeds; and the same applies to the 2+2. In both these boats there are two forward berths, a toilet compartment to starboard and sink and galley to port. Plate 2 shows the 610 and in plate 3 the 2+2, and from this it can be seen that in the 2+2 there is just that much more headroom (in point of fact 5 ft 10 ins. (1·778 m.) as opposed to 5 ft 7½ ins. (1·715 m.) in the 610).

But these boats are designed for performance, making use of long-shaft outboard motors up to 135 h.p., or inboard/outboard up to 165 h.p. Speeds of up to 39 m.p.h. can be reached. Both boats, with their hulls of deep V design, are good sea boats.

Shetland 570

Sandwiched, from the point of view of length, between the Sheltie and the 535 and the Speedwell 610 and 2+2, comes the 18 ft 8 ins. Shetland 570, the 1972 addition from the drawing board of Colin Mudie. The purpose of the Shetland 570 is to bridge what seemed to be a gap between the 17 ft 7½ ins. 535 and the 20 ft 3 ins. Shetland 2+2; or, in other words, between the day cruiser and the week-ender. I think Mudie has succeeded. On a length of 18 ft 8 ins. (5·70 m.) with a beam of 6 ft 10 ins. (2·08 m.) this boat packs in all the essentials; cabin forward with berths for two (convertible to large double berth) and large, well-protected cockpit. In performance the 570 is no les successful. Using the maximum 65 h.p. long-shaft outboard motor, she quickly reaches planing speed, and this in spite of a load of normal cruising gear aboard.

This is an interesting range of boats. Look again at the photographs. Look at the Speedwell and 610; perfect for the job. But when it comes to cruising, that sink and galley, the separate toilet, that little bit of extra space in the 2+2 makes, to anyone with any experience of cruising, all the difference. This range has something for most people.

MARINA

Most people think, and rightly, that a Marina is a man-made harbour for yachts; yet at the Boathouse, Tything Road, Kinwarton,

Alcester, England, a firm of the name is busy producing an excellent range of runabouts, small racing boats and cruisers. Let us have a look at the sportsboats first. These are illustrated in the plates 4 to 7. These illustrate the Sports G.T. Mark 2, the Continental 14 footer and the 15 ft 4 ins. Blue Fin.

The hulls are V type. Power is by outboard and make is optional; Evinrude or Mercury or whatever appeals to you. Steering is by cable. 2 to 1 reduction is normally used with engines of over 50 h.p. The builders specify from 35 h.p. to 85 h.p. long-shaft outboards. Common sense must be used clearly as to the power applied; for example, a 35 or 40 h.p. engine is perfectly easy to handle and quite adequate for water skiing, yet motors of 60 h.p. and over will turn any of these boats into something pretty lethal in the hands of an inexperienced driver.

Sports G.T. Mark 2

Let us take the Sports G.T. Mark 2 first. This is a four-seater having four back-to-back seats; but it can also be a two-seater by having two bucket seats and two ski hooks. This zippy looking little boat has had considerable success in class 4 racing as well as ski racing. A versatile craft for water skiing, racing or just running about. Dimensions of the Sports G.T. Mark 2 are: length 12 ft 7 ins. (3·82 m.); beam 5 ft 3 ins. (1·60 m.). Maximum h.p. recommended for this boat is 40; the weight is approximately 325 lb.

Marina Continental 14 Footer

The Marina Continental 14 footer is available as either a five- or six-seater. Notice in the photographs, the pronounced flair ensuring a dry ride. With this boat you can go up to 85 h.p. maximum power. Dimensions are: length 13 ft 10 ins. (4·17 m.); beam 6 ft (1·83 m.); approximate weight 450 lb.

Blue Fin

With the Blue Fin, we have a boat that will take plenty of power, suitable for ski racing, sheltered water racing and, competently handled, off-shore racing. With this boat you can spread yourself up to 100 h.p. maximum power. Dimensions are: length 15 ft 4 ins. (4·68 m.); beam 6 ft 2 ins. (1·88 m.). In addition to handling well, this is, as the photographs show, a good looking boat.

610 Safari

The Safari (illustrated in plate 8) is a four-berth cruiser; two berths in the cabin and two in the cockpit. There is a separate toilet compartment and a galley comprising a wash basin and a two-burner cooker. Dimensions of this boat are: length 20 ft 1 in. (6·10 m.); beam 6 ft 10 ins. (2·08 m.); weight is about 12½ cwt. Maximum recommended power for this boat is 60 h.p.

16 Foot Mark II

The 16 footer cruiser (illustrated in plate 9), again deep V design, is a boat of much versatility; being suitable for cruising in coastal waters, fishing, pottering about, or skiing. This is a two-berth vessel; having also a sink unit and toilet compartment up forward. Dimensions are: length 16 ft 3 ins. (4·96 m.); beam 6 ft 10 ins. (2·09 m.). Weight is about 7¾ cwt. For this boat, with her sportier performance, maximum recommended power is 100 h.p.

What she may lose in speed however, the Safari gains in comfort; headroom in the 16 footer being 4 ft 6 ins. (1·35 m.), as opposed to full 6 ft headroom aboard the Marina Safari. All these boats, moulded in G.R.P., may be had in a wide variety of attractive colours.

At risk of repetition I would point out that all the boats which I have chosen for this book are not included because the author's opinion is that they are vastly superior to any other but because they are representative of a particular type of motor boat. I would not wish the reader to be under the delusion that having spent an incredible amount of time and money testing every available known make of every type of craft in the world, I am now putting into a book the ones which I thought were the best; far from it. I am merely hoping to give the newcomer to our sport an idea of the variety of motor craft and some typical examples. In other words, I hope this book will start you off. A visit to a boat show will take you further and, joining a club, further still. But to paraphrase the 'Water Rat' there is ... nothing, absolutely nothing ... like getting behind the wheel of your own boat and feeling her go!

MADEIRA

Madeira 20

This boat has a happy sounding name with associations of sea and sunshine and indeed she is a vessel in which a family could have a very happy time. She is quite a small boat, being only 20 ft 2 ins. (6·15 m.) overall. This vessel (and her larger sister the Madeira 27 which we will be examining shortly) is designed not only for estuary or sheltered water cruising, but for making the best of the thousands of miles of the network of inland waterways; in Britain, on the continent of Europe, or wherever. Construction is in G.R.P. The hull form is in the builder's description, 'semi deep V hard-chine'. Let us look at her measurements. Overall length, as we have already seen, 20 ft 2 ins. (6·15 m.); beam 7 ft 8 ins. (2·34 m.); draft 1 ft 10 ins. (0·56 m.). Her overall height above the load water line, and this is important where one is going beneath bridges, is 7 ft 4 ins. (2·24 m.). She carries 12 gallons of fuel (54.5 litres) and the same amount of fresh water.

Look at figure 14. This shows profile and accommodation plan. It will be seen that there is a centre cockpit and a cabin aft and a cabin forward. There are lockers either side of the centre cockpit and also the galley fitment. The toilet compartment is to port and there is ample wardrobe space to starboard. Headroom in the fore-cabin is 5 ft 7 ins. (1·70 m.); in the after cabin is 4 ft 2 ins. (1·27 m.) – what the author once heard rather unkindly described as 'dwarf' headroom, but you cannot have everything in a vessel of only just over 20 ft long. To get this amount of headroom in an after cabin is verging on the remarkable. The galley mentioned earlier is designed to fold away when not in use in the cockpit. There is a two-burner cooker with grill, plastic bowl with a fresh water supply from a whale pump. Crockery etc. stows in the locker underneath. For power the Madeira 20 uses a Newage Vedette 1100 cc petrol engine.

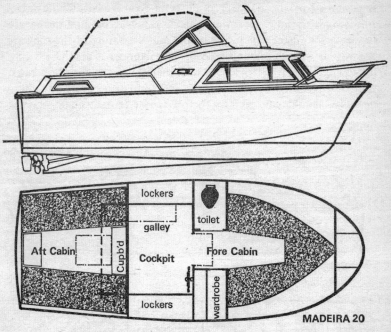

Fig. 14 'Madeira 20'

Madeira 27

Look now at figure 15. This shows that if one were tempted to think that the Madeira 27 was 'the same thing only bigger' one would be wrong. With the extra length and beam the designer has been able to do things with the accommodation plan as may be seen. Look at the measurements: length overall 27 ft (8·2 m.); beam 9 ft 6 ins. (2·9 m.); draft 2 ft 2 ins. (0·67 m.). Once again the height is given with reference to river or canal bridges and it is exactly 6 ft (1·92 m.). Headroom in the cabin is also 6 ft (1·92 m.). Instead of the 12 gallons for both fuel and water of her smaller sister the 20, the Madeira 27 carries 25 gallons (114 litres) of both.

In the cabin plan in figure 15 can be seen the substantial accommodation in this boat. A useful feature is the dining-table with two roomy fore-and-aft seats on the starboard side in the main cabin, which converts quickly into a double berth. As with the 20, the hull is described by the builders as of 'semi-deep V, hard-chine form' and is built in G.R.P. Decks also are in G.R.P. According to the use to which the vessel is going to be put and the nature of the cruising she will be doing, either single or twin Newage Captain 1·5 litre diesel engines can be fitted. As with the 20 there is an oil-operated gear-box activated by Morse single lever remote control unit. Incidentally, should you prefer a petrol engine, either single or twin

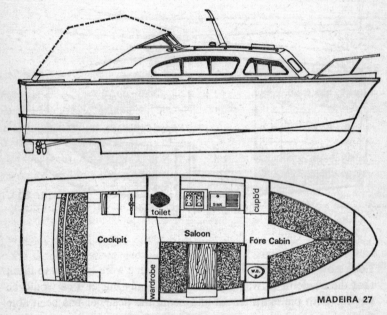

Fig. 15 'Madeira 27'

installation, the builders will supply the Newage Vedette 1100 cc. The toilet, housed in its own compartment to port just forward of the steering position in the cockpit, is a chemical one; obviously this is with inland waterways cruising very much in mind.

People to go to for the Madeira boats are J. G. Meakes Ltd who are at the Boat Centre, Marlow, Buckinghamshire.

The word yacht is descended from a Dutch word and yachting came originally from the Dutch. One would expect them to produce efficient and good-looking yachts today and Amerglass 32 is a Dutch boat. This is a very versatile yacht indeed, there being a variety of versions: the weekend cruiser, the fisherman, the offshore cruiser, even the offshore racer. Speeds vary according to power unit. For example; with one Perkins 4·236 86 h.p. diesel, 13 knots can be achieved; with two Perkins diesels, 20 knots; with two Volvo Penta 130 h.p. petrol Aquamatic engines, the speed is 27 knots.

Measurements are: length overall 32 ft (9·60 m.); length on the water-line 28 ft 4 ins. (8·50 m.); beam 10 ft 7 ins. (3·20 m.); draft 3 ft (0·90 m.). Being a centre cockpit boat with small after cabin, there is very good accommodation below, there being two berths in the after cabin, a single berth to starboard in the main saloon with double berth-convertible dinette table to port and another berth up in the fo'c'sle. The after cabin version (and incidentally the builders claim full standing headroom in that after cabin, which is quite an achievement in itself) is known as the Amerglass A K. For more sporty work, probably using the two Volvo Pentas, an open cockpit version is supplied doing away with the after cabin and this is called the Amerglass C P. Fuel capacity is 92 imperial gallons (420 litres) and the water tank, which is plastic, contains 44 gallons (200 litres). The whole hull is made in G.R.P.

A popular version is the Sport Fisherman. It has an open cockpit and an elevated and well-protected steering position, which follows the normal 'sport fisherman' trend. We should be grateful to Amerglass N.V. of Ooosterhout in Holland and J. G. Meakes for making available to us this attractive and versatile power yacht.

TREMLETT

A particular pleasure of yachting people during the boatless winter months is that of looking at drawings and plans of boats. When we look at the drawings in figures 16, 17, 18 and 19 this form of pleasure can be easily appreciated. These are not only evocative drawings, they show us four very exciting boats.

For this we are indebted to designer and builder Chris Tremlett who, at his yard at Topsham in Devonshire in England, produces a series of hot-pressed moulded wood hulls ranging from a 14 ft ski-boat right up to a 40 ft off-shore racer that can really go.

Before we examine in more detail the four boats I have chosen, let us have a look briefly at this very comprehensive range. Starting with the 14 ft ski-boat, here are some other examples. The S E A S H E L L, which can be open or decked in, can be driven by outboard

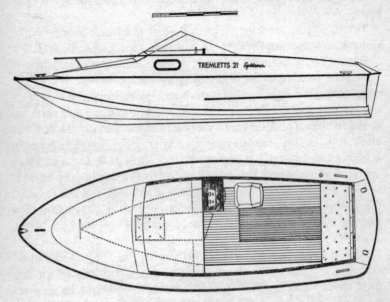

Fig. 16 Tremlett 21 ft cruiser

or by inboard/outboard 80 h.p. Mercruiser. There is a 16 ft offshore racer; this is a standard hull and powered by twin outboards. There is a 19 ft offshore racer which can be powered by twin outboards, or single, as can the 16 footer. Then we have the 21 ft offshore racer for Classes I or III; this is based on the 21 ft hull that we shall be looking at in more detail later. There is a wide range of 18 to 21 ft cruiser hulls. Then there are larger boats; the 23 footer, a cruiser or a racer as you like; there is the 25 ft offshore cruiser, the 30 ft off-shore cruiser and so on, up to the largest of the range, at present, the 40 footer.

The smallest of the boats I have chosen is the 21 footer. The

TREMLETT 30' CRUISER.

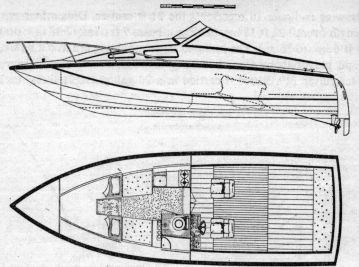

Fig. 17 Tremlett 30 ft cruiser

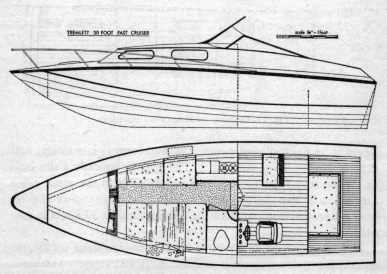

Fig. 18 Tremlett 30 ft fast cruiser

drawing in figure 16 represents the 21 ft cruiser. Dimensions are: length overall 21 ft 1½ ins. (6·47 m.); beam 7 ft 6 ins. (2·28 m.); draft 2 ft 6 ins. (0·76 m.). The hull and inner moulding are in G.R.P., with rigid polyurethane foam buoyancy between. Power comes from a Mercruiser 140. Petrol is carried in a 20 gallon (90·91 litres) tank.

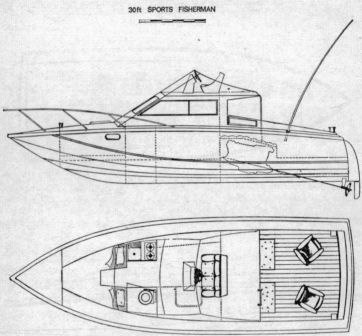

30ft SPORTS FISHERMAN

Fig. 19 Tremlett 30 ft Sports Fisherman

There is an electric bilge pump. The hull form is interesting; it is deep V but has large flat chines. The boat is basically a day-boat as can be seen from the drawing, nevertheless in the small cabin forward are two berths and sufficient stowage space for at least a weekend aboard. With the 140 Mercruiser 30 knots is possible.

We now move on to the 30 ft hull. There are three forms; the cruiser, the sports fisherman and the 30 ft fast cruiser. The three drawings in figures 17, 18 and 19 illustrate the varying profiles and accommodation plans possible on this hull. Specified power for the 30 footer comes from two Perkins diesels, two 145s. Construction is hot-moulded. Hull form as with the 21 footer is deep V.

In these days when 'doing it yourself' has been brought within the scope of anyone who can do a little home carpentry, Tremlett boats have the added attraction of being purchasable in kit form for completion by the new owner. Boats may be bought in varying stages: stage one being the shell with runners and chines pressed on outside of shell; stage two is the shell with transom, runners, chines, gunwhales and bilge stringers plus inside rails; and stage three takes the boat as far as stage two, but includes deck beams, decks, cabin sides and tops, rubbing strip, interior woodwork, longitudinal frames for bunks, bottom boards, engine bearers etc. and main bulk head.

Stage one is the stage at which hulls are normally taken off the Tremlett mould. The most popular stage for amateur building is stage two. The inside runners can be fitted for a level floor or with two parallel runners positioned about one foot each side of the hog to take seats and floor. The mahogany transom is fitted to take the standard shaft motor; it can be varied to take a long shaft or outboard/inboard. The kit of parts which are hand sawn to shape are supplied by Tremletts; they consist of woodwork for deck beams, decks, carlings, engine-well and dashboard. For the cruising boat it includes cabin sides, beams and top. The kits are cut to size and shape from ply or planed timber. There are sets of copious instructions together with stage by stage photographs showing the building up. With stage three, decks, engine-well and rubbing strip are fitted to the stage two hull; this means that the amateur builder has very little woodwork to do. For all this, a vote of thanks to Chris Tremlett, designer, builder, enthusiast and benefactor.

AVENGER

Look now at plates 10 to 12. Here we see an example of a really fast, production, racing boat. This sleek performer, which came in three sizes; 16, 19 and 21 ft overall length is sadly no longer produced, although you can obtain spares and servicing from East Kent Marine, Victory Gate Wharf, Sandwich, Kent.

The 16 footer (4·88 m.) has a beam of 5 ft 5 ins. (1·65 m.); the 19 footer (5·80 m.) has a beam of 6 ft (1·83 m.); the 21 footer (6·41 m.) has the same beam. Power is inboard, but you can have I/O or outboard if you wish. Recommended makes are Mercruiser, B.M.W. and Volvo Penta. Specified recommended horsepowers vary from 128 h.p. to 140 h.p. for the 16 footer, and from 120 h.p. to 165 h.p. for the two larger sisters. With the latter, where outboard units are concerned, 140 h.p. is recommended for single unit and up to 280 h.p. for twin units. Quite obviously, these are boats you can really race and speeds of well over 50 m.p.h. are well within compass.

Although the Avenger has gone out of production very recently, the series is continued in the 21-foot 'Tigershark' (TS. 65), built by and available from East Kent Marine.

CORONET

As the photograph shows, the Coronet boats look fun, they look exciting and they look as if they mean business. They come from Denmark; a land which is almost surrounded by water and which has produced sailormen for centuries past. But Coronet boats are more than fun; they are tough and thoroughly seaworthy; the product of years of experience at sea and of testing.

The boats are fibre-glass, laid up by hand. The bottom is laminated with eight layers; the sides of the hull having seven layers. The tough stringer system is moulded into the bottom. The transom has a 36 mm. piece of plywood moulded in and is glassed on to the stringers with heavy knees. In the Baltic, long the home of elegant wooden-built yachts, local yachtsmen may perhaps be excused for an initial dislike of fibre-glass boats. Yet how quickly has this prejudice gone and it is easy to see why, when firms like Botved Boats A/S of Vedbaek in Denmark (who build the Coronet boats) are turning out such beautiful little vessels in G.R.P.

Nevertheless, although fibre-glass is accepted everywhere nowadays and its many good points appreciated, there are still plenty of people who like to see a bit of 'wood' trimming about the place. This is not because yachtsmen are trying to kid themselves that their fibre-glass boat is really a wooden one but because wood provides below decks, a certain warmth. Varnished wood of attractive grain is pleasing to look at – it has pleased seamen for centuries. So wisely Coronet introduce into their fibre-glass boats pleasing woodwork in both cockpit and interior.

But when we come to the design of the hull here we are right up to date with deep V-hull design from the board of top American designer James R. Wynne. Such a hull needs plenty of reliable power to drive it and the Coronet boats use Volvo Penta Aquamatic engines; a Swedish product of proven reliability.

Let us now look at some boats in the Coronet range and if after this first look at some of these mouth-watering little vessels you want to know more, Dell Quay Marine Ltd of Dell Quay, Chichester, England, can tell you all you want to know.

Coronet day cruiser

This is a sporty boat with a large cockpit. Measurements are as follows: length (excluding Aquamatic engine) 21 ft (6·42 m.); beam 7 ft 8 ins. (2·34 m.); draft 1 ft 2 ins. (0·35 m.). The weight is 1250 kg. Power comes from either a single or twin 130 h.p. or single 170 h.p. Volvo Penta Aquamatic. The Coronet 21 ft day cruiser is a versatile boat. The seats for pilot and co-pilot can tilt over backwards to face the wide stern seat and by using a table a little dinette can be achieved. Furthermore, the pilots' seats when tilted, can be used for fishing. Again, the table can be used to support a third berth. It stows away under the fore-deck when not in use. Up in the fore-peak, incredible as it may seem, are ample berths for two people, both light with ventilation being provided by means of two port holes, a transparent hatch and a screened door.

Coronet 24 family cruiser

Coronet call this the 'family' boat and this compact 24 footer sleeps five people in two separate cabins. A folding table arrangement enables a dinette with two seats to be set up on the starboard side in the main cabin, the galley being to port. The toilet compartment is also to port in the fo'c'sle. The cabin top which may be seen in the photograph, gives adequate headroom in this part of the vessel.

Power as usual comes from Volvo Penta Aquamatics, either twin 130 h.p. petrol, single 170 h.p. petrol or twin 106 h.p. diesels. Electricity is provided by two 12 volt batteries. There are electric lifts for the outdrive units, an electric petrol gauge and an electric bilge pump. Measurements are as follows: length without Aquamatic 24 ft 3 ins. (7·40 m.); beam 9 ft 3 ins. (2·80 m.); draft 1 ft 4 ins. (0·40 m.). Once again, this fibre-glass hull makes use of deep V-design. There is a surprising amount of space below decks and headroom in the main saloon is 6 ft 4 ins. All in all, this is a real little ship and moreover she is fast, having with twin 130 h.p. Volvos, a maximum speed of 34 m.p.h.

Coronet 24 cruiser

In plate 13 we see a version of the 24 ft Coronet Cruiser. This boat is not unlike the 24 ft Family Cruiser but as the photograph shows the cabin top arrangement is different and indeed these boats are marginally smaller than the 'Family', being true 24 footers as opposed to 24 ft 3 ins. To be exact, the dimensions of the Coronet 24 Cruiser are: length without Aquamatic 24 ft (7·32 m.); beam 8 ft (1 ft 3 ins. less than the 'Family') (2·44 m.); draft 1 ft 7 ins. (0·48 m.). (Incidentally that is draft with the outdrive units up.) Headroom again is slightly less than in the Family Cruiser, being 6 ft (1·83 m.) exactly.

But what the 24 footer loses marginally in size she gains in speed, having a maximum, with her twin 130 h.p. Volvos, of 36 m.p.h.; which is a very presentable speed indeed for this type of boat. Once again, hull design is deep V and construction in G.R.P. with teak trim. All these craft come with a very fair and ample inventory of gear for the all-in price, and there is a formidable and mouth-watering list of extras for those with deep pockets!

BERTRAM

Look at plate 14. The general impression surely is one of boat performance and crew enjoyment; power and fun. There must be few people who have had more fun out of powerboating than Dick Bertram. A versatile sailorman, at one time heavily involved in the races for the America's Cup in 12 metre yachts, it was Bertram's meeting, and subsequent association, with designer Raymond Hunt, that led to the production of some of the fastest offshore powerboats known. The deep V constant rise hull designs of Raymond Hunt have already been discussed in this book and we have seen how the Hunt–Bertram partnership came to make a formidable mark on international powerboat racing. Bertrams of course have a wide range; they are in the boat business in a big way. Let us have a look now at some of the boats in that range. Should the reader be tempted (as is most probable) to learn more about the Bertram Boats, a letter to the Thomas Nelson Yacht Agency Ltd, Cobs Key, Hamworthy,

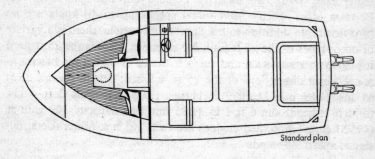

Standard plan

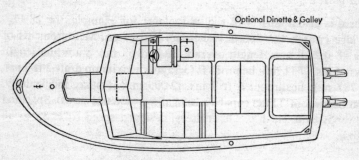

Optional Dinette & Galley

Fig. 20 Bertram 25 footer

Poole, Dorset will provide the answer; or if you are in the U.S.A. you can write direct to the Bertram Yacht Corporation, 3663 North-west 21st Street, Miami, Florida 33142.

25 Footers

Let us start with the Bertram 25 footers. The drawings in figure 20 show two plans; one the standard plan, and the other with optional dinette and galley. The boat we have mentioned in the photograph is called by Bertrams the 25 ft SPORTS CONVERTIBLE. It is a direct descendant of the famous deep V Moppie ocean racers. This boat, fibre-glass like all the Bertram boats, is as you would expect, really fast. With two outdrive engines (an optional range but Bertram often specify Mercruiser) speeds up to 40 knots are no pipe dream. In addition to the Sports Convertible, there is a variety of other types of the 25 ft hull; for example, there is the 25 ft hard top SPORT CRUISER and there is the 25 ft SPORTS FISHER-MAN. Basic dimensions of the 25 ft hull are: length overall 25 ft 11 ins. (7·89 m.); beam 9 ft 11 ins. (3·02 m.); draft 2 ft 4 ins. (0·71 m.); headroom 6 ft 1 in. (1·85 m.); fuel capacity 109 gallons (495·51 litres). Specified engines are twin 165 h.p. Mercruisers; designed speed, 39 m.p.h.

28 Footers

There is also a variety of the 28 footers: for example, the 28 Fly-Bridge cruiser, the Sports Fisherman and so on. Measurements of the 28 ft hull are: length overall, 28 ft (8·53 m.); waterline length 23 ft 4 ins. (7·11 m.); beam 11 ft (3·35 m.); maximum draft 2 ft 7 ins. (0·787 m.); headroom 6 ft 7 ins. (2·006 m.). (Notice, incidentally, that headroom!) Fuel capacity 165 gallons (750·084 litres). Specified power is twin 215 h.p. Mercruisers; designed speed from 35 to 38 m.p.h.

Bertram 31 footers

Look now at figure 21. This shows three designs based on the 30 ft 7 ins. length hull, which Bertram call the Bertram or the Bahia

(1) Bahia Mar

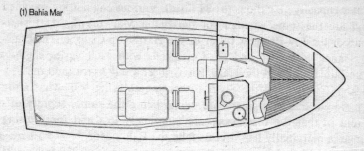

(2) Sport Fisherman

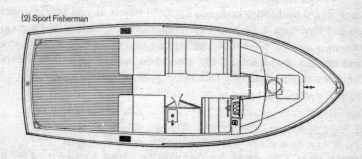

(3) Flybridge Cruiser

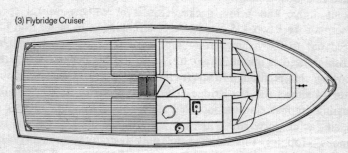

Fig. 21 Bertram 31 footers

Mar 31. Let us have the measurements straight away: overall length, 30 ft 7 ins. (9·32 m.); beam 11 ft 2 ins. (3·40 m.); draft 2 ft 7 ins. (0·78 m.). (This draft includes the propeller.) Headroom is 6 ft 2 ins. (1·87 m.); fuel capacity 170 gallons (773·01 litres); fresh water capacity 18 gallons (81·82 litres). Various engines are specified and are the same whether for the Bahia Mar, the Sports Fisherman or the Fly-Bridge Cruiser or the Hard Top Cruiser. The cruising range with each and the top speeds with each varies slightly. The Bahia Mar and the Hard Top Cruiser are the same and the Fly-Bridge Cruiser and the Sport Fisherman carrying somewhat more top weight and equipment are, while being the same, slightly different in that the top speeds are marginally less and the cruising range is marginally less. Let us take the Bahia Mar.

Two 215 h.p. Mercruisers give a cruising range of 210 miles and top speed of 35 m.p.h. With two 325 h.p. Mercruisers, the cruising range is 220 and top speed goes up to 38 m.p.h. If you prefer diesel you can have two 4/53 N h.p. General Motors' diesels giving a good cruising range of 370 miles and a top speed of 28 m.p.h. or if you want another two knots of top speed you can put in two V 470 N Cummins diesels but this will bring your cruising range down to 350 but a very fair cruising range for all that.

38 Footers

Now let us take a look at the 38 range, the SPORTS FISHERMAN illustrated in the photograph in plate 14. Figure 22 illustrates the layout above and below decks. This is a really powerful sport fisherman. Her two 325 h.p. Mercruiser engines can make it at top speed out to the fishing grounds at something around 34 m.p.h.; cruising speed is about 26 m.p.h. Notice the big cockpit aft in the drawing, this is about 110 sq. ft (10·21 sq. m.). The photograph in plate 14 shows the Fly-Bridge. The seating is shaded dark in the drawing emphasizing the fact that the skipper and four others can all sit facing forward. With her V-bottomed hull based on the famous Moppies, this boat is not only fast but thoroughly seaworthy. Her measurements are as follows: length overall 37 ft 8 ins. (11·41 m.); length waterline 32 ft 11 ins. (10·03 m.); beam 14 ft 5 ins. (4·39 m.); draft 42 ins. (1·06 m.); she carries 350 gallons (1,591·08 litres) of petrol and 100 gallons (454·59 litres) of fresh water; the inventory is as magnificently full as anyone who knows Bertrams would expect it to be.

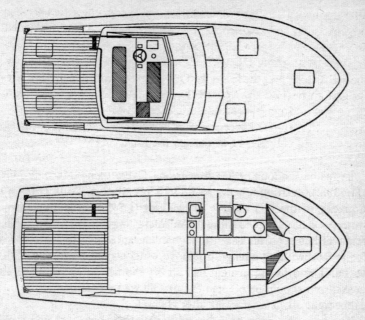

Fig. 22 Bertram 38 ft Sports Fisherman

'38' Cruiser

Slightly over 38 feet in length is the largest in the Bertram range, the '38' Cruiser. This is a fast boat. Look at the drawing in figure 23. Notice how the interior layout makes full use of the available space. As with the 38 ft Sports Fisherman 325 Mercruisers are specified. Optional if you prefer diesel are two 283 h.p. General Motors (V8 53). (Incidentally you can have these General Motors diesels in the Sports Fisherman instead of the Mercruisers if you prefer diesel to petrol.) The Mercruiser engines will send the Bertram 38 Cruiser along at 30 m.p.h.; with the diesels this will drop to about 27 m.p.h. She is not as fast as the Sports Fisherman but then she has a lot more below decks in the way of accommodation and general gear. But to be able to sleep six people in extreme comfort with a general headroom of 6 ft 3 ins. (1·90 m.), in a boat which even has its own hot water shower and still have a top speed of 30 m.p.h., is surely enough for the most demanding.

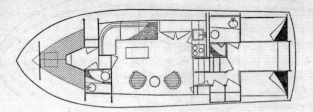

Fig. 23 Bertram 38 ft 6 ins. cruiser

Let us have a look at her dimensions. Overall length is 38 ft 6 ins. (11·63 m.); maximum beam 13 ft (3·96 m.); draft is 42 ins. (1·06 m.). Capacity of the fuel tank is 340 gallons (1,545·62 litres) and fresh water 94 gallons (427·32 litres). An interesting feature is the engine removal hatch on the cabin top, enabling an engine to be removed for repairs without having to remove windows or other parts of the vessel. The drawing in figure 23 shows the accommodation below decks, so it should be pointed out that above that sumptuous double cabin right aft, is a spacious after cockpit.

The boats which go to make up the Bertram range are fine, well-designed powerful craft and good value for money.

FAIREY MARINE

Pretty well anyone who reads the newspapers will have heard of Fairey Marine of Hamble, in Hampshire. People who do not normally even glance at yachting news find themselves interested in the now classic off-shore powerboat race from Cowes to Torquay. In this race Faireys have notched up many successes. In the first ever Round Britain Powerboat Race there were five competing Fairey Huntsmen. All finished the course taking third, fourth, fifth, sixth and twelfth places overall. Again in the race from London to Monte Carlo in 1972, Faireys chalked up more successes. Faireys believe in racing. In their view, experience gained in off-shore powerboat racing improves the design and construction of every Fairey boat. It is their boast that the man who owns a Fairey powerboat owns 'a fast boat, a safe boat and, inside, a very comfortable boat', and this boast is very difficult to contradict. I have selected here two from the range, the 30 ft Spearfish and the 31 ft 3 ins. Huntsman 31. For the record however there are four others, the SWORDSMAN 33, the HUNTSMAN 28, the HUNTRESS 23 and the new SUPER SWORDSMAN. All of these boats are tough fast boats; let us now look at one of the latest in the range, the Spearfish.

Spearfish

The dimensions are as follows: length overall 30 ft (9·1 m.); beam 9 ft (2·74 m.), draft 2 ft 9 ins. (0·84 m.); displacement is 9,500 lb. (4,320 kg.). The standard engine is the Ford 2704 E.T. turbo-charged 6 cylinder diesel rating 150 h.p. at 2,400 r.p.m. She has two of these and with them her performance is rated as 24 knots cruising speed, 29 knots maximum. You can have twin 180 h.p. engines which pushes up those speeds to 27 knots cruising; 32 knots maximum. Fuel consumption of the 150 h.p. engines is 14·2 gallons per hour, that is 64 litres per hour at top speed: 11 gallons (50 litres) per hour at cruising speed or 2,000 r.p.m. There is a separate electric system for each engine, comprising two 12 volt batteries charged by engine driven alternator. The hull is in G.R.P. with varnished teak trim. Propeller shafts are twin 138 inch stainless steel and the P-brackets which support them, are nickel aluminium bronze. Rudders are nickel aluminium bronze with 1½-in. stainless steel stocks in bronze bearings. The boat has rod steering. Although the technical specification names twin Ford diesels, other boats have been fitted with twin Perkins 6·354 U diesels, turbo-charged developing 145 h.p. and prospective owners have a choice between these two. Spearfish has two berths in the forward cabin and a toilet to port and galley to starboard. A feature is the roomy cockpit. This is a fast sporty weekend boat, race-bred. In hull form she has the real deep V design having a dead-rise of 26° from midships aft. She has a tough chine rail in addition to the three spray rails each side; all moulded in one with the hull. This is not only a good performer, she is a good looker and a great addition to the Fairey range.

Huntsman 31

Huntsman 31 is a high speed cruising motor yacht with a forward saloon and an aft cabin giving accommodation for four. She has in consequence a centre cockpit and control position. Power comes from two turbo-charged diesel engines. Unlike Spearfish the hull is not G.R.P. but hot-moulded wood; but like Spearfish the design is from Alan Burnard. The 31 is a development of the race-proved, twin diesel Huntsman 28. Let us have a look at her dimensions; length overall 31 ft 3 ins. (9·52 m.); length waterline 25 ft 8 ins. (7·85 m.); beams 9 ft 8 ins. (2·95 m.); draft 2 ft 10 ins. (0·865 m.); displacement is 9,000 lb. (4,082 kg.). Her Thames Measurement Tonnage is stated to be twelve.

Like Spearfish either Perkins or Ford engines are specified, either twin T 6·354 6 cylinder Perkins or, as with Spearfish, 150 h.p. or 180 h.p. turbo-charged Ford diesels. As with Spearfish transmission is Borg Warner, using oil operated gear-boxes installed side by side under the cockpit floor. Again like Spearfish, Huntsman 31 has a separate 24 volt starting system for each engine, supplied from two 12 volt lead–acid batteries which are located below the driving position and charged by alternators on each engine. Two 45 gallon fibre-glass tanks carry the fuel; there are separate deck fillers. This 90 gallons of fuel provides at cruising speed a range of about 150 miles working on a consumption of 13 gallons per hour, so Huntsman 31 is not all that costly to run—an important point. A 35 gallon galvanized steel tank carries fresh water.

The hot-moulding method of building a hull has long been used by Fairey Marine. Agba veneers and resin bonding is used. Engine bearers and bulkheads are mahogany; floor bearers and other structural members are either of mahogany or marine-ply. The deck is nine millimetre marine-ply. As already stated, there is accommodation for four below decks. A good looking vessel both above and below, this fast cruiser combining 27 knots with a lot of comfort below, takes a good deal of beating in her class of boat on an international scale. Her handling and sea-keeping qualities are known and proven. She is of her type, a very fine boat.

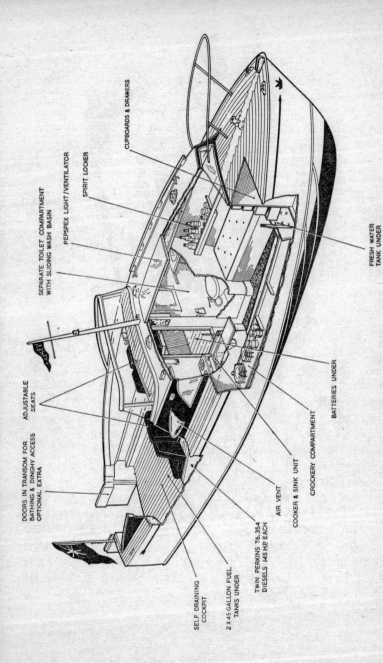

CUPBOARDS & DRAWERS

PERSPEX LIGHT/VENTILATOR

SPIRIT LOCKER

SEPARATE TOILET COMPARTMENT
WITH SLIDING WASH BASIN

FRESH WATER
TANK UNDER

ADJUSTABLE
SEATS

DOORS IN TRANSOM FOR
BATHING & DINGHY ACCESS
OPTIONAL EXTRA

BATTERIES UNDER

CROCKERY COMPARTMENT

COOKER & SINK UNIT

AIR VENT

2 X 45 GALLON FUEL
TANKS UNDER

TWIN PERKINS T6.354
DIESELS 145 H.P. EACH

SELF DRAINING
COCKPIT

Fig. 24 Fairey 28 ft Huntsman

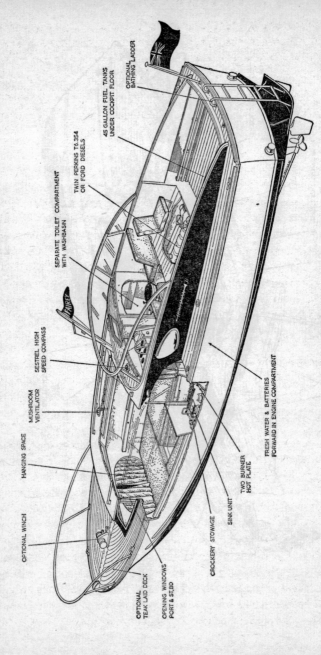

OPTIONAL WINCH

HANGING SPACE

MUSHROOM VENTILATOR

SESTREL HIGH SPEED COMPASS

SEPARATE TOILET COMPARTMENT WITH WASHBASIN

TWIN PERKINS T6.354 OR FORD DIESELS

45 GALLON FUEL TANKS UNDER COCKPIT FLOOR

OPTIONAL BATHING LADDER

OPTIONAL TEAK LAID DECK

OPENING WINDOWS PORT & ST'BD

CROCKERY STOWAGE

SINK UNIT

TWO BURNER HOT PLATE

FRESH WATER & BATTERIES FORWARD IN ENGINE COMPARTMENT

Fig. 25 Fairey 31 ft Huntsman

Super Swordsman

The Super Swordsman is the latest version of the Swordsman, a fast luxury cruiser, and is certain to be enormously popular.

The cut-away drawings in figures 24 and 25 give an idea of typical Fairey accommodation below decks and general layout. The vessels depicted are the 28 ft, and the 31 ft, Huntsman. Both of these excellent drawings are reproduced by kind permission of Fairey Marine.

HURLEYQUIN

Almost all sailing people knew Hurley Marine of Devonshire. From them came a wide range of attractive little sailing vessels from the designing board of Ian Anderson. They were built in G.R.P., attractively trimmed. The Hurleyquin is a powerboat from the same stable, a double-ender in G.R.P. trimmed with mahogany. She has a forward cabin and a large cock-pit, at the after end of which is a small mizzen mast, always useful to set a steadying sail to counteract excessive rolling or to keep the ship's head to windward in certain circumstances.

First of all, measurements: length overall, 21 ft (6·35 m.); length on the water line, 17 ft (5·18 m.); beam 7 ft 5 ins. (2·22 m.); draft 1 ft 8 ins. (0·50 m.). Displacement tonnage is 2,350 lb. (1,066 kg.). This boat has nice clean lines, an absence of fuss about the deck, cabin coaming extending aft on either side of the cockpit for protection from the weather, and a sensible layout below decks. She has wheel steering. Power can be from either outboard or inboard engine according to choice. Engines are also to customer's choice but specified are either Stuart Turner inboard 10 h.p. petrol, giving about 7 knots, or Volvo Penta 1 MD 1·1·1 inboard diesel giving about 7 knots; or outboard 6 or 9½ h.p. Evinrude, giving from 6 to 7 knots. Headroom under the raised cabin top is 4 ft 6 ins. (1·37 m.).

This is an ideal family boat; ideal for pottering about in, fishing and at the same time capable of modest cruises. She is a displacement type boat; not a planing boat and of course will not have the speed of the latter type. Nevertheless with her long straight keel and her seamanlike hull with ample beam and good freeboard, she will be able to look after herself and her occupants very adequately should the weather turn nasty.

CHEVERTON WORK-BOATS

It may be thought surprising by some to find 'work'-boats included in a book on motor yachting and boating; and if we are not careful we shall find ourselves involved in that most tricky question on definition – what is a yacht? I hope I can dispel the doubts amongst my more aesthetically-minded readers; for these powerful, sea-kindly little vessels are also extremely attractive to look at. But in the view of the author, one range of general purpose work-boats should be included and the range I have chosen is that of Cheverton work-boats which are built in Cowes, Isle of Wight. They may be built in Cowes, but you find them all over the world. They range from destroyer or frigate motor boats ordered by overseas governments as well as the Royal Navy, to a 40 ft fishery research vessel for use on Lake Tanganyika; to motor boats for the Irish Navy Fishery protection service; and so one could continue. But the real point of the Cheverton boats is that they are multi-purpose. So let us have a look at some.

Cheverton Champs

The range of smaller Cheverton Champs starts at 18 ft. Dimensions are: length overall 18 ft 9 ins. (5·70 m.); beam 7 ft 6ins. (2·28 m.); draft 2 ft (0·61 m.). This is a simple open boat with a hand start, 8 h.p. water-cooled diesel engine which will give approximately 6 knots. Figure 26 gives the general layout of the small Champ.

There are also a number of practical useful vessels in the 21 ft overall range, but let us look now at the 27 ft Cheverton which is the centre wheel-house version. Figure 27 shows elevation and other plans including the accommodation in the fo'c'sle. This little vessel is a real all-rounder. A fibre-glass hull with fore-cabin, centre wheel-house and large working cockpit, she is strongly built to a tested and well-proven design; intended for use in any weather and requiring the minimum of maintenance. A whole range of engines may be supplied giving specified speeds from 8 to 15 knots. Let us look now at the measurements. Length overall 27 ft (8·23 m.); beam 9 ft (2·74 m.); draft 2 ft 8 ins. (0·81 m.). This is a tough boat. All

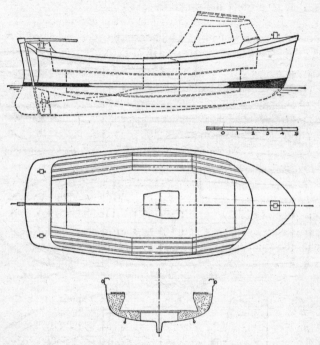

Fig. 26 Cheverton 18 ft 9 ins. launch

hull moulding is carried out under Lloyd's approved conditions. The main deck and superstructure is a one piece, heavy duty moulding in G.R.P. with additional strengthening at stress points. Around the cockpit and on the after facing edges of the wheel-house are mahogany cappings. Motive power is normally from the Perkins range of engines. The electrical system is 12 or 24 volt with the battery charged by engine-driven alternator. An electric wiper on the window of the wheel-house is standard fitting. The vessel has wheel steering on the port side of the wheel-house, the steering gear being of the cable type. The rudder is galvanized mild steel. A short tiller connects to the steering gear in the after peak and (a good point) an emergency tiller is provided. It can be seen in the drawing, that the lower bearing is formed by the skeg extending aft which also serves to protect the propeller.

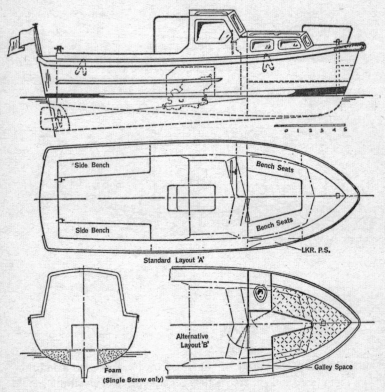

Fig. 27 Cheverton 27 ft work-boat

The 27 ft Cheverton Champ comes in three main forms: the open work-boat to standard specification, the forward control work-boat and the central wheel-house work-boat which we have been discussing. Standard equipment is very adequate but there is a long list of additional items which may be had if desired. For example: revolving clear-view screen in place of the standard wiper; an alloy mast with three stays, flag halyard and cleat; oak towing post; wheel-house extension in nylon reinforced P.V.C.; spray hoods in nylon, cockpit awning etc., etc. And of course the internal arrangements can be as sophisticated as required.

50 Footer

Chevertons who build to order are prepared to build boats to almost any length – for example a new 20 footer has been recently introduced and a number of 40 footers have been built and are now operating successfully. But when we come to the 50 ft Cheverton hull we find some very exciting vessels. Look at figure 28 which gives two ideas of what can be done on this length. Figure 29 gives

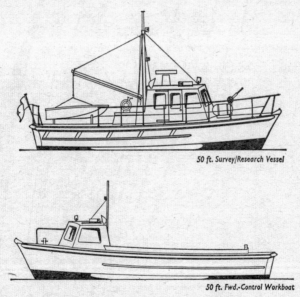

50 ft. Survey/Research Vessel

50 ft. Fwd.-Control Workboat

Fig. 28 Two Cheverton 50 footers

a typical example of a sophisticated vessel based on the Cheverton 50 ft G.R.P. hull. This excellent cut-away drawing is reproduced from *Workboat World*, the lively journal of Cheverton work-boats, with the company's kind permission. This boat is intended mainly

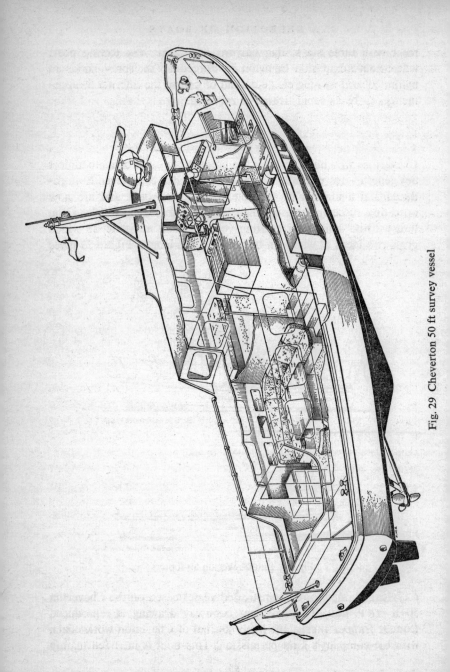

Fig. 29 Cheverton 50 ft survey vessel

for survey work in large exposed estuaries. The instrument console and survey table in the wheel-house which can be seen in the illustration are for this purpose. The saloon aft can be easily seen in the drawing. Up forward, there is sleeping accommodation for four people. The general measurements of the 50 ft hulls are as follows: length overall 49 ft 3ins. (15 m.); beam 14 ft (4·25 m.); draft 4 ft 9 ins. (1·50 m.). This is a twin-screw vessel. The two rudders can be seen in the drawing and the starboard propeller and shaft. Her designed speed is 18 knots. The accommodation as shown in the drawing is for survey work, for carrying passengers and V.I.P.s in the saloon aft and for providing accommodation for the ship's crew in the fo'c'sle; but of course you can have it any way you want.

Look now at figure 30. This gives us a good idea of the basic

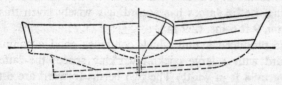

Fig. 30 Lines of a Cheverton 50 ft hull

lines of the Cheverton 50 footer, the hull is round-bilged form, one piece G.R.P. moulding under Lloyd's approved conditions. You can have single or twin-screw. In the case of single engine, specification is for up to 400 s.h.p. With a 42 in diameter propeller. With the twin-screw version, specification is up to 500 s.h.p. each. Superstructure can be in G.R.P. but also specified is either wood, or aluminium alloy. The round-bilged form is entirely suitable for this kind of vessel and Chevertons have produced not only a seaworthy hull but one which can economically be driven at speeds from 10 to approximately 20 knots.

COASTWORKER 32

Coastworker 32 (her overall length is 32 ft 6 ins. (9·9 m.)), comes from the drawing board of Mr Leslie H. James of Weymouth in Dorset, England. The hull form of Coastworker is inherited from the Sea Rider Motor Cruisers also designed by Leslie James, and is interesting. She is interesting because she represents something of a halfway-house between two relatively extreme types; the round-bilge displacement hull and the deep V form of the racing power boat.

Newbridge Boats of New Zealand Works, Church Street, Bridport in Dorset build Coastworker. They build also of course the Sea Rider Range; and they call this hull form a 'fast round-bilge form'; and it is patented under the name 'Sea Rider'. The hull has a fine entry forward with well-flared bows. So far we have nothing very unusual but the straight buttock lines on a rise of floor dihedral of 130° show the difference from the traditional round-bilge hull, and permits much higher speeds. Nevertheless Coastworker is a fishing or general purpose type and as such, she must be able to take the weather as it comes and not be subject to excessive rolling or pitching. Leslie James has accordingly wisely given this boat a good beam, 9 ft 6 ins. (2·9 m.).

He has produced a hull which combines good accommodation up forward with a large cockpit working space; the latter being 18 ft long by 8 ft in width. The two berths forward are 6 ft 6 ins. long. There is a separate toilet and galley space, and a very good point, maximum headroom in the forward cabin reaches the 6 ft mark and in the wheel-house is 6 ft 6 ins.

Coastworker is built in G.R.P. and moulding is carried out in Lloyd's approved works. If desired, completion to Lloyd's 100 A.1. can be arranged. Draft (which is of course maximum draft aft) is 2 ft 8 ins. (0·8 m.). Specified engines are 65 h.p. to a maximum of 175 h.p., single or twin diesel. With single engine, speeds of from 10 to some 14 knots should be possible. With twin engines, although it is perfectly possible to push the speed higher, one must remember that this is basically a displacement hull and fairly considerable additional power will be needed to approach the 20 knots which the makers claim.

This in point of fact, is rather a good example of what we talked about earlier in this book concerning the economics of power in displacement hulls. A displacement hull, so called because it displaces its own weight of water, has to push that water aside if it wishes to move ahead. We have also seen how moving forward through the water creates wave forms. Several factors combine to increase the resistance to a point where the maximum economical speed is reached and where, if it is desired that the vessel should go faster, this can only be achieved at a very great and quite uneconomic increase in power.

For fishing and coastal cruising it can be argued that one engine is large enough to give 12 or 13 knots (and in this connection Newbridge Boats quoted to me a 6 cylinder Ford-based 'marinized' diesel by Dolphin Marine which rated at 115 s.h.p. at 2,500 r.p.m. gave 14 knots). I should add here that a 'land' engine can be perfectly suitable for marine use if the conversion is professionally done, bearing fully in mind the erosive nature of marine use. The only thing this author does not care for too much is the verb 'marinize'. 'I marinize, thou marinizest, he marinizes' etc! It is also capable of confusion with 'marinate'! But to resume; a good reliable diesel of sufficient power to give anything from 12 to 14 knots is perfectly adequate for this kind of vessel. There is nothing of course to stop you installing twin engines but I would suggest that this should be for reasons of reliability, safety and ease of manoeuvring with twin-screws, rather than for extra speed.

There is something very likeable about Coastworker 32. She is not only a good, tough, substantial vessel, she is also very pleasing to look at. Dare one stick one's neck out and affirm that if a boat looks good she is good?

PARKSTONE BAY

An interesting range of small cruisers and fishing boats comes from Frederick C. Mitchell and Sons of Parkstone, Poole, Dorset. Based on a 21 ft G.R.P. hull, a number of different layouts are available. There is the standard Ferriboat with small cuddy forward. There is the Sea Horse which is virtually the standard Ferriboat with wheel-house roof. The latter has, in point of fact, wheel steering in the wheel-house, while the Ferriboat has tiller steering. These two versions may be seen in figure 31. More sophisticated versions may be seen in the Sea Cruiser and the Sea Fisher; the former being shown in figure 32 (2) and the latter in figure 32 (1). Basic measurements of the Parkstone Bay 21 footers are as follows: length overall 21 ft (6·4 m.); waterline length 19 ft 6 ins. (5·9 m.); beam 7 ft 3 ins.

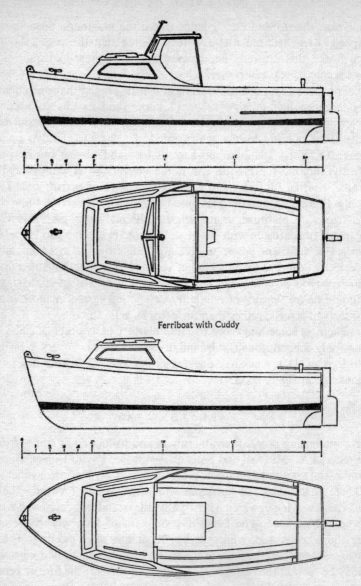

Ferriboat with Cuddy

Fig. 31 Parkstone Bay   (1) Sea Horse   (2) Ferriboat

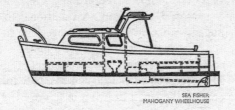

SEA FISHER
MAHOGANY WHEELHOUSE

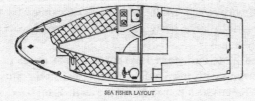

SEA FISHER LAYOUT

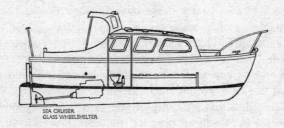

SEA CRUISER
GLASS WHEELSHELTER

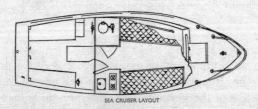

SEA CRUISER LAYOUT

Fig. 32 Parkstone Bay (1) Sea Fisher (2) Sea Cruiser

(2·2 m.); and draft 1 ft 10 ins. (0·56 m.). The vessels are robustly constructed in G.P.R. The hull is of round-bilge design and moulding is under Lloyd's approved conditions. A traditional touch is given by the solid mahogany cabin sides and coamings. The simple accommodation plan may be clearly seen in the two figures.

The Parkstone Bay Sea Horse, a development of the ordinary Parkstone Bay 21 footer, has been designed basically for sea angling and, as can be seen in the small drawing in figure 31 (1), the cockpit has a large unobstructed space in order to give ample room for six fishermen complete with their gear. Round both sides of the cockpit are mahogany slatted seats with storage space underneath. Of course this does not mean that the boat cannot be used as a cruiser and with a large party on board the roomy cockpit would come in very handy.

With these 21 ft Parkstone Bay boats a wide range of engine is possible. Starting with the smallest for example: the Stuart Turner P 66 R 2 cylinder 10 h.p. petrol engine with 2 to 1 reduction; the Stuart Turner ST 4 MR 12 h.p. 2 cylinder four-stroke with 2 to 1 reduction; the Brit 12/55 2 cylinder 12 h.p. four-stroke with direct drive; the Sabb GG 10 h.p. diesel with reverse reduction; the Lister SW 2 MGR 2 15 h.p. water-cooled 2 cylinder diesel with 2 to 1 reduction, or you can have the larger 42 h.p. Mercedes-Benz OM 636 diesel with 2 to 1 reduction. Speeds range from 6 to 9 knots, according to choice of engine. This is a displacement hull and a lot of additional engine horsepower could be merely wasteful. With the 42 h.p. Mercedes-Benz we can push the speed up to a good 9 knots. However, for her designed purpose, the Parkstone Bay 21 footer's speed range is perfectly adequate. She is both seaworthy and economical to run and must be 'just the boat' for many people.

MOONRAKER 36

This name, with (for many of us) its memories of the novel by the late Ian (James Bond) Fleming, has been well chosen for one of the most attractive of the medium-sized, fast, sea-going luxury cruisers available today. This is the Moonraker 36, the 36 referring to her overall length. Plates 15 and 16 illustrate this vessel. Notice the standard of comfort below decks, shown in the photographs of the interior. The hull in G.R.P., is moulded in Lloyd's approved conditions to designs by the well-known naval architect, R. Tucker. It it deep V forward coming aft to a 15° stepped V under-hull form. Standard power is twin Perkins 6·354 6 cylinder diesel engines, rated at 115 s.h.p. at 2,800 r.p.m.; electrics are 24 volt. Standard transmission system is Borg Warner.

Let us look now at Moonraker's dimensions. Length of the hull: 36 ft 1 in. (10·91 m.) [when the pulpit and davits are fitted, the full overall length is actually 40 ft 6 ins. (12·03 m.)]. Beam is 11 ft 6 ins. (3·50 m.) and draft 3 ft (0·91 m.). She can carry 100 imperial gallons of fresh water (477·3 litres) and 190 gallons of standard fuel (904·5 litres). Thames Tonnage works out at about 16·43. Various accommodation plans are available for from five to nine people. Different specifications include different styles of accommodation and upperworks; for example, the vessel may be fitted with a flying bridge with upper control position; she may be fitted with accommodation aft with two alternative state room plans, or she may have (in the Sportsman model) a very large, self-draining, laid teak cockpit.

This is of course not a cheap boat but you get value for money. Such refinements as two toilets with shower; treble duty dinette — four place table; large U-shaped settee; 6 ft double berth. This is in the main saloon and opposite it is another settee that does double duty as a glazed cocktail cabinet and formica bar top. You can have TV. You can have an 8-track stereo tape player and you can even have a Webasto oil-fired heating system.

But do not let all this luxury blind you to the fact that this is a thoroughly practical, fast, sea-going boat. According to the power that you put in her, she is capable of speeds from 8 to 21 knots. The people to go to are: J.C.L. Marine Ltd, of Brundall, Norwich, England.

FLEUR DE LYS

Intercontinental

Here in this 97 ft 6 ins. twin-screw diesel yacht we have real luxury. Dagless Ltd of Brigstock Road, Wisbech, Cambridgeshire, England are the people to go to if you have plenty of ink in the pen, a cheque book and the resources to match. But for all that the Fleur de Lys boats represent amazing value for the money you will have to spend. Look at figure 33 which illustrates the profile of this beautiful vessel, and let us examine her principal measurements. Length overall 97 ft 6 ins. (29·72 m.); beam 20 ft (6·096 m.); draft 7 ft 5 ins. (2·260 m.); displacement tonnage about 100 (90·625 tonnes). Power comes from twin Volve Penta engines of 320 h.p. each; in addition, there is a separate diesel generator for electricity. The vessel is fitted with Vosper stabilizers.

There are five double cabins, a deck lounge, dining saloon and galley; the fortunate owner has his own private study. There are crew's quarters for three in addition to the master's cabin.

International

But if the largest vessel in the range at present, is too much for your ambition or your cheque book, there are a number of tempting vessels smaller in dimension but each one a possession that one would dearly love to own. Coming down in the scale, we have the 88 ft International class. Her overall length is 88 ft (26·822 m.); her beam is 19 ft (5·791 m.) and her draft 7 ft 3 ins. (2·209 m.). Displacement tonnage is about 75 (67·968 tonnes). Power comes from twin Volvo Penta 240 h.p. engines. This vessel too has Vosper stabilizers. In the engine room will be found a diesel generating set, a Lucas 24 volt starter and batteries. In this vessel there are diesel tanks for 2,000 gallons (9,091·926 litres) and water tanks are for 750 gallons (3,409·472 litres). Two 12-inch (304·8 mm.) fans keep the engine room properly ventilated.

Ambassador

Coming down the scale again, we have the Ambassador class, whose overall length is 78 ft (23·774 m.). Beam is 17 ft (5·182 m.) and draft 6 ft 9 ins. (2·032 m.). This vessel displaces approximately 60 tons (54·375 tonnes). She is driven by twin Cummins engines 177 h.p. each.

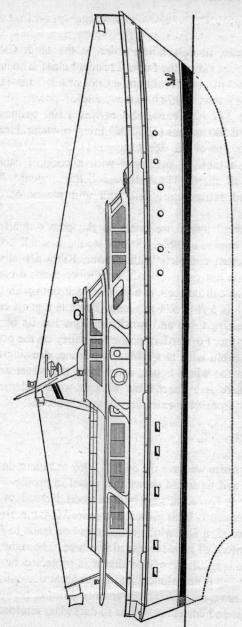

Fig. 33 Fleur de Lys 97 ft 6 ins. 'Intercontinental'—profile

Super President

Next in the scale, in descending order, is the 68 ft (20·726 m.) Fleur de Lys yacht called the Super President class. This vessel has a beam of 16 ft 3 ins. (4·953 m.) and a draft of 6 ft 3 ins. (1·905 m.). She displaces 45 tons (40·781 tonnes). Motor power comes from twin Cummins 177 h.p. each. She carries 1,100 gallons of fuel (5,000 litres) and 500 gallons (2,272·982 litres) of water. Her Thames Tonnage works out at 70 (see Chapter 1). She has three chairs, a fitted settee, a table, a sideboard with a cocktail cabinet, and a book case, all fitted. The galley is below forward. This has gas cooker and refrigerator, sink unit and plenty of cupboard space.

Moving forward again, we come to the crew's quarters. Here there are two bunks, a table, various stools, a small cooker and toilet compartment complete with shower. Right aft, there is the state room. This has double berth, wardrobe, chest, dressing-table etc. Attached, as can be seen, is a private bathroom with basin and toilet. The bath is 5 ft (1·524 m.) long. There is a guest cabin with two bunks, dressing-table and wardrobe. This has its own shower and toilet opposite. Forward, opposite the galley on the port side, is another guest cabin with two bunks, wardrobe, dressing-table and small basin. In the wheel-house, apart from the wheel and instrument panel, there is a chart table with drawers underneath. The navigational equipment is extremely comprehensive.

Continental

Finally in this range we have the 56 ft (17·069 m.) Fleur de Lys Continental class; and figure 34 shows this vessel in profile.

These Fleur de Lys vessels are built of wood. Nowadays, yachts of this size are frequently built in steel and indeed in G.R.P. But they are also built of wood, a fact which sometimes one tends to forget and here is living proof of how successful it can be. The right wood has the quality for long life. Provided that it is protected by paint and varnish its upkeep is economical and it has great durability. Yachts built of steel have to be kept continually painted because of the problem of rust and corrosion. While to date glass reinforced plastic

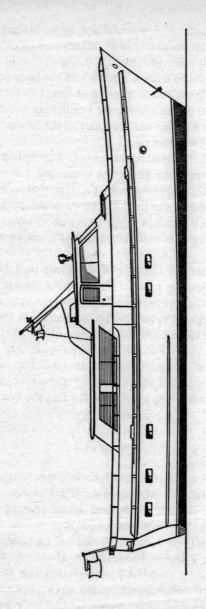

Fig. 34 Fleur de Lys 56 ft 'Continental' – profile

has been fantastically successful material for yacht building, this form of construction is still relatively in its infancy and its durability in all conditions has still to be proved.

Of course yachts have to be built of wood which has been properly seasoned. Dagless have installed a Wells kiln to complete the drying of planks up to 35 ft (10·668 m.) in length. Furthermore, the problem of bad damp winter weather has been met by the heating of the main construction bays in winter time.

It has been my practice in this book to avoid mentioning prices of boats. Experience over some years has convinced me that the effect mainly of inflation combined with the fact that a book is always six months behind by the time it appears in the bookshops, means that a book which contains much information about prices will be out of date before it is read. Nevertheless I am aware that there must be some curiosity in the mind of the reader as to what a large yacht, built in wood, of the type of the Fleur de Lys range costs. I am therefore breaking my rule on this one occasion to say that from the largest (the Intercontinental) down to the smallest (the 56 ft Continental) these vessels range, according to the price list for 1975 deliveries, from £286,500 down to £106,000. For the years which follow I would ask the reader to make his or her adjustments for inflation. It used to be said that a sailor judged a boat by a 'blow o' the eye'. If a ship looked right she probably was right and I think the reader will agree that the Dagless boats look very right indeed.

CORNICHE EXPRESS

Corniche seems to be a popular word these days. For a long time evocative to the initiates of golden summers on the French Riviera, the word has recently been used in advertising media. An example of this is that extremely luxurious motor car the Rolls-Royce Corniche. Then Lancer Marine of Lowestoft came out with the Corniche Express 10 metre. In a curious way the name suits the boat rather well but I suspect that this is only a personal impression probably caused by the sleek appearance of this vessel. But whether the name means anything or suits the boat or not, this is indeed quite immaterial beside the fact that

Lancer Marine have produced a little winner in this boat.

Figure 35 shows the profile and plan of the 33 ft Corniche Express tourer, and also, at the bottom a profile of the 32 ft outboard racer *Safari Express*. This boat comes from the board of experienced designer Robert Tucker. One would expect a seamanlike design from Mr Tucker but here, in collaboration with Lancer Marine, he has succeeded in producing a vessel distinctly out of the ordinary. Out of the ordinary because this is a production boat while at the same time being a very specialized boat and, as such, one would expect her to be much more pricey than she is. To help those with slender pockets even further, the Corniche can be bought in various degrees of construction, starting from a low sheer-line hull for outboard installation intended for racing, to complete hull super-structure assembly with bulkheads, windscreen etc. with high freeboard. Of course as is always the case, more power and more speed means more money and the model with two 120 Mercruiser outdrive engines giving 32 knots is naturally cheaper than the fastest model which, with twin 325 Mercruisers has a total horsepower of 650, which gives 52 knots. If you look again at the plans and photograph you will see that this boat has a well-protected cockpit and as one examines her it becomes increasingly obvious that from the point of view of accommodation Corniche perhaps leaves something to be desired. But there are doubtless many for whom the present accommodation, rudimentary as it is, is perfectly sufficient for coastal touring. But for those who want more room below decks for more extended cruising a G.T. version is already planned with headroom forward and an after cabin.

The Corniche Express lives up to her name. She is a fast and seaworthy boat which can make quick passages from place to place along the coast. If you want comfort you must stay ashore at night but if you don't mind or should you be caught out, the two bunks aft are perfectly comfortable and the space is adequate for the purpose. The hull is of fibre-glass reinforced plastics hand laminated in Lloyd's approved conditions. The hull form is of a 48° included angle deep V incorporating the three spray rails and a soft chine boundary. In connection with this fast hull I should point out that although the specified 650 Mercruiser twin outboard gives a 52 knots speed yet the hull design speed is in fact in excess of 70

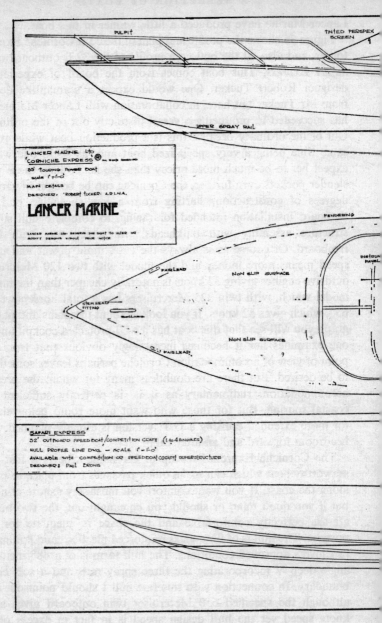

PULPIT

TINTED PERSPEX
SCREEN

UPPER SPRAY RAIL

LANCER MARINE LTD
'CORNICHE EXPRESS' ® ALL RIGHTS RESERVED
35' TOURING POWER BOAT
scale 1"=1'-0"

MAIN DETAILS

DESIGNER: ROBERT TUCKER. A.D.I.N.A.

LANCER MARINE

LANCER MARINE LTD. RESERVE THE RIGHT TO ALTER OR
MODIFY DESIGNS WITHOUT PRIOR NOTICE

FENDERING

FAIRLEAD

NON SLIP SURFACE

INSTRUMENT
PANEL

STEM HEAD
FITTING

BOLLARD

NON SLIP SURFACE

S.S. FAIRLEAD

'SAFARI EXPRESS'
32' OUTBOARD SPEEDBOAT/COMPETITION CRAFT (1 to 4 ENGINES)
HULL PROFILE LINE DWG. — SCALE 1"=1'-0"
AVAILABLE WITH COMPETITION OR SPEEDBOAT COCKPIT SUPERSTRUCTURES
DESIGNER: PAUL DRONS

Fig. 35 (1) Corniche Express 10 m.

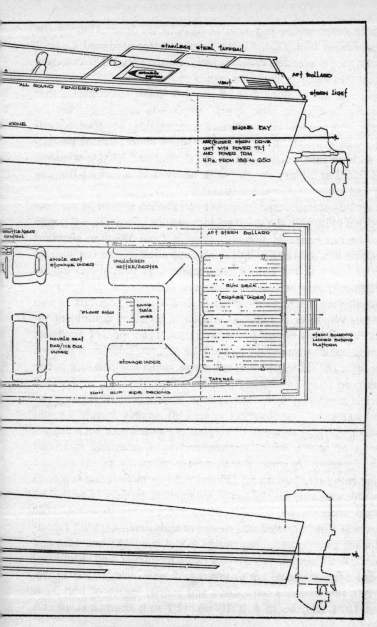

(2) *Safari Express* outboard racer

knots. In other words this boat is built to be driven, indeed the original design was taken from a South African designed Cowes/Torquay race contender, called *Safari Express*. (The 32 ft outboard racer by that name is shown in profile in figure 35.)

But if you are thinking that all this talk about speed means that she cannot be manoeuvred at low speeds you can be quickly reassured. The vessel is completely controllable at displacement speeds. The wrap-around windscreen (which apart from its practicality, adds so much distinction to the design) and its side windows are of tinted anti-glare Perspex with heavy duty anodized framing based and sealed to the super-structure.

As already stated, standard power installation is twin Mercruiser stern-drive units with the standard inclusion of power tilt and power trim. The full range of power options is from 188 h.p. standard installation to a total of 650 h.p. as we have already seen but with up to 950/1,000 h.p. for special requirements. A twin diesel engine installation, providing two turbo-charged inter cooled 210 h.p. Ford engines driving a remote mounted Walter V-drive gear-box is also available. Whatever installation you have, standard equipment includes per engine, power tilt, power trim, 1/1·5 or 2/1 propeller reduction, ignition shielding, power take offs, rev. counter, ammeter, power trim indicator, oil pressure gauge, water temperature gauge and exhaust risers (where applicable).

Fuel is contained in a steel tank of approximately 87 imperial gallons capacity. For electrical system all models feature 12 volt alternator charging separate 12 volt battery systems for each engine. There is of course wheel steering driving a rideguide rack and pinion assembly. A sophisticated note is given by power assisted steering being standard on all 255 and 325 h.p. models and is indeed optionally available on the lower horsepower models as well. The standard specification includes many more items than the basic ones which I have quoted and there are additional features; especially for the export special equipment model, ranging from radio and stereo tape to electric refrigerator with ice-maker and additional ice box! Measurements are as follows: length overall 35 ft 11 ins. (10·7 m.), this includes stern drive and pulpit; length of hull 32 ft 10 ins. (10·1 m.); beam 8 ft 10 ins. (2·7 m.); draft 2 ft 10 ins. (0·9 m.).

For those who like performance and a sleek, distinguished looking boat at a moderate price and do not want lots of comfort below decks, the standard model Corniche Express seems to me to be just the thing. But although she can seat nine or more in that big cockpit from the point of view of cruising she is a 'coast-hopper', an express 'coast-hopper', and since Corniche means coast I have to admit that she is after all very well named! And whatever they want to do with her whether to race with the low sheer race model or to cruise in the high sheer tourer I think most owners would find her ideal.

WEYMOUTH 32

This is a traditional craftsman-built boat by James & Caddy Ltd of Weymouth, Dorset in England. The G.R.P. hull is built by Halmatic in their temperature-controlled factory at Havant in Hampshire, approved by Lloyd's and under the strict supervision of Lloyd's inspectors. The hull is round-bilge form. Every Weymouth 32 is custom-built to suit the particular requirements of the purchaser. Figure 36 shows two alternative versions for either aft cockpit or aft cabin on the Weymouth 32 hull. Designer John J. Askham has as can be seen from the drawings, made the maximum use of every square inch of available space below. This is a really good boat to go cruising in. She can take the weather as it comes. The round-bilge hull gives a soft ride and in rough weather good speed can be maintained. James & Caddy quote an owner as saying, 'You can cruise this craft at 18 knots almost regardless of weather, without pounding, with the skipper and crew dry and warm and everyone's teeth happily in place.' This seems to me to be an excellent way of describing the all-round capabilities of this fine little ship. Now let us have a look at measurements.

Measurements are as follows: length overall 33 ft (10·06 m.); length waterline 30 ft (9·14 m.); beam 10 ft 10 ins. (3·30 m.); draft 2 ft 9 ins. (0·84 m.). The length of 33 ft includes the pulpit forward, the actual hull length is 32 ft (9·75 m.).

Specified power comes from twin Perkins HT 6·354 marine diesels, 6 cylinders in line, hand rotation developing 145 s.h.p. at 2,400 r.p.m. The engines have direct injection and Borg Warner oil-operated

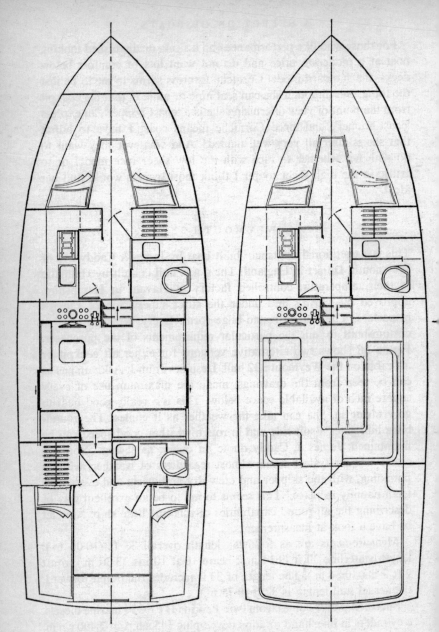

Fig. 36 Weymouth 32 ft – accommodation plans

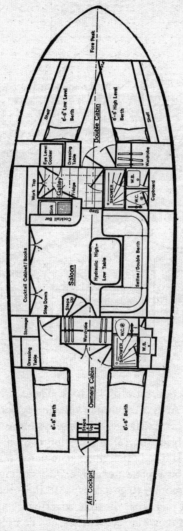

Fig. 37 Cresta K 40

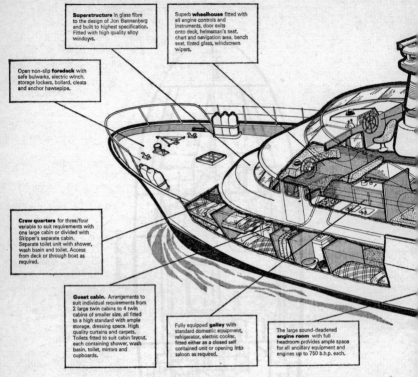

Superstructure in glass fibre to the design of Jon Bannenberg and built to highest specification. Fitted with high quality alloy windows.

Superb wheelhouse fitted with all engine controls and instruments, door exits onto deck, helmsman's seat, chart and navigation area, bench seat, tinted glass, windscreen wipers.

Open non-slip foredeck with safe bulwarks, electric winch, storage lockers, bollard, cleats and anchor hawsepipe.

Crew quarters for three/four variable to suit requirements with one large cabin or divided with Skipper's separate cabin. Separate toilet unit with shower, wash basin and toilet. Access from deck or through boat as required.

Guest cabin. Arrangements to suit individual requirements from 2 large twin cabins to 4 twin cabins of smaller size, all fitted to a high standard with ample storage, dressing space. High quality curtains and carpets. Toilets fitted to suit cabin layout, each containing shower, wash basin, toilet, mirrors and cupboards.

Fully equipped galley with standard domestic equipment, refrigerator, electric cooker, fitted either as a closed self contained unit or opening into saloon as required.

The large sound-deadened engine room with full headroom provides ample space for all ancillary equipment and engines up to 750 b.h.p. each.

Fig. 38 Savoy K 65

reverse gears, reduction ratio of 1·5 to 1. There is electric starting, fully suppressed C.A.V. alternators; voltage regulator and cut-out; also fresh water heat exchanger cooling system, water-cooled exhaust manifold, lubricating oil cooler, lubrication oil sump drain pump, water and dirt trap in fuel line, tachometer, water temperature gauge, ammeter, boost pressure gauge, Morse single lever engine controls with interconnecting cables. All this, including flexible rubber exhaust and fuel pipes, flexible coverings, engine trays, water injection exhaust fittings, starter switches, etc. complete with instruction book and parts list is standard specification for the Weymouth 32. The list of standard parts and fittings is equally impressive and

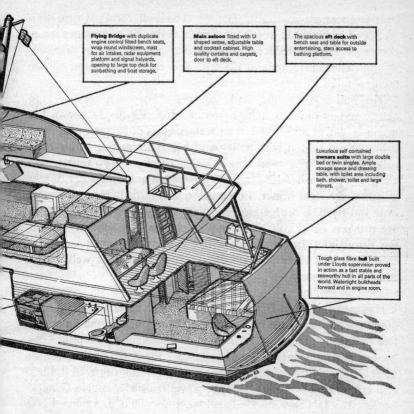

Flying Bridge with duplicate engine control fitted bench seats, wrap round windscreen, mast for air intakes, radar equipment platform and signal halyards, opening to large top deck for sunbathing and boat storage.

Main saloon fitted with U shaped settee, adjustable table and cocktail cabinet. High quality curtains and carpets, door to aft deck.

The spacious **aft deck** with bench seat and table for outside entertaining, stern access to bathing platform.

Luxurious self contained **owners suite** with large double bed or twin singles. Ample storage space and dressing table, with toilet area including bath, shower, toilet and large mirrors.

Tough glass fibre **hull** built under Lloyds supervision proved in action as a fast stable and seaworthy hull in all parts of the world. Watertight bulkheads forward and in engine room.

Studio 63

comprehensive. For example: set of toughened glass windows set in anodized aluminium frames; Kent C 11 'clear view' screen; Goad Sumlog. One might say the 'compleat' cruiser.

CRESTA K 40

This luxury cruiser is capable of 20 knots and more in normal conditions. As might be expected, her length is 40 ft (12·192 m.) and the rest of her measurements are as follows: beam 13 ft (4·0 m.); draft 2 ft 9 ins. (0·84 m.). This vessel comes from Knox-Johnston Marine Ltd, of Hamble, Hampshire in England, and the fibre-glass hull is built to Lloyd's requirements in Knox-Johnston Marine's own temperature-controlled factory. The hull form is semi-deep V. Specified power is from twin Perkin HT 6·354 diesels 145 b.h.p. each with 1·5 to 1 reduction oil operated gearboxes. Her displace- is approximately 8 tons (8·128 kg.) and she has a range of 300 nautical miles.

The hull is G.R.P. but decks are teak. This is a good-looking vessel and is built to a high specification. Figure 37 shows the accommodation which as can be seen consists of two self-contained cabins, main saloon with galley and bar. The interior furniture is teak-faced ply with solid teak edging. There are two toilets, two showers, two wash basins and pressurized hot and cold water. Water is heated by a gas heater. In the galley is a three-burner gas range, grill and oven, a refrigerator and very adequate storage. Electrics are two sets of 24 volt batteries with change over switch: 24 volt d.c. throughout. In connection with the electrical system should be mentioned that there are two electric bilge pumps as well as the manual bilge pump.

However this is, in fact, one of the smaller vessels in the Knox-Johnston Marine range of luxury motor craft and in the Smeralda and the Savoy are two more even more sumptuous examples. Let's look at measurements of the 65 ft Savoy – the K 65. Length overall 65 ft (20 m.); length waterline 58 ft 9ins. (17·9 m.); beam 16 ft 4 ins. (5·0 m.); draft 4 ft 9 ins. (1·45 m.); power comes from twin General Motors 12V71N engines. Designed speed 25 m.p.h. and range 1,000 miles. She carries 1,950 gallons (5,600 litres) of fuel and 530 gallons (2,410 litres) of fresh water. Her displacement tonnage is approximately 35 tons (35·562 kg.).

The K 65 is the result of Anglo–American cooperation. The hull of this all fibre-glass vessel was designed by American powerboat designer Jack Hargrave, while the superstructure comes from the board of British designer Jon Bannenberg. The hull is built under Lloyd's supervision by Halmatic Ltd. For a very good idea of the accommodation, let us now look at figure 38, the excellent cut-away drawing which I reproduce by kind permission of Knox-Johnston Marine Ltd. There is a gap between the mass-production motor cruiser and the extremely expensive individually built boat and it is this gap which it is the policy of Knox-Johnston Marine to bridge. bridge. It would certainly appear that they are succeeding!

GRAND BANKS

The Grand Banks are very comfortable seaworthy, tough, homely cruisers of heavy displacement. This may be seen in the drawings. The range runs from the 32 to the 50. The profiles are seen in the line drawings 39, 40, 41, 42 and 43 show the 32 standard model, the 36, the 42, and the last two, the largest, the GB 50. This range of diesel cruisers is built by American Marine Ltd whose U.S. Office is 1501 Westcliff Dr., Newport Beach, California 92660. British agents are Solent Yachts Ltd of Warsash, Southampton in England. So let us have a look at this highly individual range, starting with the smallest.

GB 32

The measurements of the 32 are as follows: length overall 31 ft 11½ ins. (9·741 m.); length waterline 30 ft 9 ins. (9·372 m.); beam 11 ft 6 ins. (3·505 m.); draft 3 ft 8½ ins. (1·130 m.). She carries 110 gallons (500·056 litres) of water and 240 gallons (1,091·031 litres) of fuel and has a range of a good 1,000 miles. Her engine is 120 b.h.p. 6 cylinder Lehman Ford diesel with Borg Warner reduction gearbox and heat exchanger cooling. Below decks, there is plenty of comfort and there are six berths all over 6 ft. There is 6 ft 4 ins. (1·929 m.) headroom. The deck saloon measures 11 ft 4 ins. (3·454 m.) by 8 ft 2 ins. (2·489 m.). She has a big roomy cockpit and, as can be seen in the drawing of the profile, plenty of freeboard; in point of fact, 6 ft (1·828 m.) forward and 3 ft 4 ins. (1·016 m.) aft. This is a good, sturdy vessel in which six people can go cruising offshore in both security and comfort.

All these Grand Banks vessels are strongly built, using selected hard-woods and silicon bronze fastenings. In these boats we are right away from light displacement, deep V and all the rest of it. Here we have fishing boat lines. The deep forefoot and long keel give an easy ride when the wind and the sea get up.

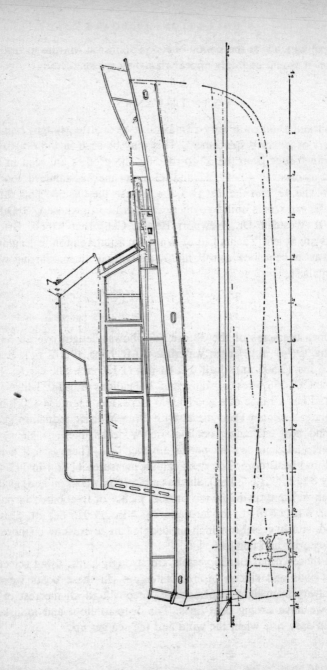

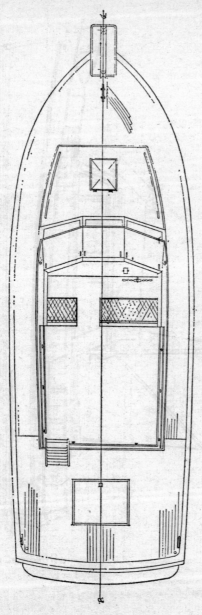

Fig. 39 Grand Banks 32

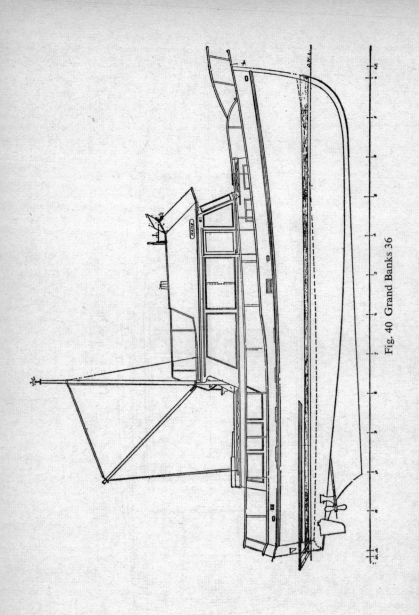

Fig. 40 Grand Banks 36

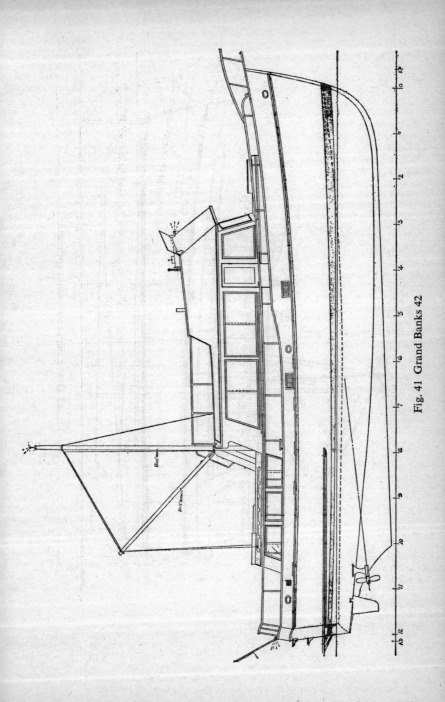

Fig. 41 Grand Banks 42

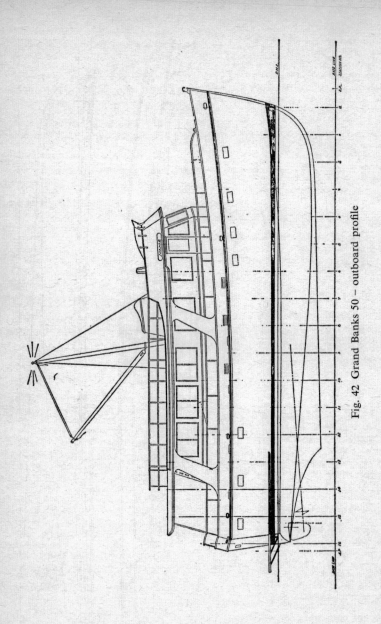

Fig. 42 Grand Banks 50 – outboard profile

GB 36

Let us now look at the 36; next in the range. Measurements are: length overall 36 ft 4 ins. (11·074 m.); length waterline 35 ft (10·668 m.) (notice the very small overhangs); beam 12 ft 2 ins. (3·708 m.); draft 3 ft 11 ins. (1·193 m.). Once again, there are berths for six people and plenty of accommodation below decks, with a headroom of 6 ft 4 ins. (1·929m.). A look at figure 40 shows that here we have an after saloon and also a mast. Also a glance at this figure will show us that here we have twin screws. The bracket and propeller can be clearly seen in the drawing as also can be the different rudder plan. All the larger boats are twin screw and follow similar design.

GB 42 and 50

With the GB 42 we now come to what is perhaps the happy medium. This vessel, while still being designed to accommodate six persons, does provide that much more comfort below for extended cruising without going to the expense of the GB 50. The difference between these two boats is perhaps more marked than overall measurements might lead one to suppose. The GB 50 is considerably roomier and more luxurious and in point of fact is virtually double the price! Perhaps it may be interesting therefore to compare the measurements of these two side by side.

	GB 42	GB 50
l.o.a.	41 ft 10 ins. (12·751 m.)	50 ft 11 ins. (15·514 m.)
l.w.l.	40 ft 6 ins. (12·344 m.)	48 ft (14·630 m.)
beam	13 ft 7 ins. (4·140 m.)	16 ft (4·876 m.)
draft	4 ft 2 ins. (1·270 m.)	5 ft (1·524 m.)
displacement	34,000 lb. (15,422·042 kg.)	59,300 lb. (26,898·023 kg.)

That should tell its own story. The deck saloon in the 42 is 15 ft (4·572 m.) by 9 ft 7 ins. (2·971 m.) whereas the deck saloon in the 50 is 20 ft 3 ins. (6·172 m.) by 11 ft 7 ins. (3·530 m.). It may not sound much but it is surprising what a difference these feet and inches can make!

For all this however, the GB 42 is a very comfortable long dis-

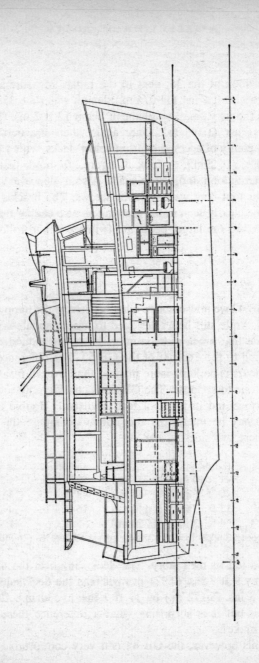

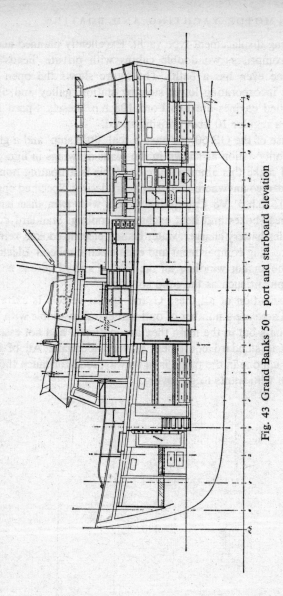

Fig. 43 Grand Banks 50 – port and starboard elevation

tance cruising displacement-type yacht. Excellently planned accommodation comprises two double cabins with private 'heads' and showers (one even has a bath). The figure shows the open plan deck house incorporating lower steering station, galley and dining area. Specified engines are two Ford 108 h.p. diesels. Speed is 12 knots with a regular 10 knot cruising speed.

In the case of the GB 50, we have a real 'little ship' and a glance at the accommodation as shown in the plans drawings in figures 42 and 43 will make this abundantly clear. This is a floating home in which you can go anywhere that your heart desires. Specified engines are twin 215 b.h.p. V8 Caterpillar diesels with twin disc handed reduction gear-boxes and heat exchanger cooling. Standard equipment includes battery charger, water heater, electric cooker, refrigerator with freezing compartment and even electric toilets! Electricity also runs the anchor windlass on the fo'c'sle and of course navigational equipment such as the echo sounder.

The specification of all these Grand Banks vessels is extremely adequate. There are a number of optional extras available with U.K. delivered boats but in the main they are 'optional' and not essential and the basic standard equipment is very adequate. All of them excellent, each one in the range is in its way, food for much thought for the man who wants to go roving.

CHAPTER 4

A Selection of Engines

WE have now examined a variety of boats and in doing so, have noted that different engines are specified by the builders in each case. Let us now take a closer look at a selection of modern marine engines.

WaterMota

This well-known firm at Newton Abbot in Devonshire, England produces a variety of marine engines from 10 to 62 b.h.p. From their fine range I have chosen three engines. Two of these are SEA WOLF and SEA TIGER, both of which are based on the Ford industrial engines 2251 E and 2254 E respectively, and both are up-to-date 'cross flow' Ford engines. These tough yet lightweight engines are water-cooled; the water-cooled manifolds, thermostats and twelve volt alternators being fitted as standard equipment. Each model is available in four different basic specifications. (1) manual marine J-type gear-box; (2) hydraulic PR marine gear-box; (3) hydraulic Borg Warner marine gear-box and (4) Perkins Z drive. The third engine I have included is the WaterMota SHRIMP.

Let us look at SHRIMP first, illustrated by figure 44, which shows the engine, her shaft and propeller. Specification is as follows. The engine is a single-cylinder four-stroke side valve, air-cooled. It starts on petrol, but runs on paraffin. Reduction is 4 to 1. Propeller is 12 ins. with 37 sq. ins. blade area. The control gear-box gives ahead, astern, neutral and optional feathering. Notice in figure 44 the gear position right aft, marked 'sail'. This is the optional feathering which is for sailing craft where the two blades can be brought into the feathering position so as to present as little

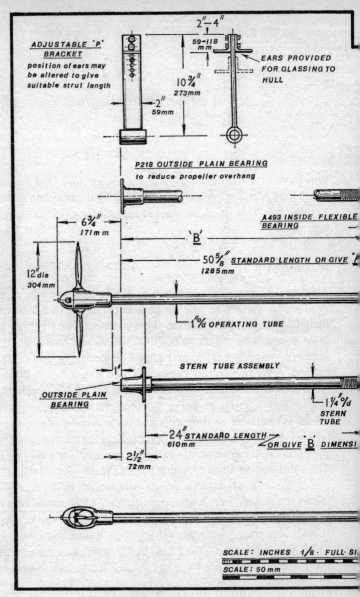

ADJUSTABLE 'P' BRACKET
position of ears may be altered to give suitable strut length

2" 59mm

2"–4"
59–118 mm

10¾" 273mm

EARS PROVIDED FOR GLASSING TO HULL

P218 OUTSIDE PLAIN BEARING
to reduce propeller overhang

A493 INSIDE FLEXIBLE BEARING

6¾" 171mm

'B'

50⅝" STANDARD LENGTH OR GIVE 'A'
1285mm

12" dia 304mm

1⅛" OPERATING TUBE

STERN TUBE ASSEMBLY

1"

OUTSIDE PLAIN BEARING

1¼" o/d STERN TUBE

24" STANDARD LENGTH
610mm
OR GIVE 'B' DIMENSI

2½" 72mm

SCALE: INCHES 1/8 · FULL SI.

SCALE: 50 mm

Fig. 44 WaterMota *Shrimp* propulsion unit

ATERMOTA "SHRIMP" PROPULSION UNIT

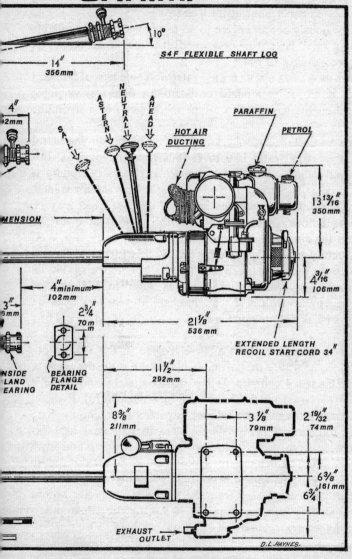

10°

S4F FLEXIBLE SHAFT LOG

14″
356mm

4″
2mm

SAIL

ASTERN   NEUTRAL   AHEAD

HOT AIR
DUCTING

PARAFFIN

PETROL

13 13/16″
350mm

...MENSION

4″ minimum
102mm

3/16″
106mm

3″
6mm

2 3/4″
70 mm

21 1/8″
536mm

EXTENDED LENGTH
RECOIL START CORD 34″

NSIDE
LAND
EARING

BEARING
FLANGE
DETAIL

11 1/2″
292mm

8 3/8″
211mm

3 1/8″
79mm

2 19/32″
74mm

6 3/8″
161mm

6 3/4″

EXHAUST
OUTLET

D.L.HAYNES.

resistance to the water as possible. Ignition is magneto. Fuel consumption is quite remarkably low, being $1\frac{1}{2}$ pints per hour at cruising speed and $2\frac{1}{2}$ pints per hour at full power.

This is obviously not an engine to go racing with but for reliable cruising in a small boat at modest speeds it is easy to maintain and extremely economical to run.

The SEA WOLF/SEA TIGER WaterMota models of inboard engine are produced in inboard/outboard (or outdrive) versions; the inboard engine has either a J-type mechanical, or a hydraulic gearbox.

This is a vertical, four-stroke, overhead valve, four-in-line petrol engine. Compression ratio is 9 to 1. It has water-cooled exhaust manifold and cylinder block with thermostat. The water pump is camshaft driven. There is a 12 volt alternator with inbuilt voltage regulator. The difference between Sea Wolf and Sea Tiger may be indicated as follows. While the bore is the same (that is to say 80·98 mm.) the stroke is different, being 53·29 mm. for Sea Wolf and 77·62 mm. for Sea Tiger. Cc for Sea Wolf is 1,098 and for Sea Tiger 1,599. By the same token Sea Tiger is heavier, being 390 lb. to 370 lb. of Sea Wolf (or 185 kg. Sea Tiger to 175 kg. Sea Wolf). The engine with a J-type mechanical gear-box, has an epicyclic gear-box with manual control, either direct drive or 2 to 1 reduction.

Let us now have a look at a diesel engine in the WaterMota range. This is the SEA SCOUT and is illustrated in the drawings in figure 45. This is a 4 cylinder, 71 h.p. marine diesel with hydraulic gear-box. It is based on the Ford 3·97 litre model 2701 E diesel engine. This is a tough marine diesel, capable of running for long periods at full power. The cooling system uses internal heat exchanger cooled fresh water system with sea water pump and fresh water circulator. The exhaust manifold is water jacketed. Electric system is 12 volt. This engine is not only tough and reliable but it is economical, as can be seen from the following full power ratings with corresponding fuel consumption; 34 h.p. 1,250 r.p.m. approximate consumption $1\frac{3}{4}$ gallons or 7·7 litres per hour; 50 h.p. 1,750 r.p.m. approximate consumption $2\frac{1}{2}$ gallons or 10·8 litres per hour; and 64 h.p. 2,500 r.p.m. consumption $3\frac{1}{4}$ gallons or 14·9 litres per hour.

Easy to start, quick to respond and capable of long periods of continuous effort, the Sea Scout has been well named.

Stuart Turner

Continuing, as we have started, with relatively small marine engines, we come to the range of the well-known firm of Stuart Turner Ltd of Henley-on-Thames, Oxfordshire, England. The Stuart range is justly famous. It is their proud boast that they cover practically every requirement for the smaller boat. For example, you cannot get much smaller than the type R3 MC, a little mini-engine for dinghies, auxiliaries, punts and 'pleasure park boats'. This little engine with centrifugal clutch and no reverse, has a fuel consumption of 0·97 pints per hour or alternately $5\frac{1}{2}$ hours per gallon. The centrifugal clutch (a Stuart patent) is automatic in action, engaging when the throttle is opened and disengaging when the throttle is closed. The R3 MC is shown in the drawing in figure 46.

Look now at figure 47, this illustrates the 5 b.h.p. petrol engine. The illustration also shows dynastart and reduction gear in dotted line. This engine is for launches, tenders, etc. As can be seen it has a 'tram handle' type gear control but it can be supplied with fore-and-aft gear lever at slightly extra cost. 6 ft remote flexible throttle and choke controls can also be supplied. With this engine, reduction gear brings the engine speed of 1,650 r.p.m. down to 805 r.p.m. propeller shaft speed.

For launches, work-boats, fishing boats etc. Stuart Turner specify the S.T. 4 engines. These are 12 b.h.p., 1,650 r.p.m. engines, having fore-and-aft gear lever as shown in the drawing. However, if the tram handle type is preferred, it is available to special order. Reduction gear brings the engine speed down to 805 r.p.m. shaft speed.

Volvo Penta

As makers of marine engines ranging from two cylinder 15 h.p. up to 6 cylinder 170 h.p., Volvo Penta have long been world famous. But perhaps of even greater, although more recent, renown is the Volvo Penta Aquamatic inboard/outboard unit, an engine of proven worth. Let us have a look at both these types.

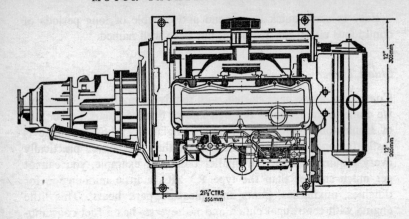

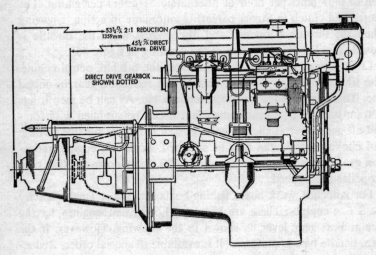

Fig. 45 WaterMota *Sea Scout* diesel engine

The home address of Volvo Penta is 405–8, Goteborg, Sweden. Those of us who live in England may go to the Bolinders Company at 150 King's Cross Road, London W.C.1. Taking the inboard marine engines first, I choose as my typical example, the BB 115 B. This is a four-stroke marine engine, designed and built for salt water operation under tough running conditions. It is particularly suitable for installation in high speed planing craft. Fuel

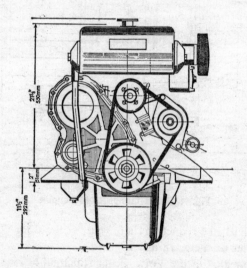

consumption is low; the engine itself is compact and light in weight. Figure 48 gives a general idea of the dimensions. This engine, the 71/115 h.p. BB 115 B, has thermostatically-controlled cooling, water-cooled exhaust manifold and elbow, amongst other standard features. You can have the model RB reverse gear-box or the Borg Warner reverse gear-box. Specified are three-bladed propellers with the following optimum diameters. For 1·91 to 1, or 2·1 to 1 reduction

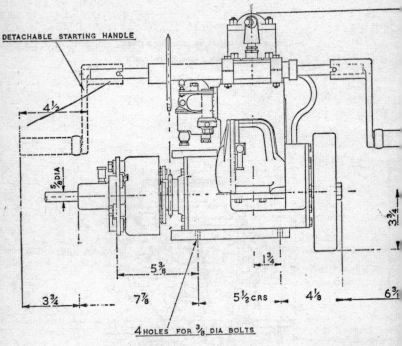

Fig. 46 Stuart Turner R3 MC engine

15 ins.; for 2·91 to 1 reduction (in the case of the Borg Warner gear-box) propeller diameter 18 ins.

Let us now look at the Volvo Penta Aquamatic. There is a wide range, both petrol and diesel. In petrol, for example, from the 115 h.p. 4 cylinder engine up to the 225 h.p. 8 cylinder engine, and in the diesel range, from the 25 h.p. 2 cylinder engine to the big 106 h.p. 6 cylinder engine. Finally, there are the two 'sports', as they are called, Aquamatics, both large and both petrol. The 155 h.p. 4 cylinder being the smallest and the 200 h.p. 6 cylinder being the largest; both of these having the special 'Slimline' outdrive.

There is a wealth of experience behind this engine. It combines

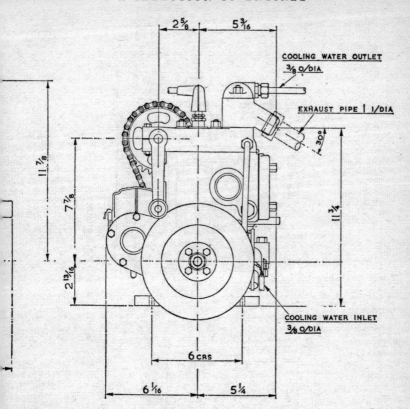

high performance with extremely economical fuel consumption and is in consequence particularly suitable for fast lightweight boats. Both the flywheel and the starter motor are completely encased, thus minimizing risk of bilge water damage. Indeed much attention has been paid to keeping this engine free from corrosion. Look now at figure 49 which gives an idea of the general dimensions. This depicts the 115 h.p. Volvo Penta, the 4 cylinder marine engine with the outboard drive model number 100. It is a four-stroke carburettor engine with overhead valves. Maximum operating speed is 5,100 r.p.m.; the compresion ratio is 9·5 to 1. The total weight of the engine is about 460 lb. (210 kg.).

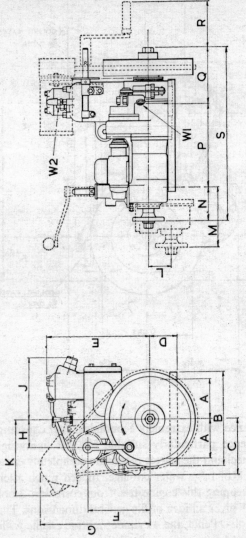

Fig. 47 Stuart Turner 5 b.h.p. engine

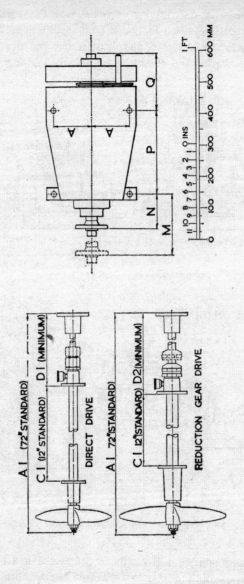

This engine is not only used in yachts all over the world but it has been also extensively used for work boat installations. The model 100 can be said to be one of the most tested and developed out-drives in the world, and tested under widely varying conditions.

DIMENSION DRAWING (engine with RB reduction/reverse gear)

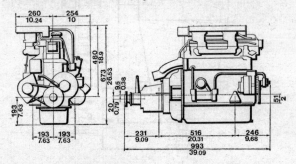

Fig. 48 Volvo Penta BB 115 B engine

DIMENSION DRAWING

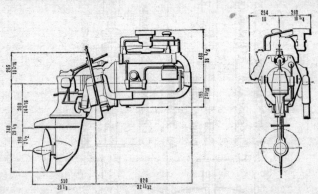

Fig. 49 Volvo Penta 115 h.p. Aquamatic I/O engine

Standard equipment of this engine includes the instrument panel with electric revolution counter, electric temperature gauge and warning lamps for charging and oil pressure. A good feature is that all electric cables are collected into one single harness between the engine and the instrument panel. There is a very comprehensive list of optional equipment and accessories for those who want them. All in all, a first class engine from a first class firm.

Gardner

The Gardner range of marine diesels needs little introduction to those in the know. Let us take the LW series. These are made in 4, 5 and 6 cylinder sizes. They are combined with the Gardner number 2 unit construction reversing and reversing/reduction gears. They can be arranged with direct drive to the propeller shaft or with 2 to 1 or 3 to 1 reduction. These first class engines have been accepted by Lloyd's and are entered on the register in the 100 A.1. classification. Let us take for our example, the 6 cylinder engine and look at figure 50 where there is a cut-away diagram of the engine and the reversing and reducing gear. This engine is of the direct injection four cycle type, having one inlet and one exhaust valve per cylinder. The valves are operated by levers, push rods and tappets from a camshaft located in the crank case. Notice in the drawing, the triplex roller chain which, running in a constant stream of lubricating oil, drives the camshaft and auxiliaries. Mounted on the port side of the engine and gear-driven from the valve camshaft is the combined fuel-injection pump and governor assembly. The engine is governor controlled at all speeds from idling to the maximum r.p.m. Exact fuel-injection timing for all loads and speeds is thereby automatically secure by inter-connection with this governor control. For the lubrication of the engine, oil is drawn from the sump by a gear type pump and delivered to an external spring-loaded relief valve which maintains constant pressure in the whole system. The LW engines have fresh water cooling, either through the medium of the sea water-cooled heat exchanger or an outboard mounted keel cooler. With either arrangement an engine-mounted fresh water header tank provides the necessary head of coolant, which is circulated through the system by the centrifugal-type water pump. The sea water is circulated through the oil cooler and heat exchanger by a separate inboard mounted, engine-driven pump. With a keel cooler system, the sea water is circulated through the oil cooler by a small auxiliary, engine mounted, plunger-type pump.

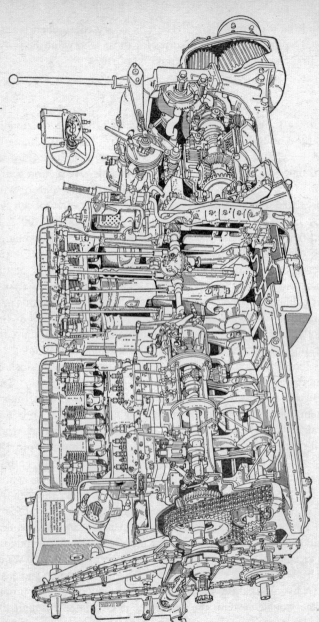

Fig. 50 Gardner 6 cylinder LW engine

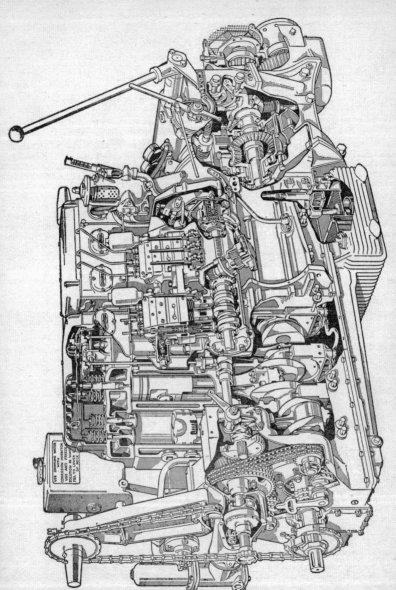

USE DRINKING WATER
WITH APPROVED
CORROSION INHIBITOR
USE ANTI FREEZE
SOLUTION IN WINTER
FILL TO LOWER
EDGE OF NECK

Fig. 51 Gardner 6 L X diesel engine

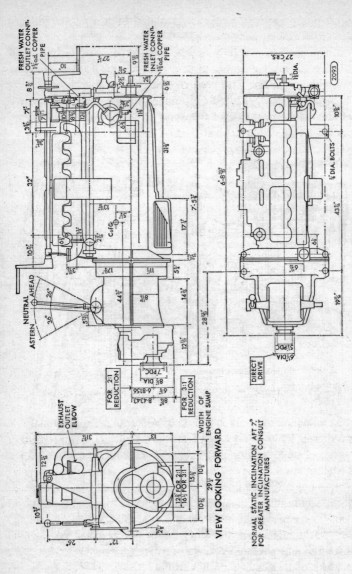

Fig. 52 Gardner 6 L X diesel engine – basic dimensions

If a bilge pump is fitted, water is circulated by a separate inboard mounted, belt-driven pump.

As can be seen from the figure, the reverse gear is constructed as a unit with the engine crank case, providing rigidity, economy in both weight and space, and ease of installation in a vessel. A 24 volt 49 amp alternator is fitted as standard equipment and is located in a cradle on the port side of the crank case. Also standard equipment is a 24 volt starter motor.

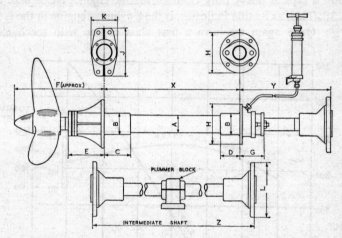

Fig. 53 Gardner 6 LX diesel engine – propeller and sterngear

Let us now look at another well-known Gardner engine, the 6 LX marine diesel. This is another first class Gardner engine with a wide range of uses; including fishing craft, customs' launches, police boats, yachts and high speed craft. In figure 51 is a cut-away drawing of this engine. It has many advantages; quiet and smooth in operation; economical fuel consumption, and great durability at excellent power to weight ratio. As with the Gardner LW series, all parts are to the highest specification. Many of them, like the pistons, are of unique and patented Gardner design.

A feature of this engine is its excellent power-to-space ratio. In this connection, the cut-away drawing in the figure, being deliberately fore-shortened, gives perhaps an erroneous impression of the compactness in this engine but a glance at the drawings in figure 52 will soon remedy this. The engine in the drawing is the 6 LX model with 3 to 1 reducing reversing gear; electric starting and chain hand-starting equipment; also additional lubricating oil pump for the oil cooler. As with the Gardner LW engine, the 6 LX unit can be ar-ranged for keel cooling instead of heat exchanger and including engine mounted, sea water pump to circulate water through the oil cooler. Again we have another first class diesel engine from Gard-ner. Figure 53 illustrates propeller and stern gear details.

For a typical heavy duty Gardner marine engine, let us take the 8L 3B. This, as its title indicates, is the 8 cylinder engine in the L 3B series. Once again we have a first class engine with mechanical

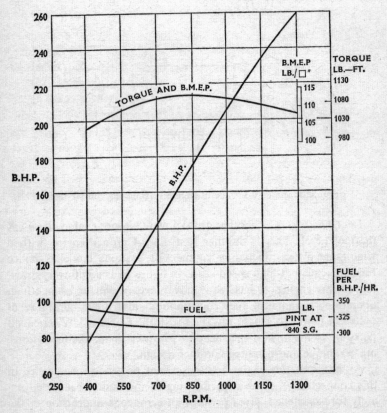

Fig. 54 Gardner 8 L 3B diesel engine – performance curves

efficiency of a high order. As with other Gardner units you can have direct drive, 2 to 1 reduction gear or 3 to 1. The graph shown in figure 54 is interesting. Here we see the performance curves of the 8L 3B engine. This is as set for high speed craft where we have 260 b.h.p. developed at 1,300 r.p.m. Notice the fuel consumption curve and how efficiency and torque is maintained over a wide speed range. This engine is suitable for all heavy duty commercial craft but it is also particularly suitable for the larger motor yacht. If you want to know more about Gardner engines, a line to Barton Hall Works at Patricroft, Eccles, Lancashire, England, will provide the answer.

Lister

From Lister Blackstone Mirrlees Marine, Dursley, Gloucestershire, England, comes an interesting water-cooled marine diesel, known as type SW 2MG/R.

Before saying any more about this engine let it be quickly stated that this is only one engine amongst a wide range of types manufactured by Lister. However, I have to make a choice, largely for reasons of space, in this book and if somebody's favourite Lister engine is omitted, I apologize. But it cannot be emphasized too strongly that the engines in this book are selected out of an enormous available range, not because I think they are better than those which are not here, but either because one has had personal experience of them, or has some knowledge of them for one reason or another, and particularly because the engines chosen are fairly representative of their type.

In the case of this Lister engine we have an excellent typical small diesel, with a 2 cylinder, water-cooled unit with a rating of 15 b.h.p. at 2,000 r.p.m.; a tough compact little four-stroke engine with a good power/weight ratio. The standard specification includes a manually operated, epicyclic reverse gear-box incorporating a cone-type ahead clutch and reverse brake band. The reduction gear is a separate unit which fits directly on to the reverse gear-box. Standard equipment also includes wet sump lubrication, sea water-cooling, fuel filter, oil pressure gauge, raised hand starting, water-cooled exhaust manifold, 24 ins. length flexible exhaust pipe etc. There are many optional fittings as well. You can, as with so many things in this life, have what you want, provided that you specify it and are prepared to pay for it!

Mercedes-Benz

Here we have, as one would expect from this famous firm, a most interesting range of water-cooled marine diesel engines. Let us have a look at three of them. I have selected two 4 cylinder and one 6 cylinder water-cooled marine diesels; 42, 80 and 125 h.p. respectively.

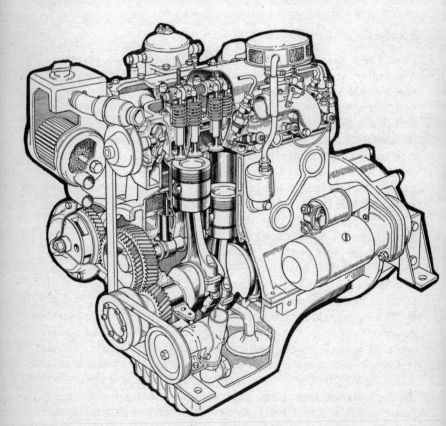

Fig. 55 Mercedes-Benz OM 636 42 b.h.p. diesel engine

The smallest of these three is the OM 636 and figure 55 shows a cut-away drawing of this engine. This 4 cylinder vertical four-stroke diesel engine has a compression ratio of 19 to 1. Fuel consumption is extremely moderate, being 2 gallons per hour maximum speed, and $\frac{3}{4}$ to $1\frac{1}{2}$ gallons per hour normal cruising speeds. Standard electrical equipment includes a Bosch 12 volt 400 watt alternator with regulator and Bosch 1·8 h.p. positive engagement starter motor. The chart shown in figure 56 shows ratings to DIN standard 6270. This

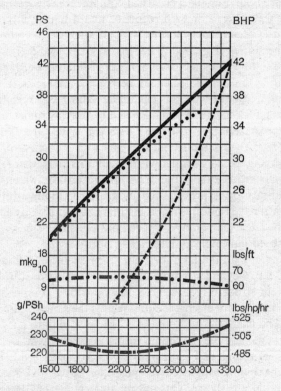

RATINGS TO DIN STANDARD 6270

●●●● = Continuous rating 36 PS at 3,000 rpm.
▬▬▬ = Intermittent rating 42 PS at 3,300 rpm.
●●▬ = Maximum Torque Curve.
▬●▬● = Specific Fuel Consumption.
▬ ▬ ▬ = Propeller Curve.

Fig. 56 Mercedes-Benz OM 636 – ratings to DIN standard 6270

is a versatile engine and is available with a choice of inboard or hydraulic drive or inboard/outboard. For more information about this and the other engines mentioned, contact Mercedes-Benz (Great Britain) Ltd, Great West Road, Brentford, Middlesex, England.

The next engine, the 80 h.p. OM 314, is a 4 cylinder vertical fresh water-cooled four-stroke direct injection diesel engine, with a compression ratio of 17 to 1. Fuel consumption at maximum speed is 4 gallons per hour and at normal cruising range, from 1 to 2½ gallons per hour. Standard electrical equipment includes a Bosch 12 volt 420 watt alternator with regulator and 4 h.p. positive engagement starter motor. As is normal with all Mercedes diesels, the long life of the starter ring, always subject to wear in diesel engines, is ensured by the starter motor pinion gear being fully engaged in the ring gear by an electric solenoid before the motor starts to turn. Standard equipment with this engine includes heat exchanger cooling, alternator, engine oil change pump, full instrumentation and Borg Warner series 71 gear-box. You can have direct drive or a choice of 1·523 to 1 reduction, or 1·909 to 1 reduction, or 2·1 to 1 reduction, or 2·57 to 1 reduction or 2·909 to 1 reduction – all being counter-clockwise, except the 1·909 to 1 gear-box, which is clockwise. Lubrication is pressure-fed by gear-type pump with replaceable element-type oil filter. The instrumentation already mentioned includes water temperature gauge, oil pressure gauge, ammeter, engine speed indicator, all electrically operated.

Coming now to the largest of our three engines we find the OM 352, 125 h.p. 6 cylinder marine diesel. This is a vertical fresh water-cooled four-stroke direct injection engine with a compression ratio of 17 to 1. Standard electrical equipment is the same as already mentioned. The chart shown in figure 57 shows rating to DIN standard 6720. Notice here the maximum rating at 2,800 r.p.m. is 125 b.h.p. Continuous rating at 2,600 r.p.m. is 105 b.h.p. As with the other graph, maximum torque curve, propeller curve and specific fuel consumption are shown. Once again this engine has Borg Warner oil-operated reverse gear-box with a variety of optional ratios. With this engine (and with the others) the water jacketed exhaust manifold incorporated in the fresh water system is standard equipment. The water jacket around the manifold reduces fire risk and noise and also high temperature in the engine compartment. To sum up,

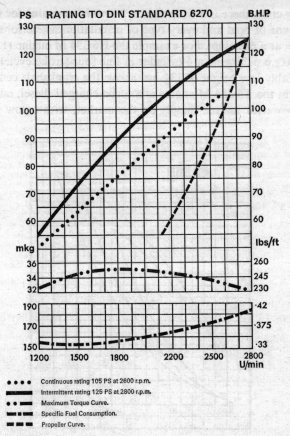

PS   RATING TO DIN STANDARD 6270   B.H.P.

- •••• Continuous rating 105 PS at 2600 r.p.m.
- ▬▬▬ Intermittent rating 125 PS at 2800 r.p.m.
- •▬• Maximum Torque Curve.
- ▬•▬ Specific Fuel Consumption.
- ▬ ▬ ▬ Propeller Curve.

Fig. 57 Mercedes-Benz OM 352 125 b.h.p. – ratings to DIN standard 6270

these compact, versatile marine engines are what one has been led to expect from this famous firm.

Perkins

Another well-known firm, this time from Peterborough, England, makes a fine range of diesel engines. From 33 s.h.p. at 2,000 r.p.m. known as the P3·152 M (a 3 cylinder in line four-stroke) to engines like the T6.354 M 175 s.h.p. a 6 cylinder in line four-stroke for fast planing craft, there is a wide choice. There is an engine for virtually every type of boat and every type of installation where for example space is at a premium. For example the H6·354 M engine (115 s.h.p. at 2,800 r.p.m. engine a 6 cylinder in line four-stroke cycle) has the remarkably low height of 13⅝ ins. above the crankshaft centre line. Or again the T6·354 M engine is a turbo-charged diesel, one of the most powerful marine diesels on the market, with a low weight/

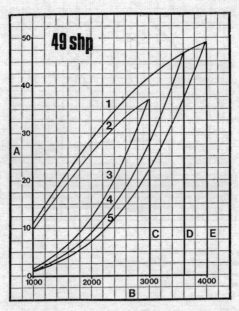

Fig. 58 Perkins 4·108 'lowline' engine – power curves

power ratio particularly suitable for high speed planing craft and off-shore powerboats. But one could continue almost endlessly with the Perkins range, so let us take three typical engines and have a look at them.

The three I have chosen are the 49 s.h.p. 4·108 M known as the lowline; the 115 s.h.p. 6·354 M diesel engine and the T 6·354 M 175 s.h.p. engine for fast planing craft, in that order. Figure 58 shows the power curve of the first type. Looking at the latter first, the key is as follows: (1) is the mean intermittent high speed output from direct drive gear-box output flange. (2) is the mean continuous output from direct drive gear-box output flange. (3), (4) and (5) are typical propeller law curves; (a) the vertical range on the graph is power in s.h.p. and (b) the horizontal axis is engine speed in revs per minute; (c) maximum continuous rated speed (and can be seen as 3,000 r.p.m.); (d) 3,600 r.p.m. and (e) maximum speed for approved high speed pleasure craft. This is a four-in-line vertical

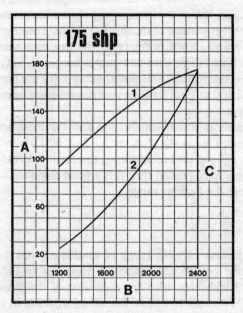

Fig. 59 Perkins T6.354 M diesel – power curves

four-stroke engine. The cooling system is heat exchanger fresh water or direct sea water. The gear-box is Thames Marine TM P 12000 mark 2, either direct drive or 2 to 1 reduction, and either rotation. The electrical equipment has a 12 volt system.

The second type of engine, the 6·354 M, is suitable for either single or twin installations in work-boats, displacement pleasure vessels or small patrol boats. It is a 6 cylinder vertical marine diesel four-stroke. Heat exchanger cooling system is by belt driven centrifugal pump; sea water circulation is by positive drive self-priming pump. Electrical equipment is 24 volt, with 31 amp alternator and regulator. There are separate sea water circulated coolers for gear-box and engine oil cooling. The gear-box is fully hydraulic with independent oil supply, eitheir Borg Warner 72 C R or self-changing MRM 350. There are various reduction gear ratios. The fuel injection is by rotary distributor type fuel pump with hydraulic governor. Maximum output of this engine to DIN standard 6270 is 94 ps at 2,400 r.p.m. rating A and 113 ps at 2,800 r.p.m. rating B.

Our third and last of the Perkins engines we are considering here, is the one for fast planing craft, the T 6·354 M. Power curve may be seen in the graph shown in figure 59 the key here being (1) mean output from direct drive gear-box output flange; (2) is typical power law curve; (a) the vertical axis power (s.h.p.); (b) the horizontal axis engine speed (r.p.m.); (c) indicates maximum rated speed, that is to say 2,400 r.p.m.

This is direct injection combustion and the induction system is turbo-charged. This is the Perkins for fast offshore racing power-boats where 100 per cent reliability is essential. International events in recent years have proved this. It is a good engine to conclude our selection from the Perkins range.

Mercruiser

Mercruiser have a very big range of marine engines, both inboard and sterndrive or inboard/outboard. Responsible for Mercruiser engines are Kiekhaefer, who are a division of the Brunswick Corporation of Wisconsin in U.S.A. For all information in Britain go to South Western Marine Factors Limited, 43 Pottery Road, Parkstone, Dorset. In the inboard engines the basic range is from 188 horse-power to 355. In the inboard/outboard or sterndrive range you start at 90 working up to 325 h.p. We have been looking at a number of diesel marine engines; the Mercruiser range are petrol driven. In fact Mercruiser claim with a good deal of authority to be the world's largest builders of four-cycle marine petrol engines. The inboard engine range is basically as follows: 188 h.p. 8 cylinder V8; 215 h.p. 8 cylinder V8; 255, 325 and 355 h.p. all of them 8 cylinder V8. Basically the compression ratio is 8·5 to 1. For the power they pack they are neat and compact engines, the smallest being $43\frac{1}{2}$ ins.

long, 30 ins. wide, 19 ins. high and $8\frac{7}{8}$ ins. depth. The largest engine, the 355 h.p., is slightly larger, equivalent dimensions being $45\frac{3}{4}$ ins., 33 ins., 22 ins., and depth 9 ins. These engines are all fresh water-cooled.

The sterndrive range is somewhat wider, the horsepowers being as follows: 90, 120, 140, 165, 188, 215, 235 and the big 325 h.p. The 90, 120 and 140 are 4 cylinder in-line. The 165 is 6 cylinder and the remaining engines are 8 cylinder V8. As with the inboard engines, electrics are 12 volt marine alternator, 42 amp in the big engines and 22 amp flywheel alternator for the 90 h.p. engine. All of them run on any regular brand of petrol.

Here, it is the sterndrives on which I am concentrating. It was back in 1962 that Mercury produced their first Mercruiser stern-drive. Since then the size and scope of the successful range they have built up speaks for itself. Let us have a look at two of them. In figure 60 is a scale drawing of the 120. This drawing gives an excellent idea of the compactness of this engine, which is no midget, sitting snugly just ahead of the transom. Let us have a look at the specification then of the 120. 4 cylinder in-line valve in head 153 cu. ins. 2,509 cc, 8·5 to 1 compression ratio. Five main bearings, hydraulic valve lifters and two barrel carburettors. Recommended revolutions are 3,900 to 4,300 r.p.m. There is dual water pump system and three point rubber engine mounts. The sterndrive itself contains power trim mechanical shift, water pump and pick-up and jet-prop exhaust. Propeller diameter is 16 ins. maximum and gear ratio is 2 to 1. Standard equipment contains full instrument panel with oil pressure, water temperature gauge, ammeter, power trim indicator, tachometer. In addition to this there is a fair range of optional accessories.

In figure 61 we have what may be termed a larger sister. The 165 is 6 cylinder in-line valve in head 250 cu. ins. 4,100 cc. Compression ratio is again 8·5 to 1 but there are seven main bearings. Recommended r.p.m. is the same as for the 120. In the sterndrive, while the maximum prop diameter is the same as for the 120, that is to say 16 ins., gear ratio is 1·68 to 1. Notice the power trim arm on the sterndrive. With this you can adjust the angle of the drive and propeller for the best performance as load and water conditions vary.

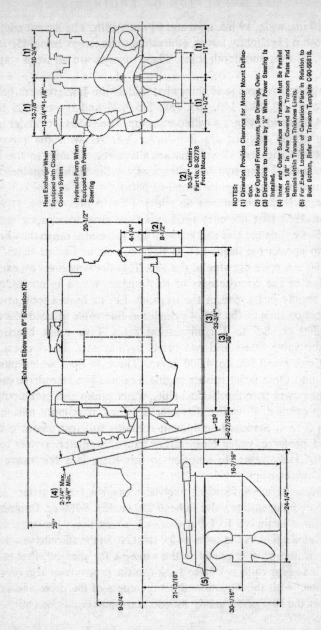

NOTES:

(1) Dimension Provides Clearance for Motor Mount Deflection.

(2) For Optional Front Mounts, See Drawings, Over.

(3) Dimensions to Increase by ½" When Power Steering Is Installed.

(4) Inner and Outer Surfaces of Transom Must Be Parallel within ⅛" in Area Covered by Transom Plates and Remain within Transom Thickness Limits.

(5) For Exact Location of Cavitation Plate in Relation to Boat Bottom, Refer to Transom Template C90-55818.

Heat Exchanger When Equipped with Closed Cooling System

Hydraulic Pump When Equipped with Power Steering

Exhaust Elbow with 6" Extension Kit

10-3/4" Centers
Part No. B-32778
Front Mount

Fig. 60 Mercruiser 120 – stern-drive

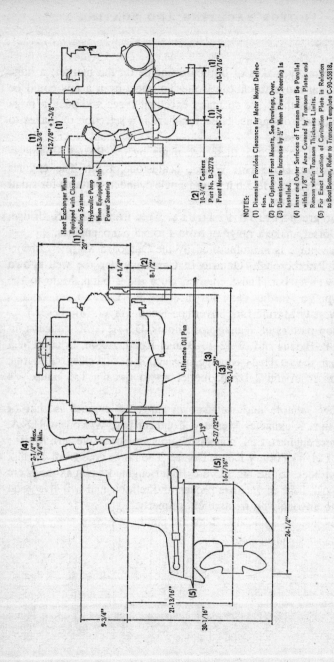

NOTES:

(1) Dimension Provides Clearance for Motor Mount Deflection.

(2) For Optional Front Mounts, See Drawings, Over.

(3) Dimensions to Increase by ½" When Power Steering Is Installed.

(4) Inner and Outer Surfaces of Transom Must Be Parallel within 1/8" in Area Covered by Transom Plates and Remain within Transom Thickness Limits.

(5) For Exact Location of Cavitation Plate in Relation to Boat Bottom, Refer to Transom Template C-90-55818.

Fig. 61 Mercruiser 165 – stern-drive

Outboard Engines

There are many makes of outboard engine on the market; a huge international range to choose from. To select even a few could be misleading, as there are so many excellent types and such a large variety of sizes of engine. However, here is a selection of makes to give you some idea.

BRITISH ANZANI: these are made by the Boxley Engineering Company, Dove Hill Works, Maidstone, Kent. The engines are quite small, of 3 to 5 b.h.p. and single cylinder. Suitable for small boats, dinghies etc.

Similar are BRITISH SEAGULL. This firm at Fleets Bridge, Poole, Dorset, make a range of from 1 to 5·5 b.h.p. engines.

A large range is manufactured by the Outboard Marine Corporation of Peterborough, Ontario in Canada under the well-known name EVINRUDE. These engines, from the 2 b.h.p. Mate to the 200 b.h.p. V6 Starflite cater for most needs. (U.K. concessionaires are University Marine Ltd, Silverdale Road, Hayes, Middlesex.)

Johnson motors of Wankegan, Illinois, U.S.A. (U.K. concessionaires E. P. Barrus Ltd of 12–16 Brunel Road, Acton, London W.3 provide, in the JOHNSON range, a selection of first class outboards. They run from the 2 b.h.p. model up to the big 135 b.h.p. V4 engine.

Another reliable and well-known range of engines is that of MERCURY. Kiekhaefer Mercury, Fond du Lac, Wisconsin, U.S.A. make these engines. U.K. concessionaires are South Western Marine Factors Ltd, 43 Pottery Road, Dorset. The range goes from 4 b.h.p. single cylinder, to the big 135 6 cylinder engine known as the Merc 1350 E. All these engines are proven and reliable and will give good service to anyone who treats them properly.

This is just a sample list, there are plenty of others.

CHAPTER 5

Examining, Buying and
Where to Keep a Boat

WE have now had a look on paper at a lot of different boats. Let us now consider the question of how we set about acquiring one. We can buy a new boat from stock. We can commission a boat to be built to a standard design, or we can commission a naval architect to design a boat for us. We can buy a second-hand boat, of which there are usually plenty advertised in the yachting papers. We can acquire a second-hand work-boat, a fishing boat say, and have her converted or convert her ourselves. We can build our own boat. Many firms supply kits of parts; you can buy the hull partly completed and finish the job yourself or you can do the whole thing. Such kits range from runabouts to cruisers. Finally, if perhaps we do not wish to commit ourselves too much to begin with, we can charter a boat for a period.

Survey of second-hand boats

There is nothing against buying a second-hand boat, provided that she has been well built to a good design and well looked after by her previous owner or owners. The way to find this out is to employ the services of a surveyor. Never think that you know enough to examine a boat for yourself. It always pays to employ a qualified professional surveyor.

A survey if it is a good one, takes time. If the yacht is lying at moorings, she will have to be slipped so that the bottom may be inspected. This will cost money and it will be you who foots the bill. You will also pay the surveyor's fee and his travelling expenses. Even so, it will be well worth your while. Since very few second-hand boats are in perfect order, the surveyor almost certainly will find faults which may help to reduce the price, and even if the vessel does prove to be 100 per cent, you then have the satisfaction of

149

being told so by a professional which will give you complete confidence in the boat you have bought.

It goes without saying that if you send your surveyor to boat after boat you can very quickly run up a sizeable bill. Before you commission a surveyor therefore, it is advisable to be fairly certain that the boat you are sending him to look at will stand a reasonable chance of passing survey. If you are buying through a yacht broker it is unlikely that the latter will offer to you a boat which has little chance of passing survey. If you, on the other hand, have selected a boat from the advertisement pages in one of the yachting periodicals, such advertisements give little idea of the condition of the vessel. The best method here is to take with you a knowledgeable and experienced friend who can at least tell you whether it is worth employing a professional surveyor for the boat you have chosen.

It will be obvious that the larger the vessel under consideration the more complicated this matter becomes. If you have joined a club and are buying a second-hand twin-screw diesel yacht described as 'seaworthy and in sound condition' then you should make every endeavour when going up to look at that boat, to make sure that you take with you a friend who knows what to look for.

So what should we look for? It depends of course whether our prospective purchase is built in wood, in steel, in G.R.P. or whatever. If built of wood the main things to look for are signs of rot. Take with you a light hammer and make frequent taps with it. This may sound like a footling exercise but it is not, since timber gives a ringing sort of sound if it is in good condition. If there is rot there, the sound is lifeless. Take with you also a spike or bradawl and push it into any suspected parts to test for soft wood.

There are certain parts of a boat which are susceptible to rot. This is largely a matter of common sense; anywhere where water collects, or anywhere where air cannot pass freely, for example. But with wooden boats we must keep our eyes out for worm in addition to looking for rot. Worms reveal themselves by tiny little holes. There are two principal types of worm liable to be met with in our British waters, the teredo and the gribble. The teredo bores straight into the planking and then after a short journey turns at right angles and continues boring along with the grain of the wood. The gribble bores in for one or two centimetres and then comes back to the surface and chooses another spot. The gribble is therefore easier to detect. In point of fact only the teredo is a worm, the gribble resembling more a louse.

If the boat we are looking at happens to be built of G.R.P. we must, in our examination, look carefully for any evidence of damage or distortion. We look for discolouration or small cracks or stains or wet patches not easily explained. By distortion I mean if there is a sudden change in the shape or size of one or perhaps more girders, girders likely to come under stress. Look out also for scratches and chafing. These may be found around fairleads and cleats and around and along the gunwhale.

If you have a knowledgeable friend who knows of a good surveyor you are in luck but if he doesn't or you are not fortunate enough to have such a friend, you can go to the Yacht Brokers, Designers and Surveyors Association or Ship and Boatbuilders Federation for these people can supply you with a list of qualified surveyors from which you can choose one who lives in the locality of your chosen boat since, in this way you will have less travelling expenses to pay. Lloyd's Register of Yachts can also help you as there are quite a number of qualified surveyors who do work for Lloyd's.

Once your surveyor has made his report then you or your yacht broker can approach the owner of the vessel and if the surveyor has unearthed some faults, suggest that the owner meets you either by reducing the price or having the faults put right.

If you have no knowledgeable friend to help you make the preliminary inspection of your boat and if you doubt your own ability to do this, it is perfectly possible to ask the surveyor to do it for a reduced fee. Most surveyors will do this and will tell you whether it is worth proceeding with a full survey.

Buying a boat out of income

When it comes to buying a boat remember that nowadays you can buy out of income. You can make use of hire-purchase, credit sale or marine mortgage. There are quite a number of finance houses who make these facilities available. In the case of hire-purchase, the finance house is the owner of the boat until you have paid the last instalment. With credit sale, you own the boat once you have made the first payment and the finance house has agreed the transaction. There are some advantages of a credit sale agreement with tax relief, enabling you to buy the boat and repay only the capital sum which has been advanced, plus the net charges after first deducting tax at the standard rate. If your relations with your bank manager are good, it is no bad idea to consult him.

With a marine mortgage you have the advantage of favourable interest rates and the fact that repayment of capital and interest can be extended up to periods of five years and the interest you pay qualifies for tax relief. This information happens to be true at the time of writing but unfortunately this is no guarantee that it may not be changed in the future. Incidentally a marine mortgage can only be written for a registered vessel.

Certificate of registry

A yacht's certificate of registry sets out her name and registered number and certain particulars if she is a registered vessel and bears somewhere upon her the official number as well as her registered tonnage. All these details will be noted in her certificate, which is her document of identity. On this certificate will be the name of her present, and also her previous, owner. If you lose this certificate, the Registrar of Shipping will give you a provisional one as also will your nearest consul. Registration is not compulsory under 15 tons gross, so that for many of the boats discussed in this book, registration is not compulsory. If you are going to do much foreign cruising however, it is useful.

Where to keep the boat

We now come to the question of where, having bought our boat, we are going to keep her. This problem obviously increases with size.

A displacement twin-screw diesel yacht is going to have to live afloat. A relatively light runabout can live afloat or on shore. The diesel yacht will have to take herself under her own steam wherever she wishes to go by water. The runabout may be transported on a trailer behind your car and I will have a word or two to say about this very important business of trailing later in this chapter. For the larger boats then we need some sort of harbour or mooring.

Harbours today are getting very crowded. This problem has to some extent been solved (though there are those who say it has been aggravated) by the building of what are known as marinas. A marina is an area of water almost enclosed apart from one or more entry/exit channels. Within are quays or pontoons parallel with each other to which vessels may lie alongside or stern to quay. Yachts in a marina remain afloat at all stages of the tide. An advantage of a marina is that in most of them all facilities are available – chandlery, fresh water, electricity, fuel, car parking space, showers, lavatories and in the more recherché marinas, telephone connections and T V!

All this of course costs money but one must remember that in a marina a vessel can lay up afloat during the winter using a winter cover over a framework on deck, which saves money by removing the necessity to find space ashore for the winter. But the vessel will have to be slipped in order to be painted and fitted-out, so perhaps the saving is not as big as it might seem. However, electricity and water being handy, it is much easier for the owner to do more of his own fitting-out and this is undoubtedly an advantage.

Some marinas are owned by yacht yards, other marinas have adjacent yacht yards. All yachts require a certain amount of fitting-out at the beginning of the season. Once again this is a question related to size. With fibre-glass boats maintenance is greatly simplified. But some fitting-out will always be necessary and there is one vital part of our vessel which will most certainly need attention at the beginning of the season and that is the engine. In this connection it will be clear that proximity to a workshop and one or more good mechanics is a great advantage and here again marinas can be useful.

There are of course many places, estuaries, rivers, where small harbours are found where a mooring can be laid or more probably rented from the local harbourmaster; but as I have indicated, these are getting harder and harder to find. I mentioned earlier the advantage of the belonging to a club and in this question of moorings a club will often prove its worth. Not that many clubs themselves own extensive moorings although most of them will own a few. It is rather that the secretary will be able to put you in touch with whatever mooring facilities there are in the area.

Generally speaking mooring charges, whether in a marina or not, are based on overall length of the vessel and in the case of marina berths where yachts lie side to side, on the maximum beam as well. The reason for this will be obvious. If there is no marina in your locality the local harbourmaster will probably be the best bet.

Offshore racing craft will have the same problems basically speaking as the cruising type of yacht we have been speaking of. Inland waters or sheltered water racing craft, hydroplanes, runabouts etc., will frequently live, so to speak, near the scene of their activities. In many cases they will be kept in the area of the club who supervises the racing. But many of these boats are trailed all over the country (and abroad) by their owners to take part in races and this brings us to this important subject of trailing.

Trailers

Of course one does not only trail to attend a race meeting. For the runabout owner a trailer can be used greatly to enlarge the scope of his boating. It is thus a very important part of the 'runabout' scene.

The runabout or sports boat trailer must be tough. The difference in weight between a 14 ft sailing dinghy and a 14 ft runabout is considerable. A lot of this comes from the weight of the engine; in other words, get a trailer which is designed and built for the job. A well-designed trailer should have its chocks so shaped as to fit the lines of your boat's hull reasonably closely; the closer the better. For the size of boat we have mentioned, a two-wheel trailer will do, but for boats over 17 ft a four-wheeler will do better. Most boats with inboard engines will require a special trailer because of the projecting propeller. Furthermore it is not possible to launch many inboard engine boats without immersing the trailer and floating them off.

In choosing your trailer consider carefully the loaded weight of the boat. With normal gear plus personal luggage the weight of engine and hull can often be doubled. A formula has been worked out giving 1¼ cwt. total loaded weight to each 100 cc car engine capacity. Trailer tyre pressures should be up to about 50 p.s.i. It is an excellent idea to have a winch for loading. With a winch fitted, one man can do the job. Trailers require flashing turning indicators, rear lamps and stop lights as well as a properly lit number plate. Speed limits vary with countries. In Britain it is 40 m.p.h. Finally, always carry a spare wheel and tyre.

CHAPTER 6

Powerboat Handling

MOTOR-CRUISERS

Propellers

I N Chapter 2 we talked about handed propellers. When viewed from astern a right-handed propeller turns in a clockwise direction when driving the vessel ahead, and a left-handed propeller turns in the opposite direction. We have already discussed pitch earlier in this book, but let us just refresh our memory. Think of the propeller as a wood screw and imagine water to be a solid like wood. When the screw turns or is turned it drives ahead a certain distance in one revolution. The distance is called pitch and the length of it is re-lated to the angle which the propeller blades make with the shaft. Calculating the distance advanced in relation to the pitch, therefore, would be simple were water a solid. But it is not and we get, be-cause it is liquid, a loss of efficiency which is called 'slip'. The vessel is not only driven forward by the movement of the rotating propeller, but a column of water, rotating itself, is forced astern. This column is termed the 'screw-race'.

A turning propeller has another effect upon the hull of a ship due to the fact that its blades are (alternately) in different depths of water. Look at figure 62. In the figure we have a simple two-bladed propeller. It is a right-handed propeller that turns with the clock. The deeper the water, the denser and the lower of the two blades will be in water of more density than the upper blade; it will be pushing against a more solid mass. Because the blades of a propeller turn slightly sideways in order to achieve the screw effect, it follows that a certain degree of sideways pressure is exerted by a revolving propeller as well as backward pressure, as in the case of going ahead.

Look back at the illustration. Remember that the lower propeller is in denser water. As the propeller revolves so the blade which is pushing to the left as we look at it is pushing against more solid mass than the top blade pushing to the right. Because of this difference in density the lower blade will have more effect than the upper, and so the stern of the ship will be pushed to the right and as we are looking from astern our ship would be pushed to starboard. From this we get a rule that with a single right-handed screw the initial thrust is to starboard when the propeller moves ahead.

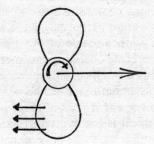

Fig. 62 Propeller transverse-thrust – ahead

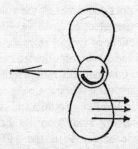

Fig. 63 Propeller transverse-thrust – astern

This transverse-thrust operates when the propeller first begins to revolve; as a boat gathers headway the transverse-thrust becomes less and less until it virtually disappears. Now if the initial thrust of a right-handed propeller going ahead is to move the stern to starboard, it will have the effect of pushing the bow to port and we shall see how important this is as we study ship-handling.

The effect of transverse-thrust is even more marked when going astern and the reason is as follows. To go astern our propeller will be revolving in an anti-clockwise direction. Look at figure 63. The bottom blade will be exerting stronger pressure than the top. The stern is now moved to port and the bows to starboard. There is, however, a difference since the column of water, instead of being moved aft away from the ship (and please remember at the moment we are leaving the rudder out of this discussion) when going astern is driven forwards in the general direction of the bows. That part of the hull ahead of the propeller is commonly known as the 'dead-wood'. The spiral column of water is not only driven forwards but upwards by the very nature of its movement and in doing so it comes up against the starboard side of the dead-wood. So we get the effect that the lower blade operating in denser water, first pushes the stern to port and then continues this movement to port by forcing water against the starboard side of the dead-wood. So with a right-handed screw going astern (that is to say, turning anti-clockwise) the initial movement is for the stern to kick to port and the bows to kick to starboard and, as we have seen, it will be a stronger reaction than when going ahead. Just as the transverse-thrust to starboard when going ahead disappeared, so when going astern, the transverse-thrust to port decreases as the ship gathers sternway.

So far we have seen the effect of a single screw propeller. When we come to look at the effect of twin-screws we will find that simple manoeuvres are simplified and complicated manoeuvres are rendered relatively simple. One can do much more with twin screws. However, there are many vessels with single screw. It is not only right to begin with single screw but readers may be surprised as we progress in this chapter at what can be done in the way of manoeuvring with single screw with the aid of such things as currents, tidal stream, wind and, of course, the rudder; the working of which we must now consider.

Rudder

When a vessel moves ahead with the rudder in the central position, the water flows past on either side of the rudder blade and the ship continues ahead with unaltered course. If the rudder is moved over to starboard for example, pressure will build up on the forward side of the rudder (that is the side which is over to starboard). This will have the effect of pushing the stern to port which in turn will cause the bows to move to starboard. If the vessel were moving astern then the water would press on the after side of the rudder (assuming that the rudder is still over to starboard). This will push the stern to starboard and the bows to port. Notice that in each case it is the stern which is initially moved by the rudder.

Now let us add the power of the propeller. We have already seen how when going ahead, with a single right-handed screw, the stern moves to starboard and the bows to port when the propeller first begins turning. If we now add to this the effect of a rudder put over (this time to port) we have a double influence to move the stern to starboard and the bows to port. We have the initial kick of the right-handed screw and the effect of the water on the fore-side and in this case the port-hand side of the rudder, both of them kicking our stern to starboard. Again we have already seen how from the propeller flows a spiral column of water. When the propeller starts turning, this column of water is projected against the fore-side of the rudder. If the rudder is put over while the engine is not in gear and the vessel has no way on, then as soon as the gear is engaged, a column of water is forced against the rudder's fore-side and the stern will kick in the opposite direction. Knowing therefore that with our right-handed screw, our stern will kick to starboard as soon as the propeller begins to revolve, if we put the rudder over to port, the kick will be greatly increased. This knowledge is later going to be useful.

Supposing however, that we wish to go astern from being stationary. Here the effect is somewhat different, although the principle involved is the same. With our right-handed screw going astern, our stern will have an initial kick to port as we have already seen. If the vessel were already travelling astern and we put the rudder over to starboard, the water would build pressure on the after-side of that rudder and force the stern to starboard. Consequently we can increase the effect of the initial kick going astern by putting our rudder over to starboard; there is however this difference.

As we have seen already, once the initial kick in either direction has been made, this effect diminishes fairly rapidly. Now the only force acting on the rudder is the water flowing on to it and past it as the ship moves astern. The propeller being located in a position forward of the rudder, will when going astern be sending its column of water past the ship's sides and away from the rudder. In consequence when going astern, once the initial kick has been felt, a rudder has very much less effect upon a ship's movement than when going ahead.

When a boat is going astern her pivoting point is right aft. If the engine is stopped and the rudder held amidships, the stern will go into the wind. The rest of the hull will blow away from the wind. This brings us to another factor which determines the movements of a ship, the wind.

Effect of the wind

It may perhaps seem strange in a book dealing with motor craft to talk about the effect of wind; nevertheless there are times when it has to be taken very much into consideration. I am not talking about the technique of handling a motor vessel in conditions when the wind is rising rapidly and beginning to blow very strongly, but when manoeuvring perhaps in either restricted or very crowded waters.

To give an example. A vessel may be moving ahead in a given direction. The gear is disengaged and she loses way. If she is built, as many vessels are, with relatively high bows and with the highest part of her superstructure forward, then her bows will fall away from the wind and if, for example, you are endeavouring to pick up a mooring buoy, the probability is that you will fail to do so! We shall later in this book be dealing with questions of anchoring and picking up mooring buoys in detail and we will learn how to manoeuvre our ship in varying conditions. The only point I am making at the moment is that had we appreciated the effect of the wind upon our movements we would have been able to have compensated by use of the rudder when picking up that buoy and achieved our objective without any trouble. Let us have a look for a moment at some examples of the sort of effect a strong wind can have on a manoeuvring vessel and what we can do about it.

Supposing that instead of going ahead as in the last example we are going astern. We know that the propeller will be kicking the stern to port. Let us also suppose that we have a fairly strong wind blowing on the port-hand side and that our vessel has high bows and that most of her upper-works are forward of the mid-ship point.

In this case the high bows and the upper-works will act like a sailing yacht with a jib set and the bows will be blown over to starboard. Here we have the propeller kicking the stern to port and the bows to starboard and the wind helping to increase this tendency. If therefore it was our intention that the stern should go to starboard and we had put the rudder over to starboard, we would find it difficult to bring this about. The wind and the screw, having the same effect, would almost certainly overpower the rudder. If on the other hand, we wanted the stern to go to port and the bows to starboard when going astern and we had the same conditions of wind, then nothing could be easier.

These extremely simple illustrations are two good examples of how the wind can act on the hull of a vessel in such a way that when combined with propeller thrust renders the rudder almost useless; and how under other conditions, it can greatly increase the rudder's effect. It is of course the principle, rather than these illustrations, that I would like the reader to bear in mind.

I have selected these two examples of a ship going astern intentionally since when going ahead the problem of handling is greatly simplified. It is when manoeuvring in crowded or cramped conditions that the knowledge of how your ship will behave when going astern and particularly if a wind is blowing becomes of vital importance.

180° turn in narrow river

Let us take this business of manoeuvring our boat a little further. For the purposes of this illustration we have a single right-handed propeller. You will remember that when going astern the vessel's stern will kick to port. We are in a river and we wish to execute a 180° turn and go back the way we have come. The river is so narrow that we cannot turn in a semi-circle; in fact there is only just room to turn our ship round in her own length, so what are we going to do?

Assuming that the boat is now stopped we put the engine ahead and the rudder hard a-starboard. This kicks the stern to port as our boat begins to move ahead. As soon as this happens, we put our engine astern but leave the rudder still hard a-starboard. The thrust of the propeller will kick the stern to port. As the ship begins to move astern we put the engine ahead again; the stern continues to go to port. We repeat this alternatively, ahead and astern, and in doing so we can turn our boat completely round on her pivoting point. It may sound complicated at first but if you think about it you will realize that we are merely using what we have learnt about the effect of propeller and rudder.

It must be emphasized that in the manoeuvre just described the ship must not be allowed to make any way through the water. As long as the vessel makes no sternway you may leave the rudder to starboard the whole time. If the boat were allowed to get way on astern, the transverse-thrust of the propeller would be nullified by the rudder being over to starboard and would result in the stern moving back to starboard, whereas what you want is for the transverse-thrust of the propeller to move it to port. It is quite often difficult to tell whether a ship is actually making way through the water when the surface of the water itself is moving as the result of wind. If therefore you can select two objects reasonably far apart on shore which can be brought into line, then, provided that they remain in line the ship is not moving and has no way upon her. This is an early example of a navigational device known as a 'transit' which we shall be discussing in a later chapter. For this instance any two easily observable fixed objects will do.

Turning vessel in her own length

It is not always easy to turn a vessel in her own length. It depends largely on two factors; the shape of the underwater body and the size of the propeller. Add to this an awkward cross-wind blowing upon high bows and forward superstructure and the manoeuvre can become virtually impossible. In such a case we can compromise by turning the ship, not in her own length, but in a relatively small area of water and this time we allow her to move astern without being checked.

We are still talking about a single right-handed screw vessel. Look at figure 64. We put the engine ahead and the rudder hard a-port. This has the effect of kicking the stern to starboard and the ship moves ahead a little, the bows going to port. We now reverse the propeller to go astern and check all movement of the vessel. Look carefully and once the stern has stopped moving to starboard, we put the helm amidships. This is position (2) in the illustration. The vessel will now begin to gather sternway and as soon as this happens we put the rudder to starboard. The stern will now begin to go to starboard (and the bow to port) as the rudder nullifies and over-whelms the transverse-thrust of the propeller. The amount which

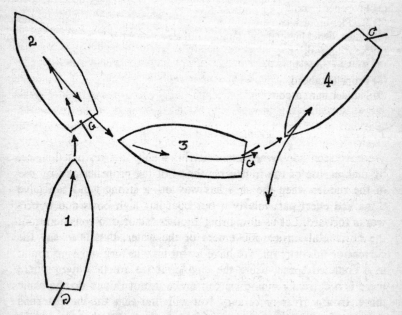

Fig. 64 Boat turning in her own length

the boat now goes astern will depend on the amount of sea room you have available. When this room has been exhausted for what-ever reason – river bank, moored craft, etc. – put the gear in the ahead position and the rudder amidships. The moment that you do this, that is to say, the moment the propeller begins turning right-handed, put the rudder hard a-port. This will give the stern a kick to starboard and the bows will move to port as may be seen in position (4) of the illustration. Each of the separate manoeuvres must be carried out exactly and in the order mentioned or the evolution will not work. The four stages of the evolution described can of course be repeated until the vessel is pointing in the direction which is desired. Before carrying it out it is as well to have the sequence firmly in your mind. You can think of it in abbreviated form as follows:

(1) Rudder hard a-port, propeller ahead
(2) Propeller neutral
(3) Propeller astern
(4) Rudder amidships
(5) When vessel has stern-way move rudder to starboard
(6) Neutral position
(7) Rudder amidships
(8) Propeller ahead
(9) Rudder hard a-port.

Turning, using the current

We have seen how, when manoeuvring a ship in a restricted space, by making use of the transverse-thrust of the propeller and by use of the rudder when the ship has way on, a strong wind can have a marked effect particularly if our boat has high bows and upper-works forward. Let us now bring another factor into consideration; the horizontal surface movement of the water, that is to say the current or tidal stream. We have learnt how to turn our ship round in a confined space, using the engine. If we are in waters where there is a current running we can make use of this to do the same thing. In any river or estuary you will find that the current runs strongest in the centre and relatively weaker near the two banks. This is of course a generalization and much depends upon geographical conditions. Look at figure 65 which shows our boat on one side of a river with a current running strongly down the centre. Let us assume that we wish to turn to starboard. Once again we have a boat with right-handed screw. If we put the engine astern this will kick the stern to port and the bow to starboard, which is precisely what we want. By using the initial kick of the propeller when putting the engine astern combined with the effect of the current on the bow, remembering that the current on the bow being in the centre of the river will be running much more strongly than the current at the

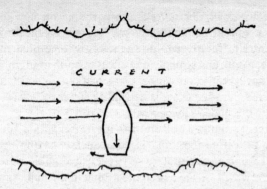

Fig. 65 Turning in a narrow river using the current (1)

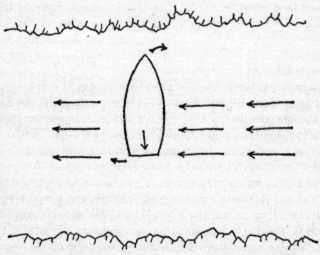

Fig. 66 Turning in a narrow river using the current (2)

side of the river where the stern is, we can turn our ship in a very small space.

Supposing however that the tide or current were moving in the other direction. Look at figure 66. Here we have the same river and the same boat and we want to turn to starboard. Notice that this time we have moved our boat over to the other bank – this is in order to get the strong current on our stern pushing it to port. Once again, a touch astern will kick our stern to port and our bow to starboard and under normal circumstances we can rely on the strong current in the centre of the river to do the rest. In some tidal rivers where the tidal stream runs strongly, the effect upon the hull in making the turn we have been discussing is very marked. It must however be remembered that this effect is dependent upon the shape of the hull or at least the underwater body.

A moment's thought will show that a vessel with a cut away bow and very little fore-foot, and in consequence having little grip on the water forward, will not be nearly so susceptible to the effect of the current which we have been describing in the first example where the current on the bow was used to turn the boat to starboard. On the other hand, a vessel with little grip on the water forward and most of its draft aft would be particularly susceptible to the turning effect in the second example, where it is the effect of the current on the stern which helps to turn the ship. For the average motor-cruiser with a reasonably long keel the manoeuvres as described are perfectly feasible.

A person in charge of a ship must be a seaman as well as a helmsman. In crowded anchorages and restricted waters it is not enough just to open the throttle and turn the wheel this way or that; the effect of the natural phenomena of current and wind must be taken into consideration as also must the knowledge of the habits and capabilities of one's own ship. For example, suppose that you had a boat which was moderately cut away and drew not very much forward and had its maximum draft well aft; and suppose that we were situated as in the first example; and let us also suppose that in addition to the tide running on our port bow we have a strong wind blowing against the tide in the opposite direction. Now here we have a problem. Because of her shape the boat has little grip on the water forward and therefore the effect of the stronger mid-stream current will be less. On the other hand our boat has high bows and most of her upper-works are forward so she is susceptible to wind effect. In such a case it will be obvious that it will be very difficult and maybe impossible to turn our boat to starboard as in the first example, and another solution will have to be found. Once however the principle of using the screw and rudder and natural phenomena has been grasped, the manoeuvring of a small ship becomes not only a relatively simple matter but because of the thought and skill involved, a matter of considerable satisfaction and pleasure.

But it may be that we are in some such position as has been described and perhaps are not achieving our manoeuvre with the facility we would have liked when we see another craft further up river performing a smart turn in her own length under identical conditions without any trouble at all and with great rapidity. Perhaps we are envious; we shouldn't be, but perhaps we are. It may be that the other yacht owner has vast experience allied to a magic touch on the wheel; but it is far more likely that he has a vessel with twin screws!

It will not need much imagination to see that if you have the

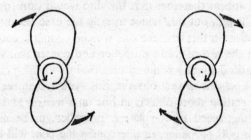

Fig. 67 Twin (handed) screws

port-hand screw going ahead and the starboard-hand screw going astern that the boat will turn round to starboard like a humming top. But in fact it is not quite as simple as that. Manoeuvring with twin screws is easier in some respects because of the greater control you have over the ship's movements, but because of the rapidity with which things can happen and because of the very fact that you have two screws to think about instead of one, in other respects it can be harder. Let us examine the difference between single and twin screws as they affect the boat's movement more closely.

Look now at figure 67. Here we have a boat with twin screws. Notice that the starboard screw is right-handed and the port-hand screw is left-handed. This is the normal arrangement; outward-turning screws – in other words the top blades of the propellers move outwards from the centre when the vessel is moving ahead.

Inward-turning screws are to be found certainly but it is generally conceded that outward-turning screws are easier to manoeuvre with.

Let us assume that we put our port engine slow ahead (with twin screws we have twin engines). At the same time we put the starboard engine to slow astern. Now what is happening? The port-hand propeller which is going ahead, being a left-handed screw, will be turning in an anti-clockwise direction. The lower blade, in the denser water, will be kicking the stern to port. The starboard propeller we have put astern and this, normally a right-handed propeller turning clockwise, will be turning anti-clockwise the same as the port propeller and it too will be kicking the stern to port. So it is easy to see that we have a double transverse-thrust.

It would appear therefore that the ship would turn round exactly in her own length but this is not usually the case because the port-hand propeller (in this case the one which is going ahead) has more power than the astern-going propeller and consequently the vessel will move ahead slightly while turning and the turning circle will be increased. You can in fact observe this (you remember before we did this by getting shore objects in line on a transit) and we can, by increasing the speed of the astern propeller, make negative the effect of the port propeller. In due course the boat will begin to go astern but once again you can check this by reducing the speed of the astern propeller.

It is perfectly simple to manoeuvre in this way and to turn the ship round in a very small space indeed. When turning in a tiny circle like this the rudder has virtually no effect and should be left amidships out of harm's way.

In the example I have given, we turn to starboard but it is equally simple to turn to port by putting the starboard engine slow-ahead and the port engine slow-astern and then varying the speed of the port engine in the manner already discussed. Notice that in this second example it is the speed of the port engine which is varied and in the first example it was the speed of the starboard engine which was varied while the port engine was maintained at a fixed speed. It is the astern-going screw which is varied in each case. The reason for this is that it is much simpler to keep one engine at a constant speed while you manoeuvre with the other. If you try playing about with both engines you are likely to find that you lose balance, shoot ahead too fast, start going astern too fast, become confused; a 'nonsense' is well on the way to being made!

Coming to and picking up a mooring

Having learnt something now of the nature of propellers and rudders let us try our hand at some simple manoeuvres. Let us assume that we have a small motor cruiser, say about 22 ft on the water line. Such a vessel may be lying alongside a quay or jetty, she may be lying to a mooring buoy or she may be lying to a buoy forward and stern to a pontoon or quay in the continental fashion. It is possible too that she might be lying to an anchor. The question is, whichever of these positions our vessel is in, how did she get there? Let us take the mooring buoy first.

With a boat of the size which we have described and with single right-handed screw, it is easy enough to get hold of the buoy rope with a boat hook from the fore-deck. A very large yacht would have to send a dinghy away or perhaps lower a man over the ship's side. Let us make our example as simple as possible and assume there is no tidal stream. Let us further assume that we have sufficient room to manoeuvre so that we can approach the buoy into the wind.

We steer a course aiming for the buoy, keeping the buoy slightly on the starboard bow. As we come to the buoy, the engine is put astern. This not only takes way off our ship it kicks the stern to port so that the bows move to starboard. We should now have the buoy just on our port bow and notice that the buoy is on the same side of the ship (the port bow) as the wind. If we had manoeuvred so that the buoy was on the starboard side the wind would tend to blow the bows over on top of the buoy, making it difficult to pick up and possibly, in strong winds, doing damage.

Supposing however, our vessel had a left-handed screw. We approach with the buoy on the port bow because now the bow will fall away to port when we put our engine astern so we finish up with the buoy and the wind on the starboard bow. Obviously with twin screws the manoeuvre is that much easier since we can manoeuvre to port or starboard equally well. It is not very important whether the buoy is finally brought under the port or starboard bow provided of course that, as in the other examples, the buoy is on the weather side of the ship. So far it would seem that there are very few snags in this manoeuvre of securing to a buoy. However we have already seen that quite a number of boats have not only

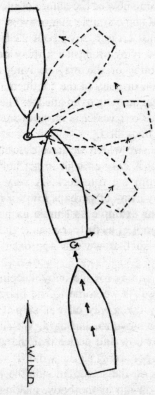

Fig. 68 Picking up a mooring in a boat with high bows and no forefoot

high bows, but they have a lack of draft forward resulting in poor grip on the water, there being nothing to grip with. In such a case, as we come up to the buoy with our single right-handed screw and as we put our engine astern to take the way off, the bow which has moved to starboard as in the first example will be caught by the wind. With her high bows and no grip forward, the vessel will be blown quickly away from the wind and if he is to reach the buoy the bow-man will need a very long boat hook and very long arms and strength to match.

In a case like this it is better to approach the matter as shown in figure 68. Notice that we are now approaching the buoy with the wind astern of us. We control our approach to the buoy by putting the engine (or engines) slow astern. Ideally the ship should stop as the buoy is under the bow. To keep the vessel in position while the buoy is secured, the engine may be kept going astern slowly and on being secured, the engine may be stopped so that the vessel can now swing with the wind and eventually she lies happily down wind. Remember that with a single right-handed screw the stern kicks to port when the engine is put astern. Remember also that in the case of the left-handed screw the stern will kick to starboard.

We shall see later in this book how experience and practice are really the only teachers in ship handling. As you come to know your boat, her capabilities, and how she reacts in different circumstances, you will know how to adapt in each case. For example in the simple sort of manoeuvres we have been describing, you will know how much room to leave between the bow and the buoy to allow for the transverse-thrust kicking the stern to port or starboard, and by the same token, the bows to starboard or port, so that the buoy is brought directly under the bow within easy reach of the bow-man's boat hook.

In tidal waters where the stream is very strong, it may well be that the effect of the tide overpowers the effect of the wind. In such a case it is simpler to approach against the current. Where the current and the wind are say at right-angles to one another the interaction of both may be noted as you approach the buoy. As we have already seen, the more grip your vessel has on the water forward, the simpler your task. With twin-screws, manoeuvring under such conditions once the general principles have been grasped, is simplicity itself. With a single screw the effect of the wind on high bows and the effect of transverse-thrust must be borne in mind as we make our approach.

171

Coming alongside a quay (I)

Let us assume however that we have no mooring buoy to pick up
and it is necessary to come alongside a quay. When cruising about,
this is something which one frequently has to do. Let us assume
that we are still in our right-handed single-screw vessel and that as
before there is no tidal stream. We are entering harbour and the

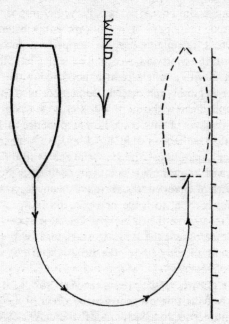

Fig. 69 Coming alongside a quay

wind is aft. Look now at figure 69. This shows at a glance the correct way of dealing with such a situation. We turn the ship 180° so
that her bows are heading into the wind. We approach the quay
slowly. As we come to it the engine is put astern to take off the way.
Remember we have a right-handed screw so the stern kicks to port
(in this instance, away from the quay). To avoid the transverse-
thrust, keeping the stern from the quay we put the rudder to port.
The bows now swing to port and the stern to starboard. We put the

engine astern. The rudder will now cause the stern to come in to the quay, overcoming the transverse-thrust of the propeller. If we had come in with the wind astern and tried to go directly alongside the quay, we would have been in trouble. There would be every chance that the wind, blowing on our stern and as we turned in to port towards the quay blowing more and more on our port quarter, would push our stern to starboard so that our bows would be driven on to the quay.

Of course, if the wind were ahead, the approach direct to the quay is the correct one. The angle of approach will depend upon both the direction and strength of this wind since its effect on our high bows will have to be watched carefully. If the wind is dead ahead or out on the port bow, the correct approach is between 25° and 35°. If the wind were well out on to the starboard bow then the angle of approach must be less – from 5° way to 15° to the quay. If the angle of approach is too broad when the wind is on the starboard bow it will push the bow round on to the quay. We must remember to stop the engine at a point where the ship, still carrying her way, will come to rest with her bows just off the quay. This kind of judgement is a matter of experience and knowing the boat. Some boats carry more way than others. Again, the stronger the wind, the quicker will way come off the ship when the wind is ahead. It will be obvious too that the more of the ship there is out of the water, the more effect will the wind have upon her especially if she is of a design that has relatively little grip on the water.

If you do make an error of judgement and find yourself in the wrong position at the quay, do not panic. It may well be advisable to go round and do it again. On the other hand the better you get to know your boat, the more you can make last minute adjustments and save the situation completely so that everybody will think it was what you meant to do in the first place!

We have so far reckoned without the tidal stream. To the landsman the tide is a seaside manifestation which goes in and out and when he wants to swim it always seems to be several miles out! The seaman knows that the tide, if its workings be properly understood, can often be turned to great advantage. Let us see what difference it makes coming alongside with our single right-handed screw boat. Just as when we were picking up a mooring buoy, the first essential is to find out whether the tide is stronger than the wind, or vice-versa. A simple way to do this is to stop the ship and note in which direction she begins drifting. You can easily tell if she is drifting against the wind and this shows you that the tide is the stronger. But there is another way. Look around you and see if there are any ships lying to a mooring buoy or single anchor. You can see whether they are lying head to wind or head to tide. Where there is not much to choose between wind and tide, sailing yachts with deep keels will tend to be tide-ridden while shallower draft motor vessels will tend to be wind-ridden. In practice, if you were cruising, you should know already what the tide is doing. We will be studying this in another chapter. By 'knowing what it is doing' I mean that you will not only know whether it is flooding or ebbing but you will know the approximate rate (that is to say speed) of the current. If it is a spring tide and running strongly then you will know in advance that the wind will have to be blowing pretty hard in order to overcome it.

But whatever method you select, the object of the exercise is to decide which is the stronger, wind or tide, and head into it just as we did when picking up the mooring buoy. Let us assume that the tide is the stronger. We approach starboard side to the quay, making sure to get our stern in before we put our engine astern. On this occasion it is a spring tide and running quite strongly, so we are careful not to approach at a wide angle because we do not want our bows to be pushed into the quay by the current. If we were coming alongside port-side-to we would not bring our stern in because it would come in of its own.

Mooring warps

Having got our vessel physically alongside a quay we must now secure her there and this we do by means of ropes known as warps. Look at figure 70. Notice that there are six warps securing the ship to the quay. There is a head rope and a stern rope, there are two breast ropes, head and stern, and there are two springs.

Look now at figure 71. This illustrates the positioning of the springs. Notice that one is led from the bow to a bollard on the quay right aft. This is the fore-spring. The second spring (the after-spring) is led from the stern to a bollard right forward. One of the main functions of the springs is to hold the ship into the quay when a strong tide is running in either direction. Let us say that we are lying with the bows to the tide. In this case the tide will be trying to push the whole ship aft; the weight of this will be taken by the after-

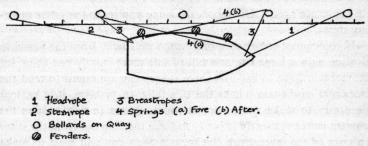

1 Headrope   3 Breastropes
2 Sternrope   4 Springs (a) Fore (b) After.
O Bollards on Quay
⊘ Fenders.

Fig. 70 Correct mooring alongside a quay

spring. The effect of this will be to haul the stern in towards the quay. The tide flowing past the bow increases this tendency and the bow would indeed come right away from the quay were it not for the fore-spring which holds it in. The tide running strongly between the ship and the quay all the time trying to move the ship away from the quay which is held in by the two springs in the manner

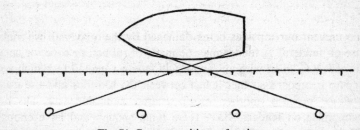

Fig. 71 Correct positions of springs

described. It will be seen that they exercise leverage as opposed to the breast ropes and head ropes which merely keep the boat into the quay. There is one very important point to remember about mooring ropes. In waters where the rise and fall of the tide is very marked, for example, the head and stern ropes should be secured as

175

far ahead and as far aft of the bow and stern as is possible. If this is not done and the yacht is moored at high water, as the tide falls and the vessel sinks, so head rope and stern rope will become increasingly taut and in an extreme case you could return from your dinner ashore to find your vessel suspended by these two ropes and in a condition that no seaman or owner would like to see; let alone an insurance agent! Of course, the same applies to the other mooring ropes.

If you cannot secure mooring warps well away from the vessel in a place with a large rise and fall of tide there is only one thing for it; you will have to see that there is someone on board to tend the lines and ease them out as the tide falls. In practice, it is seldom necessary to make use of breast ropes. Where in tidal waters the current runs sufficiently strongly to force the ship out from the quay in spite of the leverage of the springs, then you will have to make use of breast ropes to keep her in sufficiently for people to get ashore and back on board. If you are in tidal waters with a big rise and fall and you have breast ropes out, then these too will have to be tended as the tide falls and rises again. If you can secure head and stern rope well away from bow and stern and you and your whole crew wish to go ashore, then you may have to dispense with breast ropes and even springs.

Fenders

To prevent our topsides being damaged by the quay wall we make use of 'fenders'. A fender may be made of rubber, or rope, or cork, or of P.V.C. filled with air, and it will have a rope tail by which you secure it inboard so that it lies between the topsides and the quay wall or perhaps another vessel secured alongside you. Do not economize on fenders. Have them large enough and have enough of them. In a boat 30 ft long on deck you should have eight, four a side (the vessel you lie alongside never seems to have enough fenders!). You could doubtless manage with six fenders but if you were going to do much cruising, four will be too few.

These remarks on elementary ship-handling are, as we have seen, made with application to a small motor-cruiser. That is to say a

1. This Shetland Speedwell is suitable for river, canal, estuary, lake and sheltered salt-water cruising.

2. The Shetland 610 cruiser.

3. Largest of the range; this Shetland 2 + 2 in a sea/landscape to dream about in the long winter.

4. A big Mercury outboard driving the sleek Marina 15-ft Blue Fin sportsboat.

5. Another view of a Marina 15-ft Blue Fin turning; this time from the starboard bow.

6. The Marina Sports Gt Mark with plenty of thrust from the big Evinrude outboard.

7. Turning the Marina Blue Fin sportsboat; notice underwater hull form.

8. The Marina Safari 610 – excellent for river, canal and sheltered-water cruising.

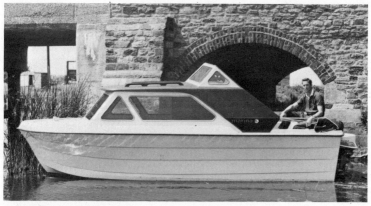

9. The Marina cabin 16 footer – a neat and speedy little motor-cruiser.

10. Avenger 16. This series is no longer in production, but the Avenger 21 is the direct forerunner of the new Tigershark (see text).

11. The clean lines of this Avenger can be seen in this photograph, with the hull at speed almost clear of the water.

12. A fine picture from above of the Avenger 21.

13. Coronet 24-ft cabin cruiser – gull's eye view.

14. Out to the fishing grounds and fast! This Bertram 38-ft Sports Fisherman looks as if she means business.

15. A cabin and toilet compartment aboard Moonraker.

16. Saloon, with dinette/double berth, etc. on board Moonraker. A well-planned interior.

17. (*Left*) Twin, three-bladed screws; notice inclination of the shafts.

18. (*Right*) In dock waiting to be cleaned up. Notice rudder extensions so as to put a rudder blade directly in the screw race.

19. To bring a large yacht like this safely into a small harbour requires considerable experience and skill, especially when, as is the case here, a strong cross wind is blowing.

20. The Le Mans type start of the Paris 6-hr. The boats roar into the first straight led by Scotti.

21. James Beard, winner overall in the Bristol Race, coasts along the straight. His boat is a Cougar, powered by an Evinrude engine. The boat is sponsored by James Latham and is called *Woodmariner*. This boat was later sold to the United States.

small cabin vessel which can do everything from potter to make coastal sea passages. It is a good form of boat to learn the elements of ship-handling and seamanship. Even for those who later branch out into one or other forms of powerboat racing, the early lessons in what is well termed watermanship will never be regretted.

Turning while alongside a quay

Supposing now that we are approaching a quay. The quay is to port of us, and the tide is with us. The wind is negligible. We know now that the right manoeuvre is to turn and steam into the tide and bring ourselves alongside starboard side to the quay.

But it may be that we have good and sufficient reason for wanting to go port side to the quay. This clearly presents certain difficulties. There are two ways of approaching the problem. The safest is to make the 180° turn and come alongside starboard-side-to. Having done this we turn the ship round short in her own berth alongside the quay. We can do this by making use of our springs and there is no need to use engine at all. Provided that the tide or the wind is ahead or astern, there is no problem; if the wind is on to the quay that is another matter and we will discuss it later.

So here we are then, lying starboard-side-to, with the tide (or the wind) ahead of us. We wish to turn the ship round in her berth so that the tide is astern of us. We lead one spring (the after-spring) from the starboard side of the stern and secure it on the quay, well ahead of the bows. The other spring, the fore-spring, is led from the port bow taken outside the vessel along the port side round her stern and secured on the quay in a position well astern of the boat. We now haul on the inboard end of the afterspring, pulling the stern into the quay and at the same time pushing out the bow –

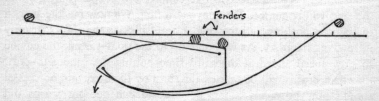

Fig. 72 Turning a boat alongside, using springs

this happens automatically. Remember to have adequate fenders between the ship's side and the quay for any manoeuvre like this. If you are alongside the quay the fenders should be out anyway.

With the bow canted out, the wind blows on the starboard bow and this increases the tendency for the bow to move away from the quay which is what we want. Look now at figure 72. We now haul in both springs. The vessel will turn completely round so that the after-spring becomes her stern rope and the fore-spring becomes her head rope. As the ship swings round, have a member of the crew handy with a loose fender guarding the stern.

Coming alongside a quay (II)

The other way to come alongside our wall port-side-to with the tide astern of us, is to make a stern-board; that is to say, we approach the quay stern first against the tide.

I have mentioned this method second because it is distinctly more difficult to do than turning the ship round in her own berth as we have just learnt. It may be that the reader is wondering why we do not simply approach the quay port-side-to; but a moment's thought will show that if we were to do this with the tide under our stern, the tide, coming on our port quarter, would swing our stern round to starboard pushing our bows directly on to the quay in the very position that we do not want to find ourselves.

So the right thing to do is to make a stern-board. We motor parallel with the quay about a couple of lengths away from it past the spot where we intend to come alongside. Look now at figure 73. We now come astern. Once again we are in a single right-handed screw ship, and so our stern kicks to port. We now put our rudder to starboard because as stern-way comes on the ship, the rudder will become effective overcoming the propeller thrust and the ship will come into the quay stern first. We now put the gear in the neutral position and the rudder amidships as she comes steadily in towards the quay. As we come up to the quay we put the engine to slow speed ahead at the same time putting the rudder to port; the effect of this will be to kick the stern off the quay and our vessel should now be nicely alongside and we can get our warps out quickly and moor. When mooring, make the stern warp fast first.

As I said, this demands a certain amount of knack and experience and unless you are sure of yourself it is easier and safer to come alongside head to tide and then move the ship round in her berth as we have already learnt.

Supposing however, that instead of coming alongside port-side-to, we want to come alongside a quay on our starboard hand, starboard-side-to. As before, the tide is with us and we have a single right-

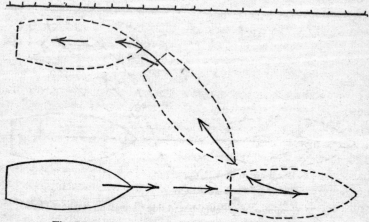

Fig. 73 Making a stern-board to come alongside a quay

handed screw boat. The method we have just described will obviously not do. We have to go about it in a different way, as follows.

Look at figure 74. Once again we motor ahead a length or so away from the quay on our starboard hand until we reach a point well ahead of the place at which we wish to come alongside. We keep closer to the quay than before. Having reached the required position, we put the engine astern and immediately our stern moves to port. As we begin to move astern we put the rudder to starboard. This, overcoming the propeller thrust, will move the stern to starboard. On approaching the quay, we put the engine in neutral and then into ahead gear at slow speed to take the stern-way off the ship. With the rudder over to starboard, the stern will kick out from the quayside and the bows will come in to starboard and there we are, alongside the quay, in the position we wanted to be.

From what we have already learnt about the action of twin-screws it will be easy to see that coming alongside a quay in a twin-screw vessel is a much simpler matter than with single-screw. To start with it makes no difference whether we wish to come starboard or port-side-to. The method when using twin screws is the same for both. Let us say we are approaching the quay on the port hand. As we come up to the quay the gears for both propellers are put into

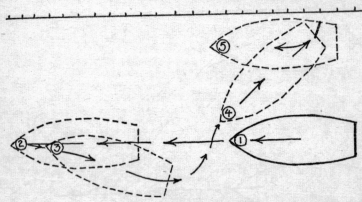

Fig. 74 Coming alongside starboard side to quay on starboard hand

neutral. The boat will continue towards the quay carrying her way. Remember once again to have plenty of fenders out on the port-hand-side. As she comes to the quay we put the outboard (in this case, the starboard) propeller astern slow. This will not only check our way but the transverse thrust will bring our stern into the quay. There is an additional useful fact in that the propeller being away from the centre line of the ship, exercises some leverage and so increases the tendency for the stern to come into port towards the quay. During this manoeuvre the helm is kept amidships. Other examples could be cited but I think I have said enough to show that with twin-screws manoeuvring should present little difficulty.

Anchors and cables

We now come to the use of that most essential and useful piece of equipment, the anchor. Before discussing the methods of anchoring and mooring and also in making use of an anchor when manoeuvring alongside a quay under difficult conditions of wind and tide, let us take a look at the basic anchoring equipment, or what is properly called ground tackle.

Let us look first of all at the anchor itself. There are a variety of types; look at figure 75, this shows: (a) the traditional Fisherman or Navy anchor, being a rigid type anchor with a stock. (The various

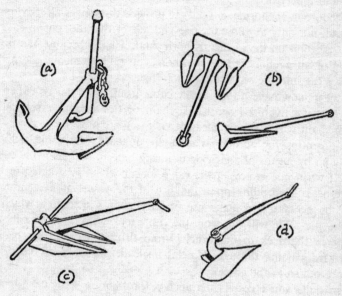

Fig. 75 Four types of anchor

parts of an anchor, stock, shank, crown, arm, fluke etc. are shown in the illustration.) (b) the Marrel anchor; notice that this is stockless, has a single shank and that the two flukes are pivoted, (c) the Danforth anchor; this again has two pivoted parallel flukes. It also has a single shank but this one has a stock. However, unlike the Navy anchor, it is at the head or crown of the anchor. Illustrated in (d) is the C.Q.R. anchor; a single plough-share fluke anchor. The fluke is pivoted, there is no stock and the anchor has a single shank.

There are quite a number of other anchors available but they are similar to the principal types I have named. The object of anchoring is to hold the ship in a more or less fixed position; 'more or less' because in point of fact the ship will swing with the movement of the tide and surface drift and wind. Theoretically, she can describe a circle about the anchor with the anchor chain or cable as radius.

In practice, this is not so because the ship should lie not so much to the anchor as to the weight of the cable itself. To ensure this we pay out plenty of cable, as we shall see when we come to study the procedure in anchoring, not only to provide the weight already mentioned, not only to allow for rise and fall of the tide, but to ensure that the pull on the anchor is horizontal. This is because the principle of all anchors is that the more you pull them, the more the flukes dig into the sea bed and hold firm.

Let us now have a look at the cable itself. This can be either of calibrated galvanized short-link chain or (for larger vessels) stud link chain which simply means that the links have cross pieces at their centres for additional strength. Inboard, the cable will be secured by means of a shackle to a ring bolt housed, as is the cable itself when not in use, in the cable locker which is situated in the fore-peak. Depending upon the size of the vessel, it may or may not be necessary to make use of an anchor winch. If a winch is used, the cable will run from the cable locker up through a hawse pipe in the deck to the winch. From there the cable can be led forward passing through a metal fairlead, probably of the roller type, and so to the anchor.

In quite small vessels the anchor (probably a light C.Q.R.) may well be housed below. The cable of light galvanized chain will be in the cable locker. It will run up through the hawse pipe and can be prevented from slipping back down into the cable locker by a simple metal cover which slots over one link holding the cable securely. When one wants to anchor, the anchor can be brought up on deck, shackled on to the outboard end of the cable and then the amount of cable required can be pulled up by hand through the hawse pipe and ranged on deck ready for running out.

Obviously the larger the vessel, the heavier the ground tackle required, and the more complicated the machinery for handling it. A large diesel yacht will certainly make use of power winches. I say winches because there will certainly be twin anchors. These may be secured on deck but will more probably be hauled taut against the two hawse pipes on either side of the bow. They will probably be of the Marrel type anchor since this type of stockless anchor can be hauled close to the hawse pipe for stowing.

Cable is traditionally measured in fathoms, that is to say six feet lengths, but will be measured equally conveniently in metres in the future. The cable should be painted at convenient fathom intervals so that it can be seen at a glance how much of it is out. Anchoring with a single anchor is termed just that but anchoring with two is known as 'mooring' and this we shall be discussing shortly. It follows, however, that in order to moor, a ship must possess two anchors. A large yacht will probably have two large anchors but any yacht capable of cruising should possess one principal anchor and a smaller anchor known as a kedge.

With a kedge anchor it is normal to use rope and not chain. Terylene and nylon ropes are the best for this purpose. We shall be discussing the merits of different types of ropes in a later section.

To sum up then, we have seen that there are various types of anchor. There are the stockless anchors which can be hove up close to the hawse pipe employed in larger yachts. There are stock anchors like the Admiralty pattern anchor, which are better for smaller vessels and there is the C.Q.R. or plough type anchor with its great holding power. We have seen that to assist us we can make use of both windlasses and capstans and they may be operated by hand, by electricity or by steam or any other suitable means. We have seen that the cable itself will be of either plain links or studded links and should be marked so that we know the amount of cable which is out. In small vessels the cable will run through the deck through a navel or hawse pipe to the cable locker below in the fore-peak where it is secured. In this connection it should be emphasized that the reason for securing the cable in the bottom of the cable locker is to prevent that unfortunate incident which has happened to more than one yachtsman where, forgetting to make the cable fast on deck and heaving the anchor over the side, the distraught mariner sees the entire chain running out through the hawse pipe with a speed and force that he is quite unable to control, and disappearing irrevocably into the sea. But in fact, the cable shackle at its end is only a 'long stop', and the cable must always be secured by some means on deck, either at the winch or by taking turns round bollards or round a sampson post.

As to the amount of cable to be veered (which is the correct term for 'let-out'), we shall be discussing this more fully in the section on cruising or passage-making. Suffice here to say that the amount we veer will depend on a number of circumstances; for example, the nature of the bottom, whether the holding ground is good or not, on the weather conditions likely to prevail and on the depth of water at the highest stage of the tide.

Anchoring

When we come to anchor we must remember to let go our anchor on the weather bow. If we do not do this the yacht's bow will blow across the cable almost certainly damaging paintwork and possibly even making it difficult to veer it. Having selected the place where we wish to anchor we must decide from information available and from observations whether the tide or wind is the stronger. Whichever is the stronger, we head the ship into it. As we approach our anchorage we put the engine into neutral and on arrival at the place where we wish to let-go we put the engine astern. If we are heading into the tide (that is to say, if the tide is the stronger) we use the rudder to bring the tide on to the bow from which we are letting-go the anchor. As we put the engine astern, it will first check our way and then the vessel will slowly move astern. The anchor is now let-go and the cable veered. In a largish vessel, it will be controlled by the brake on the winch; in a small vessel, the cable will first have been ranged on deck as already discussed and will be controlled manually (some people are adept at using their feet for this purpose). In practice, the foot method of control is not one that I would personally recommend. It is all too easy to lose control and the cable goes roaring out.

If there is much tide or wind the ship will be drifting astern on her own accord and it will not be necessary to use the engine any further so it can be put into neutral. We will already have decided how much cable to veer and noting the painted marks on the links as the cable runs out, we stop it at the appropriate place. With a moderately large vessel, with her proportionately heavy cable, the engine can be put slow ahead as the desired mark on the cable appears. The engine need only be given a touch ahead, the cable will be veered and then when the way is off the ship, the cable may be hauled in and made fast at the desired depth.

Having anchored, it is sound practice to take one or more bearings of shore objects in order to test whether the ship is dragging her anchor. The method of taking compass bearings is fully dealt with in the chapter on navigation and pilotage. If there is any danger of the boat dragging her cable over her own anchor and fouling it as she swings with the tide, or if you are going to stay for any length of time which will involve the ship swinging, it is advisable to moor with two anchors.

Another reason for mooring is restricted space. You may be in a harbour, there may be no mooring buoys which you can pick up, the anchorage may be crowded and you cannot lie to a single anchor because you would take up too much room as you swing to either wind or tide. Let us assume that we are coming into harbour against the tide. Let us say that the depth of water where we wish to anchor is three fathoms and we have accordingly decided to veer nine. We come slowly to our anchorage and motor beyond the spot at which we wish to lie when moored. Remember we are going to veer nine fathoms. We go beyond the chosen spot for about this distance and when it is reached, we put the engine astern. The moment our boat gathers stern-way we let go one anchor, let us say the port anchor. Continuing astern we are veering out the cable of our port anchor until we have let out eighteen fathoms, twice the amount we will be riding to. We now let go our starboard anchor. We heave-in on our port anchor cable and veer our starboard cable until we have nine fathoms on each, using the engine slow ahead to help us do this if necessary. The two anchors should be in line with the direction of the tide or, if there is little tide, the wind. Figure 76 illustrates in diagramatic form how the line drawn between the two anchors is either along the direction of the wind or along the tide.

It may happen, however, that having moored in the way we have described, the wind may come on to blow at right angles to the imaginary line between the two anchors, and the ship will be blown into the position illustrated in figure 77. This is called 'open hawse'.

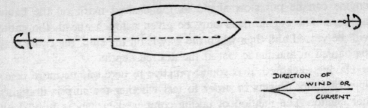

Fig. 76 Mooring with two anchors

Notice in the figure the unnatural strain on the two anchors at open hawse; there is every tendency for one or the other anchors to drag. The remedy is to veer cable. This, of course, can only be done provided that you have sea room astern of you. If it can you should veer until the angle is much more acute and looks more like the angle in figure 78.

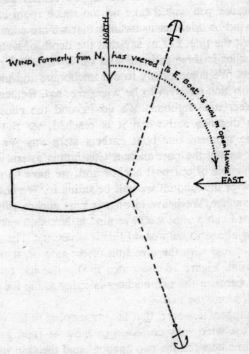

Fig. 77 'Open hawse' due to wind shaft

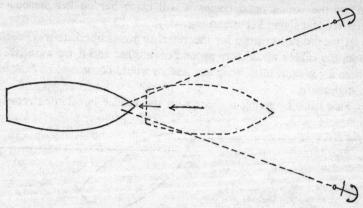

Fig. 78 'Open hawse' – action to be taken

Giving a sheer with a rudder

It may be that having moored we are likely to remain for several tides. If so we must ensure that the ship swings a different way each time the tide turns. This can usually be done by giving a sheer with the rudder. Look now at figure 79. Just before slack water, we put the rudder to port. When the tide begins to ebb, the yacht, lying in the position as is shown in the illustration because of the sheer which we have given her with the rudder, will be caught by that ebb tide on her port quarter. That is the way she will swing round. In figure 80, notice that the tide at the last of the ebb is causing the vessel to lie in the position in which the illustration shows because of the sheer given by putting the rudder this time over to starboard.

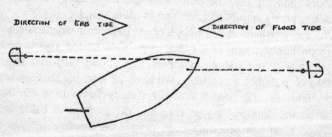

Fig. 79 Giving a sheer with the rudder (1)

When the young flood comes it will catch her on her starboard quarter and swing her round that way.

If we did not arrange for the vessel to swing opposite ways each tide, the cables would turn around each other and if we were lying there for several tides, weighing anchor would become something of a nightmare.

This trick of giving a sheer with the rudder is often extremely

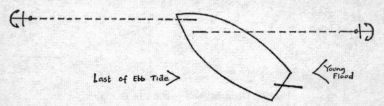

Last of Ebb Tide >

< Young Flood

Fig. 80 Giving a sheer with the rudder (2)

useful. For example: you may be lying to single anchor and when you anchored the tide was stronger than the wind, shall we say, and you began by being tide-ridden. Then the wind increases from aft and the ship begins to drive ahead towards her anchor little by little. If the wind increases more there is a danger that she may drag her cable over her anchor thereby fouling it. This can easily be averted to one side of the anchor instead of over the top of it as the boat rides forward.

The kedge anchor

For small and medium-sized vessels who may not carry two main anchors mooring may be done with the small kedge anchor. This is an extremely handy method and is quite simple.

We use normally a long rope of perhaps coir or grass line but more probably, nylon or terylene rope. One end of this is bent on to the ring of the kedge anchor using a round turn and two half hitches or possibly a bowline. (We shall be learning some seaman's knots later in this book.) We will already have done our homework on the depth of water, etc.; and the amount of cable we are likely to need has probably been ranged on the fo'c'sle. We bend one end of the kedge warp to a cleat or sampson post on the fo'c'sle. We put the kedge warp, coiled, into a dinghy. Using a dinghy is a very simple and efficient method of mooring with a kedge warp although it is perfectly possible to moor with a kedge warp, using the same principle as when mooring with two anchors. Let us in this instance assume that we are going to make use of the yacht's small tender or dinghy.

We are therefore lying to a single anchor, our main anchor. The kedge warp, coiled, is so placed in the dinghy 'capsized', so that the rope will run out freely as you row the dinghy away from the

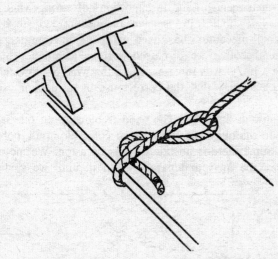

Fig. 81 Slippery hitch on dingy thwart

yacht. The anchor is put over the dinghy's stern and held with a short piece of line passing through the ring of the anchor and made fast to the thwart in the dinghy with a slippery hitch. Figure 81 illustrates a slippery hitch. It is self-explanatory. You now row astern of the anchored yacht. When the kedge warp is all paid out, we slip the hitch on the thwart, letting go the kedge. We now row back to the boat. We gather up some slack in the kedge warp and bend it to the cable of our main anchor with a rolling hitch (another knot we will learn to tie later on [See figure 102.]). Now we veer our cable a fathom or two so that the rolling hitch lies well below our keel. The main anchor and the kedge should, as in the other method of mooring with two anchors, lie in line with the tide. An important point to remember here is that when mooring with a kedge warp, the main anchor should lie towards the direction from which the greatest strain, be it tide or wind, is expected.

Using an anchor when coming alongside

Apart from the use of holding our vessel in one position for as long as we may wish, the anchor has other uses when manoeuvring. Indeed, when manoeuvring in conditions of strong winds or in a tide-way, you should always have an anchor ready to be let go. Such a small precaution has saved many a ship from damage. You will remember that we discussed various techniques of coming alongside a quay. It is in cases where the wind is blowing strongly on to such a quay that the correct use of an anchor can be invaluable.

Look now at figure 82. The wind is blowing on our starboard-hand on to the quay and we want to come alongside port-side-to. Let us assume there is no tide on this occasion. We motor along, away from the quay and parallel with it, until we come almost

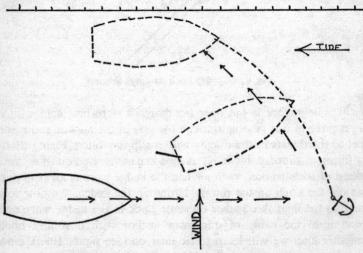

Fig. 82 Use of anchor to come alongside a quay (1)

abeam of the spot we want to go alongside. We let go our starboard anchor (see the figure). We now motor towards the quay
veering cable as we do and when the bow is close enough to the
quay we get a head rope ashore. From the figure the manoeuvre
can easily be seen. Of course this particular manoeuvre is easier
with twin-screws, since after letting go the starboard anchor, we
can stop port engine but keep starboard going ahead slowly which
will get our bows well in towards the quay.

But supposing that we are stemming the tide. The answer here
is that we let-go our anchor ahead of our intended berth having
motored past it. Look at figure 83. Notice that we have let go the

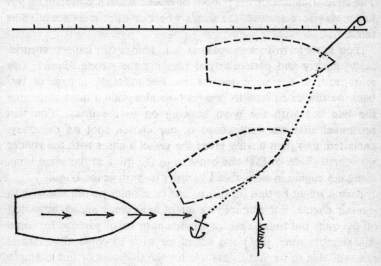

Fig. 83 Use of anchor to come alongside a quay (2)

anchor some distance from the quay. We now give our ship a sheer
by putting the rudder to port, to cant the stern to starboard. This
brings the tide on our starboard bow. We slack away on the cable
and our boat will slowly move in towards the quay.

All these examples I have given are intended to show the reader
the general principles of manoeuvring a power yacht. There would
be little point in giving example after example of ways of anchoring
or mooring or coming alongside quays in all the many and varied

conditions of wind and tide which the yacht owner is certain, at some time or other, to experience. It is sufficient to understand the principles involved – the transverse thrust of the propellers, the windage of high bows and upper-works, the use of the anchor, and the leverage which may be exercised by warps and springs.

But, of course, there is no substitute for practical experience. No amount of book-reading is as good as even just one shot at the real thing. It is very difficult for the writer to convey the manner in which any ship comes alive when under way. One cannot adequately explain the sensation of manoeuvring a boat; the throb of the idling engine, docile, yet impatient to be away as any high-spirited horse. The equestrian analogy is not out of place: when a powerful ship is under way in a seaway, the ship's wheel or tiller is as sensitive as reins.

You must learn to anticipate at sea. Things can happen surprisingly quickly and particularly if they are the wrong things! You must learn to use your imagination. For example, a page or two back we discussed how to bring a boat alongside a quay stemming the tide but with the wind blowing on to the quay. You will remember that we went ahead of our chosen spot on the quay, anchored, and then having given the vessel a sheer with the rudder we veered cable so that she came in to the quay at the same time, using the engine in slow ahead in order to push in the bows.

Now it might be that for one reason or another we did not wish to use our engine. For example we might have come ahead, anchored off the quay but found that for a moment or so, or perhaps for some considerable time, the place where we wish to come alongside is not available to us. Let us assume for the purposes of this example that the place where we have temporarily anchored is perfectly safe and we can remain there until whatever is obstructing our berth on the quay, perhaps another vessel, has left.

Let us now assume that the obstruction has gone, and we do not wish to start the engine particularly. Our dinghy is ready and available for use. We take a warp, make fast on board to a cleat or king post on the fo'c'sle, lead it out through the bow fairlead and put it, coiled and capsized so that it will run out easily, in the dinghy. We now row ashore. We make fast the dinghy painter and taking the warp with us we in turn make it fast to let us say a bollard on the quay well ahead of the position alongside we wish our boat to occupy. Alternatively we pass it, if long enough, through a ring bolt and back into the dinghy, to take back on board. We now return in the dinghy to the yacht.

We now have the yacht lying to two fixed points; the anchor by means of the cable and the bollard on the quay by means of the head rope. All we have to do now is to veer the cable and as we do so the head rope will bring the boat surely into the quay.

Having exhorted the reader to use his or her intelligence and imagination I would hope that a question has already arisen in the reader's mind. The question of course is 'what now becomes of the anchor and cable lying on the sea bed?'

As we saw earlier when discussing anchors, the whole principle of an anchor is that as long as the pull is horizontal it will bite ever more deeply into the sea-bed and hold even more firmly. Should the pull be vertical or near vertical, the anchor will break from the ground and can easily be hove-in. If therefore it is our intention to remain alongside this imaginary quay for some considerable period we should, with the dinghy, follow the cable, over-handing as we go to the point above its position in the sea-bed when an easy pull should break it free. We haul it in, sling it over the dinghy's stern (it may well be covered in mud and inadvisable to bring aboard the dinghy) and row back to the yacht. If however it is probable that in an hour or two we will wish to proceed to sea again and the wind seems likely to continue blowing strongly on to the quay, our anchor will be in an excellent position to haul ourselves clear of the quay. This can be particularly useful in the case of a vessel with single screw.

Foul anchor and slipped anchors

Two words of caution here. Take good care that you are able to veer plenty of chain so that it lies along the bottom and cannot be picked up by any passing craft. The other caution is that the use of an anchor in any circumstances whatever must always be accompanied by a virtual certainty that there is no old ground-tackle, mooring chains, etc., scattered about the ocean bed in the place where you wish to anchor. All too often the unwary yachtsman, when the time comes to weigh anchor, finds that this cannot be done because one of the flukes has caught round old mooring chains on the bottom. This foul-anchor, as it is termed, can be extremely tiresome. There are however remedies, and by far the best is to heave in the anchor as much as possible to start with. It is unlikely that you will succeed in heaving the chain round which your anchor is caught clear of the water but it is quite possible that you will be able to heave enough off the ocean bed to be able to see it. Then, by using the dinghy or a boat hook, and certainly in all cases your own intelligence and initiative, pass a line under the offending piece of ground tackle and bring the end back on board. Heave taut on this line and make well fast. Now lower the anchor clear of the ground chain after which it should be perfectly simple to bring it aboard.

Of course circumstances alter cases. A lot depends on the depth of water in which you are anchored. It may be that you would be advised to wait for low water for example. If for one reason or another your own anchor is so fouled that it is impossible to break it free and you have to leave, it may be necessary to slip. But here another strong word of caution. Unless you have a second large anchor and a second anchor cable on board (and in a small yacht this is rather unlikely) I would personally be very against slipping my cable and proceeding to sea with only the kedge anchor and kedge warp. Indeed I would put it more strongly; only the direst of emergencies should condone such action. If you do slip your cable remember to buoy the end of it, with something that not only floats properly, but which is also well marked and easily seen.

This is not really the place in the book to be discussing tactics when cruising but I should, I think, qualify my previous caution against slipping the cable by giving an example of an occasion when it is permissible. Let us say that you are anchored off a harbour which is tidal. You are waiting for the flood to give you sufficient water to enter. You are lying to a single anchor, your main anchor. Let us further assume that it is essential that you enter harbour; the wind is freshening and you are short of fuel.

When the time comes to weigh anchor the latter will not break free, try as you may. Let us assume in these imaginary and somewhat trying circumstances that the time when there is sufficient water for you to cross the bar at the harbour mouth is relatively short; in other words, time is not on your side. Once inside the harbour you will be able to lie alongside; you also have on board your kedge anchor and kedge warp made ready for any emergency in the harbour.

Under such circumstances it would be perfectly seamanlike procedure to buoy your cable and slip it and enter harbour knowing that later, after re-fuelling and when the weather had moderated, you could go back, retrieve the buoyed end of the cable and try again to break your anchor free.

Those readers who have been fortunate enough to know Erskine Childers's famous yachting novel *The Riddle of the Sands*, will remember that Davies slipped his cable under somewhat similar circumstances; and no one would suggest that Davies was not a most competent seaman!

Leaving the quay

Continuing briefly the saga of the slipped cable, no matter how snug our berth alongside the quay, the time will surely come when we have to leave it. We talked just now of making use of an anchor lying well off a quay on to which the wind was blowing. Such technique while perfectly permissible, should not normally be required, however, since we can make use of our warps and springs and our engine to do this. Even without an onshore wind we do not leave a quay by casting off warps and steaming ahead. The stern will be close in to the quay and since, because of this, we cannot use the rudder to get the ship away from the quay, all that would happen would be that we would slide along it on our fenders, quite possibly doing ourselves superficial damage. Also, there may well be other ships lying both ahead and astern of us so that we do not have much room to manoeuvre in a direction right ahead or right astern.

Of course in idyllic conditions (the kind of conditions many embryo yachtsmen visualize as they eagerly sign the cheque for their first boat) – cloudless blue sky, no wind, no tide – an elegant shove from the bows with a boat-hook may be all that is required. However for practical purposes we will probably find that the best way to leave a quay is to make use of a spring.

We are lying alongside a quay. Let us say that in this example there is no tide or wind effect to concern us. We have, however, got the problem of another yacht lying just ahead of us; both yachts are port side to quay.

Our boat is moored with head rope, stern rope, fore-spring and after-spring. There are no breast ropes out on this occasion. We cast off all lines except the fore-spring; that is to say the head rope, stern rope and after-spring. The vessel has a single right-handed screw.

The engine is ticking over in neutral. Look at figure 84. This will remind us that the fore-spring is the one leading from the bows to a

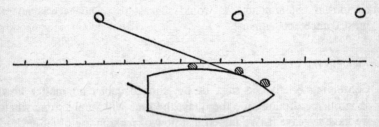

Fig. 84 Using a spring to leave a quay

bollard on the quay well aft. We will of course have fenders placed between our port topsides and the quay wall but the fender that we are particularly going to need is the one right forward on the port bow. We now put the rudder to port and the engine slow ahead. As the spring tightens, the bows are pulled in. This has the effect of moving the stern out, a movement which is assisted by the water being driven against the rudder by the propeller. With the stern well out, we put the engine into neutral and having cast off our spring, we put the engine astern.

A point to bear in mind is that with a right-handed propeller the stern (on going astern) will come in a bit towards the quay so make sure that it is well clear of any objects before engaging the gear. The manoeuvre is quite simple and with twin-screws the manoeuvre is even simpler. In that case we put the outboard (that is to say the starboard) propeller ahead leaving the helm amidships. The stern is kicked but by the starboard screw.

Let us suppose now that we have a vessel moored astern of us but the way is clear to leave the quay ahead. Once again, we will assume that we have no tide or wind. The engine is running in neutral; we cast off head rope, stern rope and fore-spring, leaving our after-spring from the port quarter to a bollard well forward of the port bow. As we put the engine astern, the spring tightens and the stern is pulled in to the quay. When we judge that the bow has come out to starboard sufficiently far, we cast off the spring and put the engine ahead, with the rudder over to port a little, to keep our stern clear of the quay wall. When executing this manoeuvre with a twin-screw vessel we use only the outer (in this case the starboard) propeller. When we put this ahead we leave the helm amidships. It is not necessary to put the rudder to port because the position of the propeller will be sufficient to keep the stern clear of the quay in this instance.

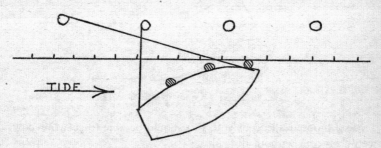

Fig. 85 Leaving a quay in a tideway (1)

Supposing, however, a tide is running. Let us imagine ourselves in the earlier position with a vessel ahead of us and a tide running under our stern in the same direction as our bows are pointing. In this case we do not cast off all lines except the fore-spring; we must also have an after breast rope and the illustration in figure 85 will explain why. The purpose of the after breast rope is to control the moving away from the quay of the stern. If it were not there, the tide pushing between the quay wall and the port side of the hull, would soon swing the vessel right round. She would then be lying facing the opposite direction from that in which she started with her fore-spring acting as a head rope and in a position relative to the vessel

now sandwiched between her and the quay wall, probably neces-
sitating diplomacy on the part of you as the skipper, and swift and
crafty work with fenders on the part of your crew! No, the beauty
of using the after breast rope is that as the tide swings the stern out,
the amount that it moves out can be controlled exactly by using the
rope. When you judge that your stern is far enough out both breast
rope and spring can be slipped, the engine put into astern and away
you go as before.

If the tide is running the other way and you are lying bows to
tide, the latter will all the time be trying to push you astern so that
if you slip all lines except an after-spring, the tide will bring the
bows right out for you. Figure 86 explains this. Even should there be

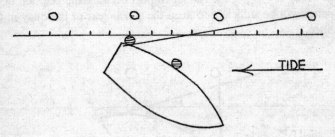

Fig. 86 Leaving a quay in a tideway (2)

a vessel moored ahead of you, you should be able to get your bows
well clear and without difficulty.

Notice that in both these examples we have made the tide do the
work of an engine by using the leverage of a spring. I can, in my
imagination, hear a reader asking 'what happens if when the
moment comes to slip, there is no one on shore to cast-off whatever
springs or breast ropes may be necessary?' Of course, this situation
quite often happens and the solution is simple. It consists primarily
of having enough rope to have long enough warps! To secure to say
a bollard, make one end fast aboard, take the other ashore, lead
it round the bollard on the quay and then back again on board
and belay it round a cleat or sampson post. If you are securing to
ring bolts in a quay wall the method is identical. When the time
comes to leave the quay you simply slip one end and haul hard on
the other.

We saw earlier in this chapter that coming alongside a quay can be turned from a simple manoeuvre into one requiring some skill by an onshore wind. Similarly, when leaving a quay an onshore wind can complicate matters.

Supposing that we are alongside port-side-to, as before, in conditions of no tide but an onshore wind blowing on to the quay and pushing us against it. You will remember how we got away ahead by making use of an after-spring, putting the engine astern so that the spring canted our bows out. With an onshore wind, however, blowing against our high bows and probably high upperworks the bow will be blown in towards the quay as soon as the engine is moved from astern back to neutral. It must be borne in mind that an after-spring exerts comparatively little leverage. The best thing to do in this case is to use a fore-spring. Put the engine ahead and let the leverage of the fore-spring pull the bow right in. The stern will now come out sufficiently to be able to get away clear. Of course if the wind were offshore your problem would cease to exist. The wind itself will push your bows out.

In connection with this whole question of mooring to and leaving quays, I must not omit that modern phenomenon, the yacht marina. People who do much continental cruising will be familiar with the technique of lying to an anchor or buoy with the boat's stern moored by two stern warps to a quay. Marinas provide just such moorings. The technique will not be difficult to learn if you have followed me so far. The anchor is let-go (or the buoy picked-up) and then the vessel comes astern to the quay veering cable. In practice marinas offer safe, sheltered and convenient berths and are much sought after.

Fouled propellers

As I said earlier, and at risk of seeming repetitious, these examples are by no means designed to cover all eventualities. They are intended simply to teach you the basic principles of manoeuvring a power vessel. In this connection it is well worth remembering that much may be done without using the engine at all. A vessel may be 'warped' from one berth to another by the proper use and combination of ropes and the elements. There are indeed occasions when it is desirable to do this. One which I have particularly in mind is where one is lying in a berth with a crowd of other vessels alongside a quay. Often in such conditions there are far too many loose mooring lines and other lines hanging, floating, dangling about perilously near to the propeller (or propellers) and it is particularly dangerous in the case of twin-screw vessels since the screws are so near the ship's sides. A propeller has an uncanny power of sucking loose line in and around it in such circumstances. Of course, in cases of this nature one must use one's own judgement. It will doubtless be advisable to have the engine ticking-over ready just in case. If you are unlucky enough to get your propeller fouled by a line the answer is usually to cut it away. Sometimes reversing helps but as a rule any movement of the screw forward or reverse tends to wrap the line round the blades of the propeller or the propeller shaft which at the best will compound the felony and at the worst can damage the screw. The best answer is to get down there with a knife and saw and unwind until the line is clear.

SPORTSBOATS

Although a lot of what has been said in the previous section may not be necessary for the small sportsboat owner to learn yet I would advise him or her to read it if only because the more you know about the boating game, the more fun it is and, incidentally, the safer. Nevertheless clearly certain matters are greatly simplified. For example leaving a quay. The small sportsboat owner is unlikely to have to kick the bows or stern out by using springs. Usually, once you have made certain that the engine is running smoothly, a turn of the wheel in the direction you wish to proceed will suffice. But just as the cruising man has to make sure that there is nothing whatever in the way in which he wishes to go, so the sportsboat driver must make sure that the way is clear for him. Making sure that the way is clear becomes particularly important for sportsboat owners or owners for that matter of any fast planing craft, since you come upon objects that much faster. So assuming that we have had a good look round, that the engine or engines are idling nicely, that all ropes are cast off and that there are no other ropes likely either to get in our way or get wrapped round our propeller, we can engage the gear. We open the throttle sufficiently to give good steerage way (say about 8 m.p.h.) and steer the boat into clear water.

Now with a light displacement planing boat, the object is to get her on the plane. First, have a good look round while driving at slow speed to see what other vessels there are in the vicinity before opening her up. Satisfied that you have got a mile or so of clear water ahead of you, open the throttle. Move the throttle up steadily to about three quarters and the boat will come up on the plane. With the boat planing in her natural designed position she will gain speed. You can let her do this or alternatively you can ease the throttle down to the boat's cruising speed while remaining on the plane. When you wish to slow her down and come off the plane do so gently, that is to say, take about a quarter of a minute – fifteen rather than three seconds. If you don't do this the boat may be swamped by her own wash.

Obviously at some point we shall have to turn around and while turning at speed is exhilarating, it is most advisable for the new owner to make his first few turns at low speed. The point of doing this is mainly to get the feel of the boat.

The principle of steering is quite simple. You turn the wheel left or to port and the boat goes left or to port and vice versa. With an outboard, the engine itself is moved by turning the wheel. This changes the direction of the screw race and produces a sharp turn. Deep V designed hulls turn particularly sharply, heeling over inwards. It is important to get the feel of the boat at slow speeds first, noticing the heel of the boat at various speeds and degrees of turn. Do not try and run before you can walk; keep at speeds of around 10 m.p.h. while you get the feel of your boat. When you are confident about turning her to both port and starboard, increase throttle up to half-speed over the hump on to three-quarter speed and beyond, to her planing position. Familiarize yourself with this feeling not only in calm water, but in conditions of slight chop. With fast driving in choppy seas the boat will tend to jump out of the water; this is perfectly normal but the beginner must remember that waves affect the boat's stability and the new driver should not drive flat out in such conditions until he feels thoroughly at home with the boat.

It is possible to create artificial wave conditions to some extent by making a turn so as to cut through your own wake. Even better is crossing the wake of another sportsboat, but remember to do this well astern of the latter. Notice how the boat bucks; notice how she feels. One point here which it may seem unnecessary to emphasize, but accidents can easily happen, is to make sure, if you intend crossing the wake of another powerboat, that the latter has no skier towing astern!

If we drive a displacement hull too fast she will squat down at the stern. In bad weather this can become very dangerous and may result in the vessel being 'pooped', that is to say taking a big sea over the stern. In the case of a planing hull, the latter generates its own lift which again is aided by the buoyancy of that part of the hull aft which is still in the water. It is on this part that the boat runs at a fixed angle of attack to the water. Now in calm sheltered water there is no problem with this but as soon as we start to get waves, as these increase, the boat tends to lose the design condition. This is where mechanically operated trim-tabs at the stern come in. The purpose of these, as we have seen elsewhere, is to keep the boat at the best angle to the water. Most offshore racing boats make use of such trim-tabs; others carry water ballast for the purpose of adjusting the trim of the vessel.

While on this question of trim, it is important if you are carrying passengers that they remain firmly in their seats and do not attempt to move about at speed. Driving a sportsboat in rough water when the wind has got up, is largely a matter of common sense. For example, ease the throttle before wave crests, notice carefully how your boat behaves in these conditions; you will probably find that while she cuts through waves met dead ahead, cross waves will have a slurring effect, and the bows tend to bump off them.

When a boat is increasing speed from slow at about half-throttle before she reaches her planing condition, she will be riding what is termed 'on the hump'. In bad weather it may be necessary to drive the boat on the hump. This has the effect of keeping the bows well up when going before the wind. I am assuming here that the boat owner has been unlucky enough to be caught out at sea and is running before big following seas for shelter. The object is to keep the bows well up and the boat ahead of the seas. Keep the speed running just above the hump. Do not let the bow go up and down (known as 'porpoising') – this is a sign of inadequate speed. The answer is to open the throttle and keep her on the hump. The boat must be moving fast enough to stop her broaching, which means to come round so that she lies across the seas – a dangerous position.

One often sees films of offshore racers showing boats leaping from one wave-top to another. This may look dramatic but it is not necessarily increasing the boat's speed, if anything the reverse, and it is certainly subjecting the hull to a terrific hammering. When driving into seas, therefore, try with the throttle to find the speed best suited to the conditions. It may be necessary (to borrow a sailing expression) to 'tack', that is to say, to drive a zig-zag course. It is sometimes advisable to do this with a heavy beam sea. It should not need emphasizing either, that turning in conditions of heavy weather requires good judgement. Watch the seas carefully and choose your moment.

Having returned to harbour, many of the principles which applied to the cruising boat are true for the sportsboat. Remember to throttle back in plenty of time but remember too that having eased down to the gentle speed required for most harbour manoeuvring, the two factors of current and wind will come into play. If there is no wind but a strong current, remember to come alongside against that current. If there is a strong wind and no current come alongside into the wind. If you have a cross wind, estimate its effect on the boat as you approach the quay.

With the enormous increase in boats of all kinds in our waters today it has become more important than ever to know what are known as the *Rules for Prevention of Collision at Sea* or colloquially 'the Rule of the Road at Sea'. These I have reproduced in full at the end of Chapter 7. Sportsboat owners can therefore extract from a quick read of these, those rules which particularly apply. The most important should be memorized.

For those sportsboat owners who want to indulge in a bit of cruising, let us now move on to Chapter 7. For those owners to whom racing has the greater appeal, Chapter 8 is the one for you.

CHAPTER 7

Powerboat Cruising; Pilotage and Navigation

'Ane skyppar can nocht gyde his schip to ane gud hevin without direction
of his compass.'

ABP HAMILTON'S *Chatechism*, 1552

A CRUISING boat may or may not go out of sight of land. Let us
assume to begin with that such passages as we are going to make are
for the most part within sight of the shore. This means basically
that we can check where we are by reference to objects which we
can see on that shore. A cruising boat must have a compass. The
compass not only tells us what course to steer and what direction to
sail in but we use it for taking bearings of the objects that we can
see on the shore and so fix our position. We fix our position on a
chart which is really a map of the sea. Conducting of a vessel from
port to port within sight of land is known loosely by a number of
names; pilotage or coastal navigation will do.

Driving a boat skilfully in a race may be called an art. Pilotage
may be called a science, for it is exact. The navigator must know
exactly where he is. An old story is told of an apprentice at sea
who, when asked to indicate the ship's position on the chart by the
captain, covered a large area with the palm of an open hand and
said, 'About here, sir.' That is not navigation in any form. To
navigate we need a chart or more exactly a number of charts and
certain instruments and publications which we will examine
presently and most of all we need a compass. Let us first take a look
at exactly what we mean by a chart.

Charts

Look at figure 87. This shows the globe which we call the earth.
Notice that it is covered with a network of lines and notice that the
line running round the centre of it is called the equator. Parallel to
the equator are a number of lines running round the globe north
and south of the equator. These are called parallels of latitude.
Notice that their circumference diminishes the nearer they get to the

two poles. The other lines, the ones which run from north to south or from pole to pole, are called meridians. The Greenwich (or prime) meridian is the one which passes through Greenwich.

You can see from the drawing that the parallels of latitude run east and west while the meridians run due north and south and that they intersect each other at right angles. The point of this network of lines on our globe is to enable us to define the exact position of

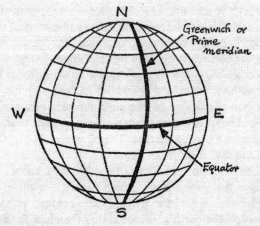

Fig. 87 Parallels of latitude and meridians of longitude

any place on it by reference to the network. We define the latitude of any place, therefore, as the angular measurement between its own parallel of latitude and the equator. This angle is measured at the centre of curvature of the earth's surface and is measured in the plane of meridian of the place. It is expressed in degrees, minutes and seconds from 0 to 90 degrees and either north or south of the equator.

So much for the latitude of a place. The longitude is the angular measurement between the meridian of a place and the meridian of Greenwich, once again expressed in degrees, minutes and seconds but from 0° to 180° east or west of the Greenwich meridian. Incidentally, when we say 'centre of the earth' we are speaking theoretically because since the earth is not a perfect sphere there is no exact centre.

We can now find the position of any place by defining it in terms of longitude east or west of Greenwich and latitude north or south of the equator. We can find two places and the distance between them can be expressed as linear measurement of latitude or linear measurement of longitude. The distance subtended by a degree of latitude on the surface of the earth is precisely the same wherever it is measured. As we have already said the earth is not a perfect sphere and each minute of latitude subtends a distance which varies from 6,046 feet at the equator to 6,108 feet at the poles. To simplify matters a mean of 6,080 feet is taken and this we call the nautical mile. When it comes to measuring longitude, the distance on the surface of the earth between any two meridians is obviously subject to considerable variation, being greatest at the equator and diminishing to nothing where the meridians all meet at the poles. The linear distance of a degree of longitude will therefore vary according to the latitude and cannot be taken as a standard measure.

Imagine now a cardboard disc. The circumference of this disc is a circle and the disc itself is the plane of that circle. Any circle whose plane passes through the centre of the earth is known as a Great Circle and is the largest circle which can be drawn on the earth's surface. The arc of a Great Circle is the nearest we can get to a straight line on the earth's surface and is therefore the shortest distance between two points on the surface of the earth. If you look again at our drawing of parallels of latitude and meridians on the globe it will be clear that a Great Circle will not cross these meridians or parallels of latitude at the same angle. It is however possible to have a circle which does cross them at the same angle and this is known as a Rhumb line.

It will be obvious that trying to draw lines or circles on the surface of a globe tossing about on the ocean is a tedious business at best and so the modern navigator makes use of charts. A chart is a flat projection of the globe or part of the globe; two projections commonly used are Mercator's and the Gnomonic.

The most commonly used is Mercator's. It is a cylindrical projection which may be described as follows. Picture a very bright light in the centre of a transparent globe which we surround with a cylinder of paper. On the surface of the transparent globe are outlined the land masses, islands and other details in black. The bright

206

light throws the shadows of this on to the inner surface of our paper cylinder. The light is bright enough to show these through the back of our paper and we trace them on. We now unroll the paper and we have the globe and the land masses upon it represented on a flat surface. Now one of two things will be immediately apparent; the distance between the parallels of latitude will increase progressively from the equator as they get nearer the poles and all features which approach the poles get distorted and extended. For example the island of Greenland is far larger than it really is. Another distortion is that the meridians appear as straight lines parallel with each other and at a constant distance apart instead of meeting at the poles. This produces a broadening of all features on the chart, the further these features are from the equator.

On a Mercator's projection, a straight line drawn on the chart will cut the meridians at the same angle; it is therefore a Rhumb line. A Great Circle, (the shortest distance between any two points), will appear as a curve. It will therefore appear to be longer than a Rhumb line joining the same two points. A ship which steers a steady course at sea moves along a Rhumb line which is not the shortest distance between any two points.

The difference between a Great Circle and a Rhumb line on a chart can, in point of fact, be ignored in the case of the very large scale charts which are used for the kind of coastal navigation we are talking about at the moment. However, when we come to make long passages in the oceans of the world the difference in distance between a Great Circle and a Rhumb line is considerable.

Another thing to remember about a Mercator chart is that we must judge distance at the correct latitude. With a Mercator's chart, degrees of longitude are marked along the top and bottom, eastward and westward of the meridian of Greenwich, while degrees of latitude are marked along the side of the chart, north or south, from 0° at the equator. Because of the distortions we have discussed, the distance must be measured along the latitude scale on the side of the Mercator chart as nearly as possible opposite to its position on the chart.

So much for Mercator's projection. The Gnomonic projection, although used less, comes into its own when you want to work out the shortest course over a long distance between any two places on the earth. When circumnavigators of recent years found themselves sailing in the forties and fifties, they used a Gnomonic chart. The distortion at high latitudes of the Mercator chart would have made such a chart quite unsuitable. A Gnomonic chart is produced by placing a sheet of paper with its centre touching either the north or south pole with the plane parallel to the plane of the equator. As in our previous example, we have a bright light shining at the centre of the globe projecting the shadows on it which can be traced on to the other side of our paper. With a Gnomonic projection, parallels of latitude become concentric circles and the meridians radiate out from the pole in straight lines.

On a Gnomonic projection, Great Circles appear as straight lines and Rhumb lines as curved ones. Degrees of longitude are marked around the perimeter from 0° to 180° each side of the prime meridian. Degrees of latitude are marked on the concentric circles from the pole outwards starting at 89° at the pole and diminishing as the equator is approached.

Such projections taken at the poles are called polar charts but in point of fact you can have a Gnomonic projection at any position on the earth's surface. Gnomonic charts are commonly called Great Circle Charts. Having worked out the shortest course over a long distance it can be transferred for navigational purposes to a Mercator's chart.

Charts fall into three main types. There are the large charts on which the whole of the proposed voyage may be plotted; these are known as passage charts. There are coastal charts which are on a larger scale, and finally, there are harbour plans. The British Admiralty publish an annual catalogue of charts. In addition to the Admiralty charts there are the Royal Cruising Club charts, the 'Y' series of charts and the Stanford charts which fold up like road maps. All these charts are excellent in their way. The important thing to remember when choosing charts is to choose enough. Coastal charts should overlap each other slightly and you must make sure that the areas into which you may be driven by bad weather are fully covered.

A first look at a chart will show you that the sea bed is dotted about with lots of little figures. These are the depths. With approaching metrication to Britain, the Admiralty charts will in future show depths in metres. But for at least five years there will be many charts around in which the depths will still be shown in fathoms; one fathom being equal to 6 ft. The depths are related to a level of the sea called chart datum, which in its turn, is a low water level below which the tide seldom falls. This brings us to a very important subject which we have met already in an earlier chapter briefly, the subject of the tide.

Tides

As many people know in these days of easy and swift air travel, and consequent familiarity with Mediterranean or Baltic resorts, there are seas which are virtually tideless. In point of fact, even in the Mediterranean there is a very slight rise and fall but by comparison with the tidal variation at, say, Dieppe during the Equinoctial spring tides, the Mediterranean may be considered to be tideless. However, most people sailing for pleasure round about the coastlines of this earth of ours are doing so in tidal waters and to them the tide matters very much indeed.

The tidal wave is caused by gravity. The sun and the moon rotate about a common centre of gravity at a speed which is sufficient to maintain the moon in its orbit round the earth, and the earth and the moon are consequently in a state of equilibrium and the gravitational forces drawing them together are thus counteracted. But anything on the earth which can move, and water is one, is affected by such forces. The gravitational force varies with the square of the distance. Nearest to the moon there is a pulling-up, a raising if you like, of the water and there is a similar raising opposite. There is another tide raising produced by the rotation of the earth about the sun but this is on a smaller scale. This rising and falling of the tide would follow the movement of the moon round the earth, varied of course in some degree, depending upon the relative positions of the moon, earth and sun, but because of the depths of the oceans and the positions and shapes of the land, this does not happen. The gravitational force we have spoken about is called the lunar generating force.

Suppose that the whole of the earth's surface were water. The two high waters are balanced by two low waters. Look at figure 88.

The moon takes about twenty-nine days to go round the earth and earth takes 365 to go round the sun. The moon therefore passes between the sun and the earth once every twenty-nine days thus causing a high tide. The earth will be in a position in line with the moon and sun every fourteen-and-a-half days (that is to say half of twenty-nine).

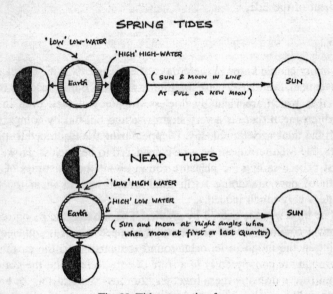

Fig. 88 Tide generating forces

Thus we have two high tides, which are called Spring tides. They are the highest high tides and at the same time the lowest low tides and this can be seen in the illustration. Twice in a month the sun and the moon will be exercising their gravitational effect on the water at right-angles to each other and the figure illustrates this. Notice that there is still a high water opposite the moon and a low water opposite the sun but, because of the sun's attraction, the high water opposite the moon is less and the low water opposite the sun is more. To explain further: the sun's attraction is about three-sevenths that of the moon since the moon is a great deal nearer than the sun and so the high water now becomes a low water to some extent and the low water now becomes a high water to some extent.

These tides are called Neap tides. Between these two tides, Springs and Neaps, the water level varies fairly regularly.

In our diagrams we have covered the whole of the earth's surface with water but in practice we know that this is far from the case. The tidal waters are affected by the land masses of the earth and results in high water and low water arriving at successive places at different times. This makes forecasting the height of the tide at any place a complicated business. It requires an analysis of much data. Luckily for the hard-pressed part-time mariner there are available formulated tide tables in which the tides of high and low water and the actual heights of the tide are given. A very good publication known as *Reed's* (after the name of Thomas Reed the publishers), contains just such tide tables. From the mass of information available you can find the time of high water and low water at any port and also the depth of water at any place, at any time, and furthermore the time at which there will be a given depth at a particular place. The direction in which the stream is running can be found and also its rate (which is the correct term for the 'speed' of a tide).

The Reed's publication I mentioned is known as *Reed's Nautical Almanack*. We are at the moment speaking of the section devoted to tidal information, but I should mention in passing that this *Almanack*, edited by Captain O. M. Watts, contains a formidable amount of nautical information for the year in question; it is an annual publication and, in the author's view, a 'must' on the bookshelf of every cruising yachtsman.

The section in it devoted to tidal predictions is divided into standard ports and secondary ports. There are fifty-two standard ports and the tidal predictions are shown twice daily, giving the time and height throughout the year. Those ports which are not standard are called secondary. The tidal differences, from which can be found the time and height of the tide to be applied to whichever is the nearest local standard port, are given on pages adjacent to that local standard port. The secondary ports are however not necessarily based on the nearest standard port geographically, but on the nearest standard port at which the tides are the most similar. It sounds complicated perhaps, but in practice it is simple. The number of the page where the secondary port data is based is shown in the standard port section so little time need be wasted in looking it up.

As we have already learnt, the depths on a chart relate to the level called chart datum. Look now at figure 89. Notice chart datum and the various levels of the tide above it. We know that low water

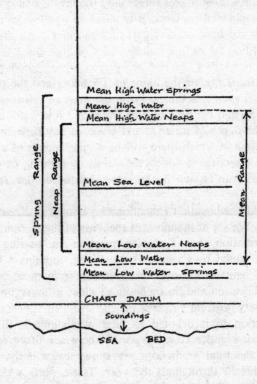

Fig. 89 Rise and range of the tide

spring tide is a 'low' low water and high water spring tide is a 'high' high water. The interval between these two levels is called the Spring range. Now look at mean low water Neap tides and mean high water Neap tides. The interval between them is called the Neap range. The mean level between all these is known as the mean sea level. Let us consider for a moment the Spring range.

Supposing that we have arrived at a port at exactly low water Springs. It will be high water in approximately six hours. The changes in the levels as they increase during these six hours are not constant but follow a sort of crescendo and diminuendo pattern. Roughly speaking this works as follows: we will begin at low water although of course we are only beginning at low water here since that is our example: we could equally well begin at high water and work down to low to complete the twelve-hour cycle. Starting then at low water; during the first hour, the tide level will rise one-sixteenth; during the second hour three-sixteenths; during the third and fourth hours increasing to one quarter. During the fifth hour, three-sixteenths and during the sixth to complete this part of the cycle, back to one-sixteenth. For practical purposes this 'sixteenths' rule is extremely useful.

We have seen that the vertical movement of the water is known as the range of the tide. When manoeuvring a vessel in shallow waters obviously the height of the tide is significant. When cruising, it is important to know the stage of the upward or downward movement of the water level. We have already seen this in our discussions on mooring alongside a quay. However, what really concerns us in making a passage of whatever length from place to place is not so much the up and down movement of the tide but the horizontal movement of it, which is known as the tidal stream.

The tidal stream is caused by the vertical undulation or tidal wave meeting resistance from the land and being turned into a horizontal advancing and retreating motion. The speed of it, which we have already learnt is properly called the 'rate', varies very much, and in some virtually inland seas, like the Baltic and the Mediterranean, is almost non-existent. In exceptional circumstances it can be found to run at seven or eight knots, but generally speaking, three to four knots is a fair average for a tidal stream at its fastest.

In the middle of the great oceans of the world, the tidal movement is a vertical undulation. It only becomes a horizontal movement as the land is approached. It will be obvious that when manoeuvring in harbour, anchoring, picking-up a buoy, coming alongside a quay, etc. the direction and rate of the tide is important. It may not be so clearly realized however that it is as important at sea.

To a motor-cruiser capable of maintaining an average economical cruising speed of 12 knots, a tide running at 4 knots may not seem of much account. However if you think about it, if that tide is running with you, then your speed over-the-ground is not 12 but 16 knots and if that tide conversely is against you then your over-the-ground speed is reduced to 8 knots. Clearly the faster your boat can go the less, on a passage, need you take the tidal stream into consideration, but the wise (and indeed the efficient) navigator always knows what the tide is doing.

The nautical almanack contains a great deal of information about the hourly rate and 'set' (that is to say, direction) of the tidal stream. *Reed's Almanack* contains excellent tidal chartlets. You can also use a tidal atlas or you can get the information from the chart itself.

Compass bearings

Let us now turn our attention to the compass and its usage. A 'true' bearing is that which relates to 'true' north. A compass bearing is the bearing obtained by looking at a ship's compass. A magnetic bearing is a bearing which relates to magnetic north which is not by any means the same as 'true' north. The bearings shown on a chart relate to true north. A very large motor yacht will have a gyro, or gyroscopic compass, which works on true bearings. More modest vessels will use a magnetic compass of some sort or other. Let us examine therefore for a moment or two, what we mean by a magnetic compass.

Take a piece of iron, rub it with another magnet or suspend it in a magnetic field and you have a magnet. This magnetized bar will have at either end of it, a red and blue pole which are terms given not because of their colour but for the sake of definition. If we approach two red poles they will move away from each other, likewise two blue, but take two magnets and approach the blue end of one with the red end of another and they will not only approach, they will come together and stay there.

Now the earth may itself be considered as a magnet and the two poles north and south can be the poles of that magnet. If we suspend a magnetic bar in the earth's field so that it can revolve freely, then the red end of this magnet will point towards the blue pole of the earth and the blue end of the magnet to the red pole of the earth. So far all you will know is where the two poles lie since one end of our magnet will be pointing to one pole and the other to the other pole. If however we fix a circular compass card on top of our magnetic bar, marked out in points and degrees, or just in degrees, we now have a simple compass capable of showing us the direction of magnetic north and of any of the cardinal and inter-cardinal points round the compass.

A good yacht's compass is a lot more sophisticated than that but even a really good compass may not necessarily point to magnetic north. In the factory it may but when it is put in the vessel, because of the presence of other metals, it may deviate one side or another from magnetic north, and this error is what we call 'deviation'. Sometimes such a deviation error is surprisingly large. In the bigger compasses the deviation error can be greatly reduced by inserting small compensating magnets. It is a skilled job and is carried out by a compass adjuster. But even so errors are likely to remain.

However there is no need for despondency. As long as the errors are known we have only to correct on their behalf and we can navigate perfectly efficiently. I say errors in the plural because it will be found in practice that the deviation will vary according to the ship's head. It will be necessary, therefore, to know what the errors are, not only when our ship's head is in one direction but right round the compass. The simplest way to do this is to make a deviation graph. To do this we need a definite known bearing. A simple and certain way of finding this is to make use of what is known as a transit. Two clearly visible objects on shore which, when brought into line, will give a definite known bearing, and make a transit.

Let us assume that we are fortunate enough to have found not only a perfect transit but a transit visible from a sheltered anchorage in which we can 'swing' our ship. Having got our transit all we need to do now is to turn our vessel slowly round, holding steady on each cardinal and inter-cardinal point for long enough to plot them on a graph. We should end up with a table like that below. The left-hand column shows the ship's head by our compass. The second column shows the compass bearing of the transit, that is to say the bearing that we got when the two objects were in line by our ship's compass. The third column is always the same because it is the known

magnetic bearing of the transit and the fourth column is the difference between columns two and three, which as you can see
shows the deviation.

DEVIATION TABLE

Vessel's Head by Compass	Compass Bearing of Transit	Magnetic Bearing of Transit	Deviation
North	199°	200°	1°E
NNE	198°	,,	2°E
NE	197½°	,,	2½°E
ENE	198°	,,	2°E
East	198½°	,,	1½°E
ESE	199°	,,	1°E
SE	200°	,,	NIL
SSE	201°	,,	1°W
South	202°	,,	2°W
SSW	203°	,,	3°W
SW	203½°	,,	3½°W
WSW	203½°	,,	3½°W
West	203°	,,	3°W
WNW	202½°	,,	2½°W
NW	201½°	,,	1½°W
NNW	200°	,,	NIL

Now we take a piece of graph paper and mark the degrees of
deviation along the horizontal axis along the top east or west of a
zero line down the centre. The points of the compass are marked on
the left along the vertical axis. We now plot the various deviations
and join them up in a curve. In point of fact you will see it is a
double curve and this is normal. It is now easy to see that we can
find the deviation for any compass course.

But how is this going to work in practice? Supposing that we are
sailing a given course and we wish to plot that course on our chart.
We get our deviation graph (which, incidentally, should always be
kept handy to the chart table, or according to the size of the boat,
wherever the navigator works his magic) and we look at it to check
whether there is any deviation for the course we are steering. If
there is, this must be applied before we plot it on the chart. On the

chart at various points there will be what are known as compass roses. These show us true and magnetic north. On a pre-1972 Admiralty chart, these show us two rings; the true bearings from 0° to 360° on the outer ring and the magnetic bearings from 0° to 360° on the inner ring. On Admiralty charts from 1972 onwards, only the true ring is printed, but magnetic north is still shown. On some other charts, like for example the Stanford charts, the compass rose printed is the magnetic. We use these compass roses either to draw in bearings or to take bearings of objects on the chart and for this purpose we use some form of parallel rule. Two pieces of equipment which the navigator must have are some form of parallel rule and a pair of dividers to measure distance. It goes without saying that he must also have at least one sharp-pointed, hard pencil. Now if there were no deviation on the course we are steering, we would simply take the bearing read from the ship's compass say 010°, run our parallel rule over to the nearest compass rose to the area in which we are sailing on the chart, measure 010°, run the parallel rule back and draw in our course.

If, however, on 010° there is some deviation, this must be applied to the bearing (either added to it or subtracted from it) before we put our parallel rule on the compass rose and before we mark in the course on the chart. Having done this the course that we will have drawn in on the chart will be our compass course. Conversely, if from a given point on the chart, we wish to head say, due north, we have now a magnetic course 'due north'. We look at our deviation graph and we find there is 1° of easterly deviation. This must be applied to the magnetic course to give us the compass course which will be our 'course to steer'. If we had steered due north without applying deviation we would not be steering the proper compass course. Look now at figures 90 and 91, which illustrate the principle of the application of deviation.

Both figures show a bird's eye view of a boat. In figure 90, the line A B represents the direction in which we are sailing, that is the direction of our ship's head. The angle BAD is the compass course while the angle BAC is the magnetic course. We have already learnt that deviation is the difference between a compass and a magnetic course. We have also learnt that the degrees of a compass run clockwise from 0° to 359° and with this in mind we call easterly deviation 'plus' and westerly deviation 'minus'. Accordingly we either add or subtract our deviation from our compass course which is measured at an angle clockwise around the compass. Look again at the first figure.

Notice that the magnetic course is less than the compass course by the amount of the westerly deviation. To find the magnetic course therefore we simply subtract the westerly deviation from the

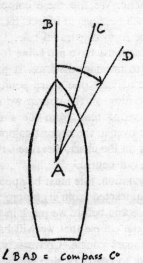

∠ BAD = Compass C°
∠ BAC = Magnetic C°

Fig. 90 Principle of applying deviation (1)

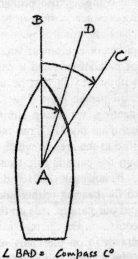

∠ BAD = Compass C°
∠ BAC = Magnetic C°

Fig. 91 Principle of applying deviation (2)

compass course. Now look at the second figure: in this, the magnetic course is larger than the compass course and by the amount of easterly deviation. Accordingly, we add easterly deviation to the compass course in order to get the magnetic course. From these two examples we can see that when the deviation is easterly the compass needle is deflected counter-clockwise. To convert a magnetic course to a compass course therefore we apply westerly deviation clockwise and easterly deviation counter-clockwise. This could be shortened to a rule of thumb, for example: 'magnetic to compass, westerly clockwise'. In other words, if our course on the chart is due north and we have one degree of westerly deviation we apply the rule and our compass course will now be 1° east instead of north, or in terms of three figure notation, 001°. Similarly, if we wish to convert a compass course (the course which we have taken from our ship's compass) into a magnetic course (that we wish to plot on the chart), the same rule of thumb gives us 'westerly deviation counter-clockwise', and of course 'easterly deviation clockwise'.

In learning about deviation we have been discussing the difference between magnetic bearings plotted on, or taken from, the chart, and compass bearings from our ship's compass. We learnt earlier in this chapter that a true bearing is a three figure bearing based on true as opposed to magnetic north. The difference, albeit of a few degrees, can be seen when we look at any compass rose on the chart. There will also be marked some information about the variation. This might read: 'variation so many degrees and minutes easterly' and also the fact that it is 'increasing by so many minutes annually'. Provided you have an up-to-date chart these increases of variation are so small that you can afford to ignore them. They are in fact caused by the movement of the magnetic field as represented by the poles in relation to true north. In practice, the compass rose will be corrected quite accurately enough for variation in a small yacht – unless you have got some charts of such antiquity that they were better off in a maritime museum! In other words, you can for all practical purposes use the magnetic rose on the chart, working from magnetic north as shown. If you are using a modern Admiralty chart it is easier to use the true rose and correct for variation in order to obtain the magnetic bearing. With the older type chart, you can, as I have indicated, use the magnetic rose, and this also applies to charts like the Stanford charts which print the magnetic rose.

If your yacht is of a size to carry a gyro-compass then you will be using the true north axis on the compass rose on your chart since the gyro compass reads true north. But magnetic compasses require correction. In order to correct for variation we apply the same rule as for deviation. The application of deviation converts a compass to magnetic course. The application of variation converts a magnetic course to a true course, and of course vice-versa. We apply variation to the magnetic course using the rule 'easterly variation clockwise; westerly variation counter-clockwise'. If we were taking a true course from the true rose on the chart and we wished to convert this to a magnetic course then we would apply 'clockwise variation for westerly and counter-clockwise for easterly'.

Plotting a course

Having learnt something about charts, about tides and tidal streams and about deviation and the application of it let us now get down to the pleasant business of doing a little chart work. Let us assume that we are at a position on the chart called A. We wish to sail to another position called B. We, or our helmsman, wants to know what course to steer to arrive at B. We take the parallel rule and a good sharp pencil and we draw a line from A to B. This is known as the course to make good. We put one edge of the parallel rule against this course and then move the rule across the chart to the nearest compass rose from which we read off the bearing on the magnetic ring. We write it down and we have the course to make good. We must now get our deviation graph and see whether there is any deviation to be applied for this particular course. For the sake of simplicity in this example let us assume that there is not.

Now if there were no tidal stream in the waters in which we are cruising all we would have to do is to tell the helmsman to steer the course to make good and we should eventually arrive at point B. However we are in tidal waters. From the chart itself or from the nautical almanack or from a tidal atlas we have found out what the tide is doing: that is to say, its direction and its rate during this particular passage we are making.

We find that the tide will be setting us at an angle away from the course we wish to make good and it will therefore have to be compensated for. Of course, if it were setting at exactly the same direction as the course to make good, then no correction would be necessary. We would merely get to B that much faster. Similarly, if the tide were running directly against us we would take longer to arrive at B by the amount of the rate of the tide. What we have to do when the tide is setting at an angle to our course, is to make a simple calculation on the chart to give us a course to steer through the water which in practice will make good the course over the ground that we want and will bring us safely to B.

Look at figure 92. Our course is due east; (090° magnetic). This is the course we wish to make good. We are in a small motor-cruiser capable of 12 knots but whose economical cruising speed is 9 knots. We are motoring at 9 knots (9 nautical miles per hour). We have ascertained that the tide will be setting us to the south of our course, 090°. It is in point of fact setting due south. The rate of the tide is 3 knots. A moment's reflection will show that if we were to motor due east for one hour at 9 knots and during that hour the tidal stream would be setting us due south at a rate of 3 knots, we would

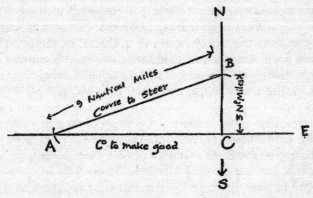

Fig. 92 Laying off a course, allowing for tidal effect

finish up not where we wanted to be, but to some point to the south of that.

We draw in our course to make good and at a point along it, any point, mark in c. From c draw a line due north; this represents the current. The current line is being drawn in the opposite direction to that in which it is running. We now take our dividers and measure off 3 nautical miles. The place on the chart where we measure is the latitude scale along its vertical edge, but it is important that we measure in the same latitude as that place on the chart on which we are working, for the following reason. The minutes of latitude on the scale represent one sea mile each of 6,080 feet or 1.15 land miles. We saw earlier in the section on charts how a Mercator's chart is a flat projection of part of the spherical surface of the earth and how the minutes of latitude increase in size as the poles are approached from the equator. In consequence, when we are measuring on the latitude scale the middle of our dividers should come over the latitude of the mid-point in the magnetic course to be laid off, and in this way we average out the inequalities of this scale.

With 3 nautical miles on our dividers we cut-off a point B along the tide or current line. With centre B and 9 nautical miles (our speed) we cut the course to steer giving us a point A. We now have a triangle ABC. AC represents the course to make good, CB is the current line and is also the rate of the current and AB is the course to steer.

By steering AB we will, if we have done our calculations correctly, arrive at C. We will be moving along the line AC with our bows pointing along the line AB, a sort of 'crabbing' movement. The important point is that it is AC along which we shall be moving, this is our course over the ground and it is the same as our course to make good. Notice that it is slightly shorter than AB. This shows that to travel the distance over the ground AC, we must motor a little further as represented by the distance AB because of the tide's effect. Had the tide been setting us in the same direction as our course we should have merely progressed that much faster over the ground; in this particular instance it would have been 12 knots.

It will be clear that the faster the craft you have, the more you can ignore the effect of the tidal stream. I am speaking in the main here for the many thousands of owners of small power craft used for pottering, fishing and coastal cruising; craft with a cruising speed range of say 8 to 20 knots. Apart from the racing powerboats you will find that most motor-cruisers of almost all sizes fall, in the case of speed, between these two figures. And if you think that you can ignore a 3 knot tide when you are cruising along at 15 knots you are making an error! You could for example be holding a steady course for three hours at 15 knots at the end of which you would have covered 45 miles over the ground. Let us assume that you were travelling due west. If during those three hours you were being set to the south by a 3 knot tide, at the end of the third hour you will be 9 nautical miles south of your intended position and such an error could be more than tiresome, it could be dangerous. Of course with coastwise cruising, where one can check one's position by reference to objects, land-marks, headlands etc. on shore, adjustments from time to time can be made, but one is not always cruising within sight of land and there are such things as fogs. In the British Navy, the navigation officer always knows what the tide is doing. It is a perfectly sound rule for the motor yachtsman.

But if that is a 'sound' rule, there is another rule which is 'golden' – '*Always know the ship's position*'. Whether by day, or by night, in thick weather or in clear, this is the golden rule. The certain knowledge of a ship's position is marked on the chart by a circle and is known as a 'fix'. An estimated position (E.P.) which, while quite possibly being laudably accurate, is nevertheless not an absolute certainty, is marked on the chart by a triangle. As a vessel proceeds on her way, it will be marked at intervals on the chart by a series of dots surrounded with either triangles or circles.

In this book we are dealing with simple coastal navigation and in this context the difference between an E.P. and a fix is best illustrated as follows. A vessel leaves harbour. Once outside, the navigator takes two or more bearings of objects identifiable on the chart. These bearings he draws in on the chart in the form of lines, known as position lines. Where they meet in the middle gives him his fix which he marks with a circle. From here he lays off his course and works out the course to steer which he gives to the helmsman (or it may be that he himself is the helmsman). The vessel proceeds on her way; the course steered has made allowance for a tidal set in a given direction at a given rate. At the end of an hour's motoring the navigator, with the three pieces of data necessary – the set and rate of the tidal stream and the speed of his ship – can mark on the chart a position round which he puts a triangle. At the end of another hour's motoring he does the same thing.

But he has by now crossed a bay and is once more in sight of land and being able to identify two or more objects on the shore and on the chart he takes his bearings, marks his position lines on the chart and gets his fix round which he puts a circle. Alongside all fixes and E.P.s must be put the time when the bearing was taken in the case of a fix or, in the case of an E.P., the time of calculation. The navigator is now in a position to compare on the chart his fix and his E.P. This will show him amongst other things, the accuracy of his navigation, the accuracy of his tidal allowance, and indeed, although who are we to doubt such pundits, the accuracy of the tidal predictions! If our navigator were going to be out of sight of land for several days, he would still be able to fix his position by making use of the art of celestial navigation or navigating by heavenly bodies, or to put it more simply by taking bearings of the stars at night and of the sun by day. Perhaps I should mention that it is eminently possible to make use of the moon in this connection as well although it is a somewhat esoteric branch of celestial navigation. At night, the position lines obtained will give him a perfectly good fix which he can compare with his estimated position on the chart. This, although I have very much simplified it, is what navigation is all about.

When navigating by heavenly bodies, the navigator makes use of a sextant; a delightfully mysterious looking collection of arms and segments and scales and mirrors, but which is in point of fact an efficient device for measuring angles. The coastal navigator on the other hand, makes use of a compass. The navigator sights along the top of the compass. From his eye an imaginary line passes the centre of the compass and runs straight to the shore object. Let us say the line cuts the compass at due east (090°). The navigator now knows that the bearing of the particular object at which he is looking is 090°. But, nothing in navigation is *that* simple! The course we are steering may be carrying some deviation and if our deviation graph proves this to be so, then that deviation must be applied according to the rule of thumb we have already learnt. The navigator now has a magnetic bearing of the object and by using the magnetic rose on the chart and the parallel rule as we have learnt to do, he can draw in his position line from the object on shore so that it cuts his estimated course line. If that was the only bearing he was able to take, he would have to put an E.P. triangle not a circle, because all that the single bearing or single position line can do is to tell him that his vessel is somewhere along that line. In other words since there is still room for error it is an E.P.

To get a proper fix therefore he needs at least one other position line. Let us say that the coastline abounds in easily identifiable objects (a circumstance all too rare!). He selects three, deliberately spaced well apart. The navigator must remember to take the bearing on the bow first as opposed to the bearings more on the beam. This is because the beam bearings will change more quickly as the vessel moves past. These position lines he now plots on the chart and where they cross we put a circle to show that it is a fix and we write the time alongside. However it is my sad duty to point out that such position lines seldom all meet together. They usually meet forming a small triangle which navigators term a 'cocked hat'.

Look now at figure 93. Here we see a fix by three position lines. Notice that we have a cocked hat, but notice particularly where the fix is. This is because the navigator has very correctly marked his fix at that point on the cocked hat nearest to danger; manifest in this instance by the rocks shown in the illustration.

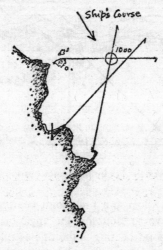

Fig. 93 Fix by three position lines

I spoke just now of the possibility of there being only one identifiable object on shore and in consequence only one available position line. Provided that this is identified in time it is perfectly possible to fix the ship by making use of what is known as a four-point bearing. Checking carefully with our compass we note the time when this object is four-points that is to say 45° on the bow. We maintain our course and steady speed. When the object comes abeam we note the time. We know our speed through the water and consequently the distance travelled. It may be that this will have been affected by tidal set and will not necessarily be the course and distance made good over the ground so, as we have already learnt to do, we must take the tide into consideration. The course with which the two bearings make an angle must be the course made good, and the distance factor must be calculated by the same token, from the speed made good and not the speed through the water. Look at figure 94. If we assume for the purposes of this illustration that the line A B represents the course made good, then at B, when the object on shore C, is four-points, the distance B C will equal A B. Since we know A B, we know B C, and B is our position.

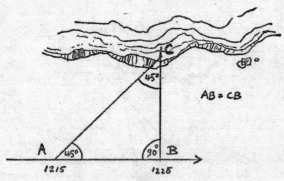

Fig. 94 Fix by four-point bearing

It is not necessary to use a four-point bearing; another similar method is that known as 'doubling the angle on the bow'. Having learnt what a four-point bearing is the title of this speaks for itself. You take the bearing of your shore object at some point on the bow, say, 30°. Look now at figure 95. This shows that we have taken our second bearing B C when the angle has been doubled, in other words 60° on the bow. As with the four-point bearing the distance run will be the same as the distance from the object on shore when the latter bears (in this example) 60°. Once again, due allowance must be made for the tide and the navigator must work from the course and speed made good. In both these examples, the bearing taken was either on the bow in both cases, or on the bow and the beam. There is another useful method making use of a slightly different principle, known as a 'running fix'. With the running fix we take our first bearing of our single object and note the time. We continue

226

motoring a steady course and speed for, let us say, half an hour. We now take our second bearing, again noting the time. The two bearings are now drawn on the chart, making any corrections which may be necessary for deviation. The principle of the running fix is as follows.

We know that at the time of the first bearing, our vessel was at some point along that position line. We also know that at the time

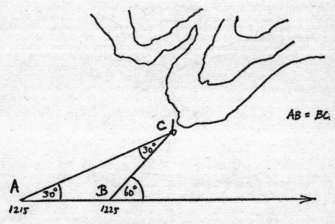

Fig. 95 Doubling the angle on the bow

of the second bearing, she lay somewhere along that second position line. Between the two bearings she has maintained course and speed. Now, if we can find a line equal to the distance made good, that is including the effect of the tide (if any) and running in the same direction as the course made good, then the two points at the end of this line where it meets the two position lines will give us our fixed position on those two lines. Look now at figure 96.

Our course is east (090°). Our speed a steady 9 knots. At 10.00 hours we take our first bearing of a lighthouse bearing north-east. At 10.30 hours we take our second bearing. These two bearings we will call E A and E B. The tide direction is east-north-east and let us say it is a good spring tide of rate 4 knots. Having laid-off our two bearings on the chart we take a point X on E A and from it we draw a line due east 090°. Taking our dividers we measure along this line from x of $4\frac{1}{2}$ nautical miles, which we have taken from the latitude scale on the chart (remembering to use that part of the scale opposite the area we are working in). We take $4\frac{1}{2}$ nautical miles because our speed is 9 knots and time between the two bearings was half an hour. The new point we will call P and x P represents the course we have steered and the course and the distance sailed through the water. From the point P we draw a line east-north-east.

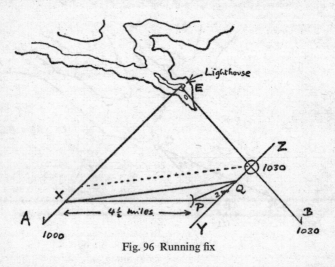

Fig. 96 Running fix

This is the tide line, just as we took only a half-hour of speed so we take half-hour of tide rate and with our dividers we measure off two nautical miles from the point P. This gives us a new point Q and a new line, the current line P Q. Now join x Q. Look carefully at x Q. It is the course and the distance made good. Now we get our parallel rule and putting it on E A we run it over to E B so that it just touches at the point Q. This new line we will call Y Z and where Y Z cuts E B is our ship's position at 10.30 hours. A useful check of accuracy is obtained as follows. Take the parallel rule and place it along x Q. Run it up until it touches E B at the new found fixed position at 10.30. The distance between the two new points where it cuts E B and E A should equal x Q.

Look now at figure 97. This explains the principle of the transferred position line. Notice here the difference between the four-point bearing, doubling the angle on the bow and the running fix. In each of these cases the first bearing was taken well before the object, the single object on shore, was abeam. In the illustration I have drawn a position line taken when the object was abaft the beam. Of course we could have taken it before the beam but I have done the illustration in this way to emphasize a point. The transferred position line is extremely useful in dense weather. As in the illustration, you might have two headlands with single identifi-

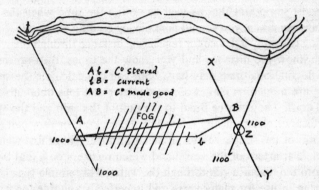

BZ = Error or difference between Estimated Position B and Position Z obtained by transferring position line.

Fig. 97 Transferred position line

able objects on each one. You might have been in dense weather which clears, allowing you to obtain a bearing of the first object. Then you run into fog again and when the fog lifts you are able to get a bearing of the second object. You, as navigator, are naturally anxious to fix your position as soon as possible. This you can do by transferring the first bearing you took, over to the second and where it cuts, will give you a position. The method is as follows.

We will assume that our two position lines have been drawn in on the chart with the times marked alongside them. We take a point on the first position line and call it A, we do not take any old point but at the point where we estimate our ship to be at that time. From A we plot our course made good in the same manner as the running fix and this gives us the line A B. Taking the parallel rule we place it along the first position line and run it across until it touches the point B. This gives us a new line X Y and where this line cuts the second position line will give us our fix at Z and at the time when the second bearing was taken.

It will be appreciated that the accuracy of this fix depends very much upon a steady course and speed being maintained between A and B. It may well be, that in the intervening fog, you have had to slow down. At times, the vessel may have almost been stopped. In cases like this, where a constant known speed cannot be maintained, it is most important that as well as noting the time when the two bearings are taken, you should note the log reading of the two times.

A log is simply a device for registering distance through the water. If you know the distance and you know the times, then no matter what fluctuations there may have been you can calculate the speed. There are numerous makes of speedometer and logs obtainable for small craft. They can be fitted to the hull of the ship and the speed and distance electronically relayed to the cockpit; or they can be in the form of the simple rotator, a metal arrangement of fins which is towed 75 ft astern of the vessel and which registers on a dial on the transom the distance run through the water. This simple type of log has been in use for many years and is perfectly suitable for vessels of modest and medium speed.

But the point which I am making here is that particularly in the case of the transferred position line, the speed between the two points A and B must be known as accurately as possible; otherwise the point Z in our figure will not be a fix but very much an E. P.

Furthermore, it will doubtless do no harm to reiterate that for the scheme to work A B must be the course and distance made good over the ground and not just through the water.

In *Reed's Almanack* will be found extremely useful Time, Speed and Distance tables from which you can find the distance run in a given time at speeds of from $2\frac{1}{2}$ knots to 22 knots. Also you will find other tables, such as the table giving a boat's average daily speed in twenty-four hours from noon to noon; and another useful table is the Log speed table for use with the towed log we have been discussing.

Electronic instruments and radio beacons

Today's motor yacht can have the advantage of electronically-operated logs and speedometers and indeed the modern navigator is lucky in that there is such a wide range of electronic aids. These aids to navigation are of course extremely useful but it should be emphasized that they are 'aids' and in no way a substitute for the normal practice of navigation and pilotage.

The oldest of the radio aids to navigation, that is to say the one which has been in existence for the longest time, is that which is called D.F. or W/R.D.F. or Radio Direction Finding. The principle involved is quite simple. The yacht which is at sea obtains two or more bearings of R.D.F. stations; these are plotted on a chart like the position lines we learnt about, and a fix obtained. The point to remember, of course, is that the fix may be obtained out of sight of land and whatever the visibility, in fog, or by night.

Nowadays, radio beacons can be found dotted around most of the coastlines of the world. These beacons send out signals round the clock and they are an enormous boon to the yachtsman and other users of the sea. The signals can only be picked up by vessels which are equipped with a direction finding apparatus. This need not be expensive since quite small sets are now available.

A typical small D.F. set is the 'Heron'. The Heron incorporates a magnetic compass for the direct measurement of the D.F. bearings of the beacons. This means that the bearing obtained (after any necessary correction for deviation has been applied) will be the magnetic bearing of the beacon. I mention this because another excellent small D.F. set, the 'Beme Loop' produces in the first instance a bearing relative to the vessel's fore and aft line. This, having been corrected if necessary for any error, can then be applied to the yacht's true heading to give the true bearing of the beacon.

In both these cases, bearings when plotted on the chart, give you a position line. You merely repeat the procedure with one or more additional selected radio beacons. Your cross bearings will then give you your fix.

Reed's Nautical Almanack which we have already mentioned contains a lot of useful information about both marine and aeronautical beacons and gives their identification signals. Moreover, not only are beacons in the waters of the United Kingdom given but also those in the Atlantic Ocean, Bay of Biscay, Ushant to Gibraltar and the western and eastern Mediterranean.

These beacons vary slightly in operation, some working in thick weather and fog only, while others work for periods of six minutes, two or four times an hour. But most of them operate continually throughout twenty-four hours. In British waters they operate on the 285 to 315 kilocycle band or 1053 to 952·4 metre band: that is, on the long wave band of any radio set. Because of the abundance of these radio beacons and also the relative simplicity of the equipment necessary, I would have no hesitation in placing them as the principle radio navigation aid for small vessels.

Radar

When it comes to larger vessels, there are a number of both interesting and useful installations. Such a one is radar; which stands for Radio Direction and Range. The principle here is that a wave is transmitted and its echo from any solid object is received. The time between the transmission and reception of the echo can be measured. This is proportional to the range of the object. As any one knows, who has seen a small radar set operating, the beam of the transmission may be rotated and so relative bearings can be obtained. A screen shows the yacht in the centre. This is the plan position indicator. On it all solid objects which will produce an echo surround the centrally placed yacht on the screen. Radar is in consequence extremely helpful as a position indicator relative to objects moving or stationary in darkness or poor visibility. Many navigational buoys are nowadays fitted with radar reflectors and these are picked up by the beam. The same applies to port radar installations ashore. There are a fair number of types of yacht radar installation available. The technical equipment is distinctly expensive.

Consol

Let us now consider 'Consol'. Consol is a long range navigational aid. The Consol beacon transmits a radiation pattern consisting of alternate dots and dashes. These are separated by a continuous note formed by the dots and dashes merging. The operator counts the number of dots and dashes to obtain a bearing by the following method. The dots and dashes add up to 60. In the merging of the dots and dashes in the middle, some of the characters are lost. The operator counts, then subtracts the total coming from 60 and then adds half of the difference to each of the dots and dash counts. He then refers to the Consol tables or Consol chart. The merging of the dots and dashes is known as the equi-signal. The number and type of character, that is to say dots or dashes before the equi-signal, is referred to the Consol chart; also the time at which the equi-signal is heard. The wise operator listens several times before referring to the chart. Before taking the bearing, it is advisable to make sure by reference to the Consol map, which dot or dash sector the yacht is in. This can easily be done from the dead-reckoning position on the chart. The receiver is tuned to the required Consol beacon and the station identified by its call sign. The operator then counts the characters and refers the true count to the Consol chart or tables. Position lines from two Consol stations will give a fix. It must be emphasized that Consol is a long range system; the maximum range being about 1,200 miles by day, to 1,500 miles by night.

Decca and Loran

Two other position finding systems are Decca and Loran. Loran which stands for Long Range Navigational Aid has about 650 miles range by day to 1,400 miles by night. With Loran a special receiver is needed and the operator uses latticed charts. Decca, on the other hand, is a medium range system and like Loran, requires a special receiver. The coverage and accuracy of the Decca system makes it particularly useful for coastal navigation and fishing vessels make considerable use of it. A feature is that the Decca Navigator is not difficult to operate. As with Loran and other radio beacons, much useful data about Decca may be found in *Reed's Nautical Almanack*. The Decca system has a particularly large coverage, indeed, it can be said to be world-wide.

Buoyage system

In pilotage waters there is a system of buoyage, which has been agreed internationally. This system is as follows:

The term STARBOARD HAND refers to buoys which must be left on the *right* hand when entering an estuary, a river, or harbour from seaward; or when going with the main Flood Tidal Stream.

The term PORT HAND refers to buoys which must be left on the *left* hand.

STARBOARD HAND MARKS

Shape: Conical.
Colour: Black, or Black and White Chequers.
Topmark (if any): Black Cone (point upwards), or, for purposes of differentiation, a Black Diamond – except at entrance to a channel.
Light (if any): White, showing 1 or 3 or 5 flashes – 'odd' numbers.

PORT HAND MARKS

Shape: Can.
Colour: Red, or Red and White Chequers.
Topmark (if any): Red Can or, for purposes of differentiation, a Red 'T' – except at entrance to a channel.
Light (if any): Red, showing any number of flashes up to 4 (or White showing 2 or 4 or 6 flashes – 'even' numbers).

MIDDLE GROUND MARKS

Shape: Spherical.
Colour: Red and White Horizontal Bands where main channel is to the right or the channels are of equal importance. Black and White Horizontal Bands where main channel is to the left.
Topmarks (if any):
  (*a*) Main channel to right.
      Outer end: Red Can.
      Inner end: Red 'T'.
  (*b*) Main channel to left.
      Outer end: Black Cone.
      Inner end: Black Diamond.

(c) Channels of equal importance.
　　　Outer end: Red Sphere.
　　　Inner end: Red St George's Cross.

Light (if any): As far as possible lights will be distinctive but no colours will be used other than White or Red, and neither colour nor rhythm will be such as to lead to uncertainty as to the side on which the mark shall be passed.

MID CHANNEL MARKS

Shape: Distinctive and different from the principal shapes (conical, can or sphere).
Colour: Black with Vertical Stripes or Red with Vertical Stripes.
Topmark (if any): Distinctive shape other than cone, can or sphere.
Light (if any): Different from nearby lights or marks at the sides of the channel.

ISOLATED DANGER MARKS

Shape: Spherical.
Colour: Wide Black and Red Horizontal Bands separated by a narrow White Band.
Topmark (if any): Sphere Black or Red, or half-Black and half-Red, horizontally.
Light (if any): White or Red with flashing character.

LANDFALL MARKS

Shape: In accordance with rules for channel marking.
Colour: Black and White or Red and White Vertical Stripes.
Light (if any): Flashing character.

UNIFORM SYSTEM OF MARKING WRECKS OFF THE COAST OF GREAT BRITAIN

Whenever a vessel is placed to mark a wreck off the coasts of England, Wales, Scotland, Ireland and the Isle of Man, the topsides shall be coloured Green with the word 'Wreck' painted in White letters thereon.

(a) *to be passed on Mariner's starboard Hand:*
Buoy: Conical, Green, 'Wreck' in White letters.

Lightbuoy: Conical, Green, giving a triple Green flash every 10 or 15 seconds.

Lightvessel: painted Green. 'Wreck' in White letters, with 3 Green lights vertical from the end of a cross yard. Deep-toned fog bell giving 3 strokes in succession at intervals of not more than 30 seconds.

(*b*) *to be passed on Mariner's Port Hand:*

Buoy: Can, Green, 'Wreck' in White letters.

Lightbuoy: Can, Green, giving a double Green flash every 10 seconds.

Lightvessel: painted Green, 'Wreck' in White letters, with 2 Green lights vertical from the end of a cross yard. Deep-toned fog bell giving 2 strokes in succession at intervals of not more than 30 seconds.

(*c*) *to be passed on Either Side:*

Buoy: Spherical, Green. 'Wreck' in White letters.

Lightbuoy: Spherical, Green, giving a single interrupted quick Green flash every 5 seconds.

All Trinity House spherical wreck marking lightbuoys in future will show interrupted quick-flashing Green (flashes rapidly at the rate of 240 per minute for 7 seconds and is then totally obscured for 3 seconds in a 10 second cycle).

Lightvessel: painted Green, 'Wreck' in White letters, with 4 Green lights (2 Green lights vertical from each end of a cross yard). Deep-toned fog bell giving 4 strokes *in succession at intervals* of not more than 30 seconds.

The day marks for wreck-marking lightvessels (shown between sunrise and sunset) are Green balls or shapes corresponding in number and arrangement to the Green lights.

A wreck-marking vessel shall not carry the ordinary riding light of a vessel at anchor.

Various Port Authorities may have regulations that differ in detail from the foregoing, but the buoy, light or signal used must have the above significance attached to it.

I conclude this chapter with those extracts from the Rule of the Road at Sea (the International Collision Regulations) which particularly apply to all power craft. The complete Rules will be found in *Reed's Nautical Almanack* or they may be obtained separately. It is essential that every man or woman in charge of a vessel, of whatever size, should be familiar with the Rule of the Road at Sea and know how to act promptly when the occasion demands.

EXTRACTS FROM THE INTERNATIONAL REGULATIONS FOR PREVENTING COLLISIONS AT SEA

To operate from September 1st, 1965

PART A – PRELIMINARY AND DEFINITIONS

Rule 1

(*a*) These Rules shall be followed by all vessels and seaplanes upon the high seas and in all waters connected therewith navigable by seagoing vessels, except as provided in Rule 30. Where, as a result of their special construction, it is not possible for seaplanes to comply fully with the provisions of Rules specifying the carrying of lights and shapes, these provisions shall be followed as closely as circumstances permit.

(*b*) The Rules concerning lights shall be complied with in all weathers from sunset to sunrise, and during such times no other lights shall be exhibited, except such lights as cannot be mistaken for the prescribed lights or impair their visibility or distinctive character, or interfere with the keeping of a proper look-out. The lights prescribed by these Rules may also be exhibited from sunrise to sunset in restricted visibility and in all other circumstances when it is deemed necessary.

(*c*) In the following Rules, except where the context otherwise requires:

(i) the word 'vessel' includes every description of water craft, other than a seaplane on the water, used or capable of being used as a means of transportation on water;

(ii) the word 'seaplane' includes a flying boat and any other aircraft designed to manoeuvre on the water;

(iii) the term 'power-driven vessel' means any vessel propelled by machinery;

(iv) every power-driven vessel which is under sail and not under power is to be considered a sailing vessel, and every vessel under power, whether under sail or not, is to be considered a power-driven vessel;

(v) a vessel or seaplane on the water is 'under way' when she is not at anchor, or made fast to the shore, or aground;

(vi) the term 'height above the hull' means height above the uppermost continuous deck;

(vii) the length and breadth of a vessel shall be her length over-all and largest breadth;

(viii) the length and span of a seaplane shall be its maximum length and span as shown in its certificate of airworthiness, or as determined by measurement in the absence of such certificate;

(ix) vessels shall be deemed to be in sight of one another only when one can be observed visually from the other;

(x) the word 'visible', when applied to lights, means visible on a dark night with a clear atmosphere;

(xi) the term 'short blast' means a blast of about one second's duration;

(xii) the term 'prolonged blast' means a blast of from four to six second's duration;

(xiii) the word 'whistle' means any appliance capable of producing the prescribed short and prolonged blasts;

(xiv) the term 'engaged in fishing' means fishing with nets, lines or trawls but does not include fishing with trolling lines.

PART B – LIGHTS AND SHAPES

Rule 2

Lights for Power Vessels or Seaplanes

A power-driven vessel when under way shall carry:

(i) On or in front of the foremast, or if a vessel without a foremast then in the forepart of the vessel, a white light so constructed as to show an unbroken light over an arc of the horizon of 225 degrees (20 points of the compass), so fixed as to show the light $112\frac{1}{2}$ degrees (10 points) on each side of the vessel, that is, from right ahead to $22\frac{1}{2}$ degrees (2 points) abaft the beam on either side, and of such a character as to be visible at a distance of at least 5 miles.

(ii) Either forward or abaft the white light mentioned in sub-section (i) a second white light similar in construction and character to that light. Vessels of less than 150 feet in length, shall not be required to carry this second white light but may do so.

(iii) These two white lights shall be so placed in a line with and over the keel that one shall be at least 15 feet higher than the other and in such a position that the forward light shall always be shown lower than the after one. The horizontal distance between the two white lights shall be at least three times the vertical distance. The lower of these two white lights or, if only one is carried, then that light, shall be placed at a height above the hull of not less than 20 feet, and, if the breadth of the vessel exceeds 20 feet, then at a height above the hull not less than such breadth, so however that the light need not be placed at a greater height above the hull than 40 feet. In all circumstances the light or lights, as the case may be, shall be so placed as to be clear of and above all other lights and obstructing superstructures.

(iv) On the starboard side a green light so constructed as to show an unbroken light over an arc of the horizon of $112\frac{1}{2}$ degrees (10 points of the compass), so fixed as to show the light from right ahead to $22\frac{1}{2}$ degrees (2 points) abaft the beam on the starboard side, and of such a character as to be visible at a distance of at least 2 miles.

(v) On the port side a red light so constructed as to show an unbroken light over an arc of the horizon of $112\frac{1}{2}$ degrees (10 points of the compass), so fixed as to show the light from right ahead to $22\frac{1}{2}$ degrees (2 points) abaft the beam on the port side, and of such a character as to be visible at a distance of at least 2 miles.

(vi) The said green and red sidelights shall be fitted with in-board screens projecting at least 3 feet forward from the light, so as to prevent these lights from being seen across the bows.

Rule 3

Lights for Power Vessels or Seaplanes, Towing or Pushing

(*a*) A power-driven vessel when towing or pushing another vessel or seaplane shall, in addition to her sidelights, carry two white lights in a vertical line one over the other, not less than 6 feet apart, and when towing and the length of the tow, measuring from the stern of the towing vessel to the stern of the last vessel towed, exceeds 600 feet, shall carry three white lights in a vertical line one over the other, so that the upper and lower lights shall be the same distance from, and not less than 6 feet above or below the middle light. Each of these lights shall be of the same construction and character and one of them shall be carried in the same position as the white light, prescribed in Rule 2 (i). None of these lights shall be carried at a height of less than 14 feet above the hull. In a vessel with a single mast, such lights may be carried on the mast.

(*b*) The towing vessel shall also show either the stern light specified in Rule 10 or in lieu of that light a small white light abaft the funnel or aftermast for the tow to steer by, but such light shall not be visible forward of the beam.

(*c*) Between sunrise and sunset a power-driven vessel engaged in towing, if the length of tow exceeds 600 feet, shall carry, where it can best be seen, a black diamond shape at least 2 feet in diameter.

Rule 4

Vessels not under Command

(*a*) A vessel which is not under command shall carry, where they can best be seen, and, if a power-driven vessel, in lieu of the lights required by Rule 2 (i) and (ii), two red lights in a vertical line one over the other not less than 6 feet apart, and of such a character as to be visible all round the horizon at a distance of at least 2 miles. By day, she shall carry in a vertical line one over the other not less than 6 feet apart, where they can best be seen, two black balls or shapes each not less than 2 feet in diameter.

Rule 5

Lights for Sailing Vessels and Vessels Towed

(*a*) A sailing vessel under way and any vessel or seaplane being towed shall carry the same lights as are prescribed in Rule 2 for a power-driven vessel or a seaplane under way, respectively, with the exception of the white lights specified therein, which they shall never carry. They shall also carry stern lights as specified in Rule 10, provided that vessels towed, except the last vessel of a tow, may carry, in lieu of such stern light, a small white light as specified in Rule 3 (*b*).

(*b*) In addition to the lights prescribed in section (*a*), a sailing vessel may carry on the top of the foremast two lights in a vertical line one over the other, sufficiently separated so as to be clearly distinguished. The upper light shall be red and the lower light shall be green. Both lights shall be constructed and fixed as prescribed in Rule 2 (i) and shall be visible at a distance of at least 2 miles.

(*c*) A vessel being pushed ahead shall carry, at the forward end, on the starboard side a green light and on the port side a red light, which shall have the same characteristics as the lights described in Rule 2 (*a*) (iv) and (v) and shall be screened as provided in Rule 2 (vi), provided that any number of vessels pushed ahead in a group shall be lighted as one vessel.

(*d*) Between sunrise and sunset a vessel being towed, if the length of the tow exceeds 600 feet, shall carry where it can best be seen a black diamond shape at least 2 feet in diameter.

Rule 6

Lights for Small Vessels

(*a*) When it is not possible on account of bad weather or other sufficient cause to fix the green and red sidelights, these lights shall be kept at hand lighted and ready for immediate use, and shall, on the approach of or to other vessels, be exhibited on their respective sides in sufficient time to prevent collision, in such manner as to make them most visible, and so that the green light shall not be seen on the port side nor the red light on the starboard side, nor, if practicable, more than 22½ degrees (2 points) abaft the beam on their respective sides.

(b) To make the use of these portable lights more certain and easy, the lanterns containing them shall each be painted outside with the colour of the lights they respectively contain, and shall be provided with proper screens.

Rule 7

Lights for Small Vessels

Power-driven vessels of less than 65 feet in length, vessels under oars or sails of less than 40 feet in length, and rowing boats, when under way shall not be required to carry the lights mentioned in Rules 2, 3 and 5, but if they do not carry them they shall be provided with the following lights:

(a) Power-driven vessels of less than 65 feet in length, except as provided in sections (b) and (c), shall carry:

(i) In the forepart of the vessel, where it can best be seen, and at a height above the gunwhale of not less than 9 feet, a white light constructed and fixed as prescribed in Rule 2 (i) and of such a character as to be visible at a distance of at least 3 miles.

(ii) Green and red sidelights constructed and fixed as prescribed in Rule 2 (iv) and (v), and of such a character as to be visible at a distance of at least 1 mile, or a combined lantern showing a green light and a red light from right ahead to 22½ degrees (2 points) abaft the beam on their respective sides. Such lantern shall be carried not less than 3 feet below the white light.

(b) Power-driven vessels of less than 65 feet in length when towing or pushing another vessel shall carry:

(i) In addition to the sidelights or the combined lantern prescribed in section (a) (ii) two white lights in a vertical line, one over the other not less than 4 feet apart. Each of these lights shall be of the same construction and character as the white light prescribed in section (a) (i) and one of them shall be carried in the same position. In a vessel with a single mast such lights may be carried on the mast.

(ii) Either a stern light as prescribed in Rule 10 or in lieu of that light a small white light abaft the tunnel or aftermast for the tow to steer by, but such light shall not be visible forward of the beam.

(c) Power-driven vessels of less than 40 feet in length may carry the white light at a less height than 9 feet above the gunwhale but it shall be carried not less than 3 feet above the sidelights or the combined lantern prescribed in section (a) (ii).

(d) Vessels of less than 40 feet in length, under oars or sails, except as provided in section (f), shall, if they do not carry the sidelights, carry, where it can best be seen a lantern showing a green light on one side and a red light on the other, of such a character as to be visible at a distance of at least 1 mile, and so fixed that the green light shall not be seen on the port side, nor the red light on the starboard side. Where it is not possible to fix this light, it shall be kept ready for immediate use and shall be exhibited in sufficient time to prevent collision and so that the green light shall not be seen on the port side nor the red light on the starboard.

(e) The vessels referred to in this Rule when being towed shall carry the sidelights or the combined lantern prescribed in sections (a) or (d) of this Rule, as appropriate, and a stern light as prescribed in Rule 10, or, except the last vessel of the tow, a small white light as prescribed in section (b) (ii). When being pushed ahead they shall carry at the forward end the sidelights or combined lantern prescribed in sections (a) or (d) of this Rule, as appropriate, provided that any number of vessels referred to in this Rule when pushed ahead in a group shall be lighted as one vessel under this Rule unless the overall length of the group exceeds 65 feet when the provisions of Rule 5 (c) shall apply.

(f) Small rowing boats, whether under oars or sail, shall only be required to have ready at hand an electric torch or a lighted lantern showing a white light, which shall be exhibited in sufficient time to prevent collision.

(g) The vessels and boats referred to in this Rule shall not be required to carry the lights or shapes prescribed in Rules 4 (a) and 11 (e), and the size of their day signals may be less than is prescribed in Rules 4 (c) and 11 (c).

Rule 10

Stern Light

(*a*) Except where otherwise provided in these Rules vessel when under way shall carry at her stern a white light, so constructed that it shall show an unbroken light over an arc of the horizon of 135 degrees (12 points of the compass), so fixed as to show the light 67½ degrees (6 points) from right aft on each side of the vessel, and of such a character as to be visible at a distance of at least 2 miles.

(*b*) In a small vessel, if it is not possible on account of bad weather or other sufficient cause for this light to be fixed, an electric torch or a lighted lantern showing a white light shall be kept at hand ready for use and shall, on the approach of an overtaking vessel, be shown in sufficient time to prevent collision.

Rule 11

Lights for Vessels at Anchor

(*a*) A vessel of less than 150 feet in length, when at anchor, shall carry in the forepart of the vessel, where it can best be seen, a white light visible all round the horizon at a distance of at least 2 miles. Such a vessel may also carry a second white light in the position prescribed in section (*b*) of this Rule but shall not be required to do so. The second white light, if carried, shall be visible at a distance of at least 2 miles and so placed as to be as far as possible visible all round the horizon.

(*b*) A vessel of 150 feet or more in length, when at anchor, shall carry near the stem of the vessel, at a height of not less than 20 feet above the hull, one such light, and at or near the stern of the vessel and at such a height that it shall be not less than 15 feet lower than the forward light, another such light. Both these lights shall be visible at a distance of at least 3 miles and so placed as to be as far as possible visible all round the horizon.

(*c*) Between sunrise and sunset every vessel when at anchor shall carry in the forepart of the vessel, where it can best be seen, one black ball not less than 2 feet in diameter.

(*d*) A vessel engaged in laying or in picking up a submarine cable or navigation mark, or a vessel engaged in surveying or underwater operations, when at anchor, shall carry the lights or shapes prescribed in Rule 4 (*c*) in addition to those prescribed in the appropriate preceding sections of this Rule.

(*e*) A vessel aground shall carry the light or lights prescribed in sections (*a*) or (*b*) and the two red lights prescribed in Rule 4 (*a*). By day she shall carry, where they can best be seen, three black balls, each not less than 2 feet in diameter, placed in a vertical line one over the other, not less than 6 feet apart.

Rule 12

Signal to Attract Attention

Every vessel or seaplane on the water may, if necessary in order to attract attention, in addition to the lights which she is by these Rules required to carry, show a flare-up light or use a detonating or other efficient sound signal that cannot be mistaken for any signal authorized elsewhere under these Rules.

Rule 14

Vessel under Sail – Using Power also

A vessel proceeding under sail, when also being propelled by machinery, shall carry in the daytime forward, where it can best be seen, one black conical shape, point downwards, not less than 2 feet in diameter at its base.

PART C – SOUND SIGNALS AND CONDUCT IN RESTRICTED VISIBILITY

Preliminary

1. The possession of information obtained from radar does not relieve any vessel of the obligation of conforming strictly with the Rules and, in particular, the obligations contained in Rules 15 and 16.

Rule 15

Sound Signals for Fog

(*a*) A power-driven vessel of 40 feet or more in length shall be provided with an efficient whistle, sounded by steam or by some substitute for steam, so placed that the sound may not be intercepted by any obstruction, and with an efficient fog-horn, to be sounded by mechanical means, and also with an efficient bell. A sailing vessel of 40 feet or more in length shall be provided with a similar fog-horn and bell.

(*b*) All signals prescribed in this Rule for vessels under way shall be given:

(i) by power-driven vessels on the whistle;

(ii) by sailing vessels on the fog-horn;

(iii) by vessels towed on the whistle or fog-horn.

(*c*) In fog, mist, falling snow, heavy rainstorms, or any other condition similarly restricting visibility, whether by day or night, the signals prescribed in this Rule shall be used as follows:

(i) A power-driven vessel making way through the water, shall sound at intervals of not more than 2 minutes a prolonged blast.

(ii) A power-driven vessel under way, but stopped and making no way through the water, shall sound at intervals of not more than 2 minutes two prolonged blasts, with an interval of about 1 second between them.

(iii) A sailing vessel under way shall sound, at intervals of not more than 1 minute, when on the starboard tack one blast, when on the port tack two blasts in succession, and when with the wind abaft the beam three blasts in succession.

(iv) A vessel when at anchor shall at intervals of not more than 1 minute ring the bell rapidly for about 5 seconds. In vessels of more than 350 feet in length the bell shall be sounded in the forepart of the vessel, and in addition there shall be sounded in the after part of the vessel, at intervals of not more than 1 minute for about 5 seconds, a gong or other instrument, the tone and sounding of which cannot be confused with that of the bell. Every vessel at anchor may in addition, in accordance with Rule 12, sound three blasts in succession, namely, one short, one prolonged and one short blast, to give warning of her position and of the possibility of collision to an approaching vessel.

(v) A vessel when towing, a vessel engaged in laying or in picking up a submarine cable or navigation mark, and a vessel under way which is unable to get out of the way of an approaching vessel through being not under command or unable to manoeuvre as required by these Rules shall, instead of the signals prescribed in subsections (i), (ii) and (iii) sound, at intervals, of not more than 1 minute, three blasts in succession, namely one prolonged blast followed by two short blasts.

(vi) A vessel towed, or, if more than one vessel is towed, only the last vessel of the tow, if manned, shall, at intervals of not more than 1 minute, sound four blasts in succession, namely, one prolonged blast followed by three short blasts. When practicable, this signal shall be made immediately after the signal made by the towing vessel.

(vii) A vessel aground shall give the bell signal and if required, the gong signal, prescribed in sub-section (iv) and shall, in addition, give three separate and distinct strokes on the bell immediately before and after such rapid ringing of the bell.

(viii) A vessel engaged in fishing when under way or at anchor shall at intervals of not more than 1 minute sound the signal prescribed in sub-section (v). A vessel when fishing with trolling lines and under way shall sound the signals prescribed in sub-sections (i), (ii) or (iii) as may be appropriate.

(ix) A vessel of less than 40 feet in length, a rowing boat, or a seaplane on the water, shall not be obliged to give the above-mentioned signals, but if she does not, she shall make some other efficient sound signal at intervals of not more than 1 minute.

(x) A power-driven pilot-vessel when engaged on pilotage duty may, in addition to the signals prescribed in sub-sections (i), (ii) and (iv) sound an identity signal consisting of 4 short blasts.

Rule 16

Speed to be moderate in fog

(a) Every vessel, or seaplane when taxi-ing on the water, shall in fog, mist, falling snow, heavy rainstorms or any other condition similarly restricting visibility, go at a moderate speed, having careful regard to the existing circumstances and conditions.

(*b*) A power-driven vessel hearing, apparently forward of her beam, the fog-signal of a vessel the position of which is not ascertained, shall, so far as the circumstances of the case admit, stop her engines, and then navigate with caution until danger of collision is over.

(*c*) A power-driven vessel which detects the presence of another vessel forward of her beam before hearing her fog signal or sighting her visually may take early and substantial action to avoid a close quarters situation but, if this cannot be avoided, she shall, so far as the circumstances of the case admit, stop her engines in proper time to avoid collision and then navigate with caution until danger of collision is over.

Part D – Steering and Sailing Rules

Preliminary – Risk of collision

1. In obeying and construing these Rules, any action taken should be positive, in ample time, and with due regard to the observance of good seamanship.

2. Risk of collision can, when circumstances permit, be ascertained by carefully watching the compass bearing of an approaching vessel. If the bearing does not appreciably change, such risk should be deemed to exist.

3. *Mariners should bear in mind that seaplanes in the act of landing or taking off, or operating under adverse weather conditions, may be unable to change their intended action at the last moment.*

4. Rules 17 to 24 apply only to vessels in sight of one another.

[*Rule 17 is for sailing vessels and therefore not included here.*]

Rule 18

Two Power Vessels meeting

(*a*) When two power-driven vessels are meeting end on, or nearly end on, so as to involve risk of collision, each shall alter her course to starboard, so that each may pass on the port side of the other. This Rule only applies to cases where vessels are meeting end on, or nearly end on, in such a manner as to involve risk of collision, and does not apply to two vessels which must, if both keep on their respective courses, pass clear of each other.

The only cases to which it does apply are when each of two vessels is end on, or nearly end on, to the other; in other words, to cases in which, by day, each vessel sees the masts of the other in a line, or nearly in a line, with her own; and by night, to cases in which each vessel is in such a position as to see both the sidelights of the other.

It does not apply, by day, to cases in which a vessel sees another ahead crossing her own course; or by night, to cases where the red light of one vessel is opposed to the red light of the other or where the green light of one vessel is opposed to the green light of the other or where a red light without a green light or a green light without a red light is seen ahead, or where both green and red lights are seen anywhere but ahead.

(b) For the purposes of this Rule and Rules 19 to 29 inclusive, except Rule 20 (b) and Rule 28, a seaplane on the water shall be deemed to be a vessel, and the expression 'power-driven vessel' shall be construed accordingly.

Rule 19

Two Power Vessels Crossing

When two power-driven vessels are crossing, so as to involve risk of collision, the vessel which has the other on her starboard side shall keep out of the way of the other.

Rule 20

Power and Sailing Vessels meeting

(a) When a power-driven vessel and a sailing vessel are proceeding in such directions as to involve risk of collision, except as provided for in Rules 24 and 26, the power-driven vessel shall keep out of the way of the sailing vessel.

(b) This Rule shall not give to a sailing vessel the right to hamper, in a narrow channel, the safe passage of a power-driven vessel which can navigate only inside such channel.

Rule 21

Vessel to keep course and speed

Where by any of these Rules one of two vessels is to keep out of the way, the other shall keep her course and speed. When, from any cause, the latter vessel finds herself so close that collision cannot be avoided by the action of the giving-away vessel alone, she also shall take such action as will best aid to avert collision (see Rules 27 and 29).

Rule 22

Vessels to avoid crossing ahead

Every vessel which is directed by these Rules to keep out of the way of another vessel shall, so far as possible, take positive early action to comply with this obligation and shall, if the circumstances of the case admit, avoid crossing ahead of the other.

Rule 23

Vessels to alter speed

Every power-driven vessel which is directed by these Rules to keep out of the way of another vessel shall, on approaching her, if necessary, slacken her speed or stop or reverse.

Rule 24

Vessel overtaking another

(a) Notwithstanding anything contained in these Rules, every vessel overtaking any other shall keep out of the way of the over-taken vessel.

(b) Every vessel coming up with another vessel from any direction more than 22½ degrees (2 points) abaft her beam, i.e., in such a position, with reference to the vessel which she is overtaking, that at night she would be unable to see either of that vessel's sidelights, shall be deemed to be an overtaking vessel; and no subsequent alteration of the bearing between the two vessels shall make the overtaking vessel a crossing vessel within the meaning of these Rules, or relieve her of the duty of keeping clear of the overtaken vessel until she is finally past and clear.

(c) If the overtaking vessel cannot determine with certainty whether she is forward of or abaft this direction from the other vessel, she shall assume that she is an overtaking vessel and keep out of the way.

Rule 25

Power Vessels in narrow channels

(a) In a narow channel every power-driven vessel when proceeding along the course of the channel shall, when it is safe and practicable, keep to that side of the fairway or mid-channel which lies on the starboard side of such vessel.

(b) Whenever a power-driven vessel is nearing a bend in a channel where a vessel approaching from the other direction cannot be seen, such power-driven vessel, when she shall have arrived within one-half ($\frac{1}{2}$) mile of the bend, shall give a signal by one prolonged blast of her whistle, which signal shall be answered by a similar blast given by any approaching power-driven vessel that may be within hearing around the bend. Regardless of whether an approaching vessel on the farther side of the bend is heard, such bend shall be rounded with alertness and caution.

(c) In a narrow channel a power-driven vessel of less than 65 feet in length shall not hamper the safe passage of a vessel which can navigate only inside such channel.

Rule 26

Vessels to avoid Fishing Vessels

All vessels not engaged in fishing, except vessels to which the provisions of Rule 4 apply, shall, when under way, keep out of the way of vessels engaged in fishing. This Rule shall not give to any vessel engaged in fishing the right of obstructing a fairway used by vessels other than fishing vessels.

Rule 27

Special Circumstances

In obeying and construing these Rules due regard shall be had to all dangers of navigation and collision, and to any special circumstances, including the limitations of the craft involved, which may render a departure from the above Rules necessary in order to avoid immediate danger.

PART E – SOUND SIGNALS FOR VESSELS IN SIGHT OF ONE ANOTHER

Rule 28

Sound Signals for Power Vessels

(a) When vessels are in sight of one another, a power-driven vessel under way, in taking any course authorized or required by these Rules, shall indicate that course by the following signals on her whistle, namely:

One short blast to mean 'I am altering my course to starboard'.

Two short blasts to mean 'I am altering my course to port'.

Three short blasts to mean 'My engines are going astern'.

(b) Whenever a power-driven vessel which, under these Rules, is to keep her course and speed, is in sight of another vessel and is in doubt whether sufficient action is being taken by the other vessel to avert collision, she may indicate such doubt by giving at least five short and rapid blasts on the whistle. The giving of such a signal shall not relieve a vessel of her obligations under Rules 27 and 29 or any other Rule, or of her duty to indicate any action taken under these Rules by giving the appropriate sound signals laid down in this Rule.

(c) Any whistle signal mentioned in this Rule may be further indicated by a visual signal consisting of a white light visible all round the horizon at a distance of at least 5 miles, and so devised that it will operate simultaneously and in conjunction with the whistle-sounding mechanism and remain lighted and visible during the same period as the sound signal.

(*d*) Nothing in these Rules shall interfere with the operation of any special rules made by the Government of any nation with respect to the use of additional whistle signals between ships of war or vessels sailing under convoy.

PART F – MISCELLANEOUS

Rule 29

The Ordinary Practice of Seamen

Nothing in these Rules shall exonerate any vessel, or the owner, master or crew thereof, from the consequences of any neglect to carry lights or signals, or of any neglect to keep a proper look-out, or of the neglect of any precaution which may be required by the ordinary practice of seamen, or by the special circumstances of the case.

Rule 30

Reservations of Rules for Harbours and Inland Navigation

Nothing in these Rules shall interfere with the operation of a special rule duly made by local authority relative to the navigation of any harbour, river, lake, or inland water, including a reserved seaplane area.

Rule 31

Distress Signals

When a vessel or seaplane on the water is in distress and requires assistance from other vessels or from the shore, the following shall be the signals to be used or displayed by her, either together or separately, namely:

(i) A gun or other explosive signal fired at intervals of about a minute.

(ii) A continuous sounding with any fog-signal apparatus.

(iii) Rockets or shells, throwing red stars fired one at a time at short intervals.

(iv) A signal made by radiotelegraphy or by any other signalling method consisting of the group ...————... (SOS) in the Morse Code.

(v) A signal sent by radiotelephony consisting of the spoken word 'Mayday'.

(vi) The International Code Signal of distress indicated by N.C.

(vii) A signal consisting of a square flag having above or below it a ball or anything resembling a ball.

(viii) Flames on the vessel (as from a burning tar barrel, oil barrel, etc.).

(ix) A rocket parachute flare showing a red light.

(x) A smoke signal giving off a volume of orange-coloured smoke.

(xi) Slowly and repeatedly raising and lowering arms outstretched to each side.

NOTE – Vessels in distress may use the radiotelegraph alarm signal or the radiotelephone alarm signal to secure attention to distress calls and messages. *The radiotelegraph alarm signal, which is designed to actuate the radiotelegraph auto alarms of vessels so fitted, consists of a series of twelve dashes, sent in 1 minute, the duration of each dash being 4 seconds, and the duration of the interval between 2 consecutive dashes being 1 second. The radiotelephone alarm signal consists of 2 tones transmitted alternatively over periods of from 30 seconds to 1 minute.*

The use of any of the foregoing signals, except for the purpose of indicating that a vessel or a seaplane is in distress, and the use of any signals which may be confused with any of the above signals, is prohibited.

CHAPTER 8

Racing in Powerboats

THIS, one of the most exciting forms of motor boating, should be approached with sensible caution. I do not mean because the sport is dangerous but because a lot of the beginners' time and money can be wasted. I would *emphasize*, right away, that the difference between this and cruising, is similar to that between touring in a car and motor-racing. It cannot be learned from a book either. The best way to start, unless you already have friends in the game, is to join a club. You can learn all about clubs by writing to the Royal Yachting Association, Victoria Way, Woking, Surrey. This is, of course if you are in Great Britain. Elsewhere, you write to the national authority of the country in which you are living. The R.Y.C. publish a list of affiliated clubs, giving their secretaries and addresses, and the classes of boats that they race. This information can be bought but I would strongly recommend becoming a member of the R.Y.A. It is by no means expensive, gives you a lot for your money and, furthermore, if you are taking powerboat racing seriously and should happen to get as far as International class, then you will have to be a member of the R.Y.A. anyway!

But if you are interested in powerboat racing, you probably do have one or more friends who are already doing it and through them you should be able to join the club of your choice. Once you are a member, you start talking to other members and watching races and looking at boats and being given a great deal of advice.

Here let it be said that in the area of small powerboat racing there is a difference from the point of view of the newcomer to say that of sailing dinghy racing. In the case of the latter, a good way to learn to sail is to go along as crew. By handling the sheets of a dinghy much can be learnt about sail trimming. Even so, it does not teach you to steer and neither does going as crew passenger in a power-boat. In other words, you are going to have to get a boat of your own. Once you have a boat you can enter club events and see how you get on. It is here, too, that belonging to a club can help you. Members of clubs are always changing boats and you should be able, with the right advice, to pick a boat in the class of your choice. Now let it be admitted straightaway that racing in power boats is not cheap. You can spend between £4 and £5 on petrol at one meeting alone. Multiply this by the number of meetings you would like to attend and you will see what I mean. Expense varies of course with size of boat.

History of the sport

The Royal Yachting Association is our national authority which controls the affairs of motor boat racing in Britain and also can speak for Britain when it comes to international competition. But it wasn't always like this. Way back in 1902 when British motor boat racing was in its infancy, an association was formed to look after it called the Marine Motoring Association. It was not a strong child and it grew slowly and its growth was seriously inhibited by the First World War. But by the late 'twenties the sport could be said to have got under way.

The sort of boats which were used were hydro-planes. They had quite small inboard engines, about 1.5 litres, and outboard engines of 1.5 litres and under. A typical race was the Duke of York Trophy. This was an annual race, sometimes on Southampton Water, sometimes elsewhere. The boats were hydro-planes, outboard-engined up to 500 cc. The rules were the rules of the 1921 International Motor Yachting Union.

The International Motor Yachting Union is nowadays referred to as the U.I.M., that is by its French name – the Union Internationale Motonautique. It was the U.I.M. who in the 'thirties defined a hydro-plane as '. . . a boat whose propeller acts in or against the water, and which has one or more breaks in the longitudinal continuity of the immersed surface forming more than one lifting surface against the water'. These breaks in the longitudinal continuity were known as 'steps' and gave lift to the hull.

Early designers

The first boat in the world to achieve a speed of 50 knots had five steps; she was called Maple Leaf IV. When competing in the 1912/13 races for the B.I. or Harmsworth Trophy, Maple Leaf defeated all comers. She was designed and built by S. E. Saunders. Between the years 1906 and 1909, an ex-patriot American from Chicago living in France, William Henry Fauber, had taken out nine British patents for hydro-plane craft. One of these patents taken out in 1908 by Fauber was used by Saunders in Maple Leaf IV.

Saunders had already been designing hydro-planes and had amassed considerable knowledge. He applied his own ideas to Fauber's patent, reducing the number of steps (Fauber's patent had eight steps) to five. The bow in Fauber's design was flat; Saunders drew a convex V-section bow. In Saunders's design the V gradually moved to about $2\frac{1}{2}°$ rise of floor at the forward step. Fauber had actually designed a fore-keel to extend over the first two steps. This fore-keel Saunders did away with. Broadly speaking, though, Maple Leaf IV is designed to Fauber's patent; all the steps having the same rise of floor and all the points on a straight line.

Maple Leaf IV belongs to the days long before construction in marine-ply or G.R.P. She was built of Honduras mahogany, her bottom and top-sides having three skins, the two inner skins double diagonal and the outer skin, fore-and-aft, and all sewn together with copper wire. Enormous developments have taken place in glues, in metal, and in plastics since the days when Maple Leaf was built, enabling boats to be not only lighter but stronger, yet craft of the same size, with the same horsepower, go no faster today, length for length and horsepower for horsepower.

S. E. Saunders had vision in more ways than one. In 1929 he said 'We must give racing boats the credit for the immense strides which have been made in the design and construction of hulls and the development of the internal combustion engine. Recent events go plainly to show that the motor boat, and especially the high speed craft, has caught on with the sporting public in a manner almost undreamed of.'

Another pioneer of powerboat racing was Hubert Scott-Payne. In the 1920s Scott-Payne founded Super Marine Ltd, a firm building sea-planes of the float type; the main interest in which focused in the annual Schneider Trophy sea-plane races. When the Schneider Trophy series finished in the early 'thirties, Scott-Payne wound up Super Marine Ltd and on the same site started the firm which came to be known as the British Powerboat Company. It was almost inevitable that he should meet S. E. Saunders at Cowes. He went on to develop the 'hard-chine' principle upon which Saunders had put so much work. To increase lift beyond that given by the stepped hull, Saunders had produced the chine design. The fore part of the hull which, until Saunders changed it, had been rounded, became V-shaped. The sections were Vs, sweeping up to the stem. The effect of this was to lift the bow as soon as the boat moved ahead. As speed increased, so did the lift. This together with the step produced tremendous lift. It virtually produced flying lift and, indeed, in the First World War Saunders was one of the first men to design a flying boat. It is no exaggeration to say that the famous Saunders–Roe flying boats were able to function at all because the hydroplane step coupled with the V-sections forward, gave the necessary dynamic lift to enable the flying boat to take off. Although the sea planes of Scott-Payne's Super Marine were of the float type yet from the point when Scott-Payne founded the British Powerboat Company he concentrated on the hard-chine hulls which Saunders had developed. In the early 1930s he started producing a range of fast motor boats powered by many different kinds of engine. These were wooden boats and all of hard-chine design, and they were enormously popular.

The great knowledge of designers Hubert Scott-Payne of the British Powerboat Company and of Peter du Cane of Vosper's Ltd was to be of tremendous importance in the design and production of the light coastal force craft – motor torpedo boats, gun boats and air sea rescue vessels in the 1939–45 war, all of which were based on the chine principle. During the war much research was done by another designer John Hacker, who experimented in what is known as rise-of-floor; the principle being that the more rise-of-floor in a vessel throughout her length there is, the easier she will cut through the waves. This theory formed the basis of the very successful designs of the American, Raymond Hunt.

The post 1939–45 war period has seen a tremendous expansion of the sport of powerboat racing in all its forms. There have been significant advances in engine design and manufacture, both with petrol and diesel engines, and reliability has greatly improved. In the design of hulls great advances have been made. A development in this connection has been the introduction of the concave instead of the convex form in the chine at the bows. This eliminates the hard hammering of the chine in rough water. Another trend is that the after-sections are now deep-V'd, like the bows, instead of being relatively flat. The American designer Ray Hunt and the builder Dick Bertram have been in the fore-front of this development. This form of a deep-V of almost constant 25 per cent rise of floor is very suitable for a boat designed to be driven so hard that she will jump out of the water, for this shape not only eases the shock of the vessel plunging back into the water but the shock of the waves striking her bottom at high speeds. There is some loss of stability and lifting power and in consequence of this such boats are given more beam.

Post-war years

The Second World War stopped all British powerboat racing and it was to have an unfortunate aftermath. For fuel rationing went on until the early 1950s. Moreover, in this period, the period in which powerboating was going ahead strongly both in Europe and America, there was no proper organization concerning itself with powerboat racing in Britain. On the continent such racing was controlled by the Union Internationale Motonautique whose headquarters were in Belgium. The old Marine Motoring Association of 1902 had disappeared with the war. However in 1956 Cyril Benstead founded the London Motor Boat Racing Club, a club which was to become the centre of the sport in Britain. Other clubs sprang up quickly and then suddenly food and consumer goods were freed from rationing – and petrol too – and the post-war motor car and motor boating boom began.

Modern authorities

The development of glass-fibre-reinforced plastics and marine ply-woods for boat-building coupled with production-line techniques assisted the boom. As the sport grew, the British Powerboat Union was formed in 1961. But it soon became apparent that the right national authority for the sport would be the Royal Yachting Association and a powerboat division was formed. This consisted of a committee with sub-committees for runabout racing, hydroplane racing, offshore racing and technical matters; so there is now a single national authority controlling the whole sport of motor-boat racing in Britain and with, moreover, a voice in international competitions. Modern powerboat racing is divided into various types for example: runabounts, racing outboards, utility outboards, pleasure craft, offshore; and within these types are a number of different classes. Let us start then by having a look at these classes, rules and regulations governing the sport which I reproduce* by permission of the Royal Yachting Association.

Powerboat clubs

The invaluable little handbook published by the R.Y.A., free to members and very reasonably priced to non-members, gives full information concerning the racing rules of powerboat racing. Anyone intending to take up the sport will need it, but better still, join the R.Y.A. – you will get far more than a handbook; useful though *The Powerboat Racing Handbook* (PB1) may be! With the Association's generous permission I am quoting from the handbook certain information for the benefit of those readers who want to take up this branch of motor boating.

First of all then: where is it done? The following is a list of powerboat clubs, their addresses and the classes they race.

Key: OP – Offshore Powerboat   S – Sportsboat (Inboard and Out-
    OH – Outboard Hydroplane   board).
      I – Inflatable   IH – Inboard Hydroplane

* The R.Y.A. make the point in *The Powerboat Racing Handbook* (PB1/73) that the information contained is '. . . correct at the time of going to press, but may be subject to alteration.'

Circuit racing clubs are limited to a certain number of boats on the water at any one time, details of which are given with the club venue.

Club	Locality	Class
Abersoch Powerboat Club	Abersoch	OFF
Allhallows Yacht Club Brett Marine Club	Allhallows-on-Sea	OFF
Bristol Channel Powerboat Association	Bristol Channel	OFF
Bristol Hydroplane Racing Club	Hill's Gravel Pit, South Cerney, Cirencester. Long course/ European course, for a max. of 18 boats for scratch events. Long course/European, for a max. of 24 boats for handicap events. Short course for a max. of 12 boats for scratch events. Short course for a max. of 18 boats for handicap events.	O
British Outboard Racing Club	(1) Princes Water Ski Club, Clock-house Lane, Bedfont, Middlesex. (2) Welsh Harp, Brent. A max. of 20 boats for scratch racing. If more than 20, start to be split between 350 cc and 500 cc; at least 5 secs. split.	H
Brixham Yacht Club	Brixham, Devon	OFF
Chasewater Powerboat Club	Max. of 35 boats on handicap. Max. of 30 for scratch events on the normal start line. Max. of 45 boats on a 3 buoy course of 1¾ miles.	SH
Cotswold Motor Boat Racing Club	Whelford Road, Fairford, Nr. Cirencester. Max. of 24 boats.	SH
Elie and Earlsferry Sailing Club	Elie	OFF
Essex Hydroplane Racing Club	South Ockendon, Essex. A max. of 10 scratch racing, a max. of 15 group and individual handicap.	H
Essex Powerboat Club	(a) South Ockendon. Max. of 12 boats not including more than 2	SH

Club	Locality	Class
	boats exceeding an engine capacity of 1,000 cc. Max. of 14 boats with no boats exceeding an engine capacity of 1,000 cc. (b) Ness Road. Max. of 20 boats on handicap for club course. Max. of 40 boats on handicap for national course, provided there is a min. of 5 rescue craft for the national events if there are more than 25 entries. If less than 25 entries there is a min. of 3 rescue craft.	
Exe Power Boat and Ski	Lyme Bay	OFF
Gorey Yacht Club	Royal Bay Grouville	OFF
Guernsey Yacht Club	St Peter Port	OFF
Jersey Powerboat and Water Ski Club	—	OP
Kent Boat and Ski Club	Isle of Sheppey	OFF
Lancashire Powerboat Racing Club Limited	(a) Carr Mill Dam, Nr. St Helens. Max. of 24 boats.	SH
	(b) Fairhaven Lake, Lytham St Anne's. Max. of 20 boats under 1,000 cc.	SH
Lincolnshire Speedboat Club	Tattershall. Max. of 12 boats with a max. of 4 boats exceeding an engine capacity of 1,000 cc. Max. of 16 boats up to 1,000 cc. Max. of 8 boats over 1,000 cc.	S
London Motor Boat Racing Club	Woodland Lake, Iver Heath, Buckinghamshire. Max. of 24 boats (all classes) or max. of 30 boats up to 1,000 cc.	S
Loughor Boat Club	Loughor	OFF
Lowestoft and Oulton Broad Motor Boat Club	Oulton Broad, Nr. Lowestoft. Max. of 20 boats in all classes, but with a max. of 6 of these to be 'F' class hydroplanes of over 1,000 cc runabouts.	OH/IH SH

Club	Locality	Class
Midland Hydroplane Club	Bodymoor Heath, Kingsbury, Nr. Tamworth, Staffordshire. 24 boats in handicap races, a max. of 16 boats in scratch races (Hydroplanes), 20 boats with 5 only over 1,000 cc (mixed racing). 24 boats up to 1,000 cc (outboard) (Sportsboats).	SH
North Sea Powerboat Racing Association	Whitby	OFF
Nottingham Speedboat Club	—	S
Offshore Powerboat Club of Great Britain	Various	OFF
Pembrokeshire Yacht Club	Milford Haven	OFF
Plym '70' Sailing and Powerboat Club	Plymouth	OFF
Porthcawl Motor Boat and Ski Club	Porthcawl	OFF
Racing Inboard/Outboard Club	Essex	H
River Towy Yacht Club	River Towy	OFF
Royal Motor Yacht Club	Poole	OFF
Royal Southern Yacht Club	Hamble	OFF
South Devon Watersports Club	Approval and limitation pending	OFF/S
Southern Inflatable Powerboat Club	Various	I
Stewartby Powerboat and Hydroplane Racing Club	Stewartby. A max. of 30 boats. Scratch racing or handicap racing (Hydroplanes). A max. of 24 boats of all classes, or max. of 30 boats up to 1,000 cc (Sportsboats).	S/H
Stone Water Ski and Powerboat Club	—	OFF
United Kingdom Offshore Boating Association	Various	OFF

Club	Locality	Class
Varne Boat Club	New Romney	OFF
Wallasey Powerboat and Ski Club	(a) Marine Lake, Southport. Max. of 36 boats. (b) Marine Lake, Wallasey. 8 boats up to 1,000 cc. (c) River Mersey. Unlimited provided adequate rescue boats.	S
Wells Hydroplane Club	Wells Harbour. Approval and limitation pending.	SH
Windermere Motor Boat Racing Club	Lake Windermere. Max. of 20 boats on handicap events for short course of 0·75 miles, providing there is a min. of 3 rescue craft. Max. of 30 boats on handicap events for the long course of 1·25 miles with a min. of 5 rescue craft if more than 20 boats are racing. For Grand Prix, 50 boats on 3·2 mile course with min. of 5 rescue craft.	S

Licences and insurance

That completes the handbook list at the time of going to press. You will need a licence to race; also personal accident cover. And if you wish to race abroad, you will need overseas cover for accidents and also any medical expenses. The R.Y.A. give the following information about licences.

Application: Application for R.Y.A. powerboat licences and compulsory third-party cover should be made on the appropriate form available from the R.Y.A. Secretariat. The form must be countersigned by the applicant's club, as proof of his membership of the club. Licence fees for the various categories are shown on the form.

Personal Accident Cover: This cover is available to licence holders, covering all racing in the United Kingdom for a whole season. Full details are given on the licence application form. Premiums are: £7 to members, £10 to non-members.

Overseas Personal Accident and Medical Expenses Cover: The United Kingdom Personal Accident cover can be extended for overseas racing. This cover includes medical expenses, and is also valid for a whole season. Full details are given on the licence form. Premiums are: £21 to members, £24 to non-members.

The Powerboat Racing Rules can be divided into sections. There are first the General Rules. Then there are the Offshore Powerboat Racing Rules. In addition, if international racing is what you are aiming for, you will need to study the International Offshore Powerboat Racing Rules too. Alternatively, for the U.I.M. international racing series (if you remember U.I.M. stands for Union Internationale Motonautique) then those rules which govern the U.I.M. series will have to be studied. Then there are the Class IV Rules which give the basic rules and definitions for outboard powerboats only which have been designed for use in coastal waters.

So one way and another, you may have quite a bit of reading to do! In each and every case the R.Y.A. booklet will give you what you need. Meantime let us have a 'condensed' look at these various rules to give us an idea of the way boats are classified and how the various branches of the sport are controlled generally.

First then, the Powerboat General Rules, as laid down in the *R.Y.A. Handbook*.

POWERBOAT GENERAL RULES

1. AUTHORITY

The Royal Yachting Association is the only recognized authority for powerboat competitive events in the United Kingdom, and all events shall be organized in accordance with the national safety rules and recommendations, the class rules and the rules hereafter set out. The rules of the Union Internationale Motonautique as may be applicable shall not be altered.

2. DEFINITION

Competitive events are divided into:

(*a*) International competitive events which are those inscribed on the international calendar published by the U.I.M. and open to competitors holding an international licence as issued by their national authority.

(*b*) National and open invitation competitive events which are those inscribed on the national calendar published by the R.Y.A. and open to competitors holding a national licence as issued by the R.Y.A.

(*c*) Club competitive events which are those open only to members of the organizing club. Inter-club races or competitive events shall rank as club races or competitive events provided no more than two U.K. clubs participate.

(d) Basic competitive events which are those open to members of the organizing club. Such events may only take place on a restricted course as laid down by the R.Y.A. For club and basic competitive events competitors shall hold R.Y.A. basic licences.

In the case of offshore races the R.Y.A. may require competitors to hold an international or national licence depending on the severity of the course irrespective of the status of the event.

3. CONTROL

(*a*) COMPETITORS – All competitors must have valid licences and Third Party Insurance issued by their National Authority, before entering or participating in any race. For all offshore classes there must be at least two correctly licensed drivers per boat, with the exception of basic, non-championship races, where only the actual driver need be licensed. Full details of licence categories, etc., are shown on the R.Y.A. Powerboat Licence and Third Party Insurance application form.

For the purposes of licensing and control sportsboat and hydroplane racing shall be divided by the following classes:
Sportsboat racing: Classes SJ to SZ; S1 to S00; National Stock Outboard Series; Junior Sportsboats; Classes OF, OI, ON, and OZ.
Hydroplane Racing: Classes OJ to OD, Racing inboards.

(*b*) ORGANIZING CLUBS – All organizing clubs must be affiliated to the R.Y.A. and must have R.Y.A. Third Party Insurance cover. A club organizing international and national competitive events shall send to the R.Y.A. the advance programme (and such other particulars as shall be required in the R.Y.A. application form) for approval.

For offshore powerboat racing these particulars shall also be provided for club and basic races and competitive events.

(*c*) All boats entered for racing shall be subject to the direction and control of the race committee, but it shall be the sole responsibility of each entrant to decide whether or not to start or to continue the race. Water approval must be given by any two members of the Hydroplane Racing Committee. This approval is then subject to ratification at the next Hydroplane Racing Committee meeting.

4. FIXTURE CALENDAR FEES

For international, national or open invitation events the appropriate fee shall be paid to the R.Y.A.

5. RULES OF THE ROAD – RIGHT OF WAY

When two boats are approaching one another so as to involve risk of collision, one of them shall keep out of the way of the other as follows:

(*a*) When two boats are meeting end on, each shall alter her course to starboard.

(*b*) When two boats are crossing, the one which has the other on her own starboard side shall keep out of the way.

(*c*) Where by any of these rules one of the two boats is to keep out of the way, the other shall keep her course and speed.

(*d*) Every boat, which is directed by these rules to keep out of the way of another boat shall, if the circumstances of the case admit, avoid crossing ahead of the other.

(*e*) Every boat which is directed by these rules to keep out of the way of another boat shall on approaching her, if necessary, slacken her speed, or stop or reverse.

(*f*) Every boat overtaking any other shall keep out of the way of the overtaken boat.

(*g*) Every vessel coming up with another vessel from any direction more than 2 points (22½ degrees) abaft her beam, i.e. in such a position, with reference to the vessel which she is overtaking, that at night she would be unable to see either of that vessel's sidelights, shall be deemed to be an overtaking vessel; and no subsequent alteration of the bearing between the two vessels shall make the overtaking vessel a crossing vessel within the meaning of these rules, or relieve her of the duty of keeping clear of the overtaken vessel until she is finally past and clear.

(*h*) When two boats are turning a buoy alongside each other, the boat on the outside shall give sea-room to the inside boat.

(*i*) An overtaking boat cannot set course for a turning mark until clear ahead of the overtaken boat.

In obeying and construing these rules, due regard shall be paid to all dangers of navigation and collision, and to any special circumstances which may render a departure from the above rules necessary in order to avoid immediate danger.

The international regulations for preventing collisions at sea shall be strictly adhered to at all times.

6. POSTPONEMENT

The procedure for postponement shall be clearly defined in the advance programme and/or race instructions.

7. PREMATURE STARTERS

Boats making a premature start shall not be recalled, but may be penalized at the discretion of the race committee.

8. ANCHORING, AGROUND OR FOUL OF AN OBSTRUCTION

A boat may anchor during a race but shall weigh and recover her anchor again, and not slip.

A boat grounding, fouling a buoy, vessel or other obstruction may use her own anchors, warps, or other gear to clear herself.

9. FINISHING A RACE

A driver who finishes a race or heat shall withdraw from the circuit without hindering the boats that are still in the race.

This constitutes an exception to rule 5 – right of way.

A vessel shall be timed for completing a race when her stem crosses the finishing line. After thus finishing a race she shall continue to observe any special regulations, prescribed by the race committee, as to keeping clear of the finishing line and course.

For circuit races, boats shall be deemed to have finished a race (regardless of number of laps completed) when they cross the finishing line after the leading boat has received the chequered flag, except in the case of long distance and duration races when instructions to the contrary shall be included in the advance programme and/or racing instructions.

10. PRE-RACE INSURANCE INDEMNITY DECLARATION FORM

All drivers and crew members shall sign an R.Y.A. indemnity form which shall be made available by clubs. All competitors who are under eighteen on the day of the race will be required to submit written consent of their parent or guardian to their taking part in the race·and confirming their acceptance of the rules governing the race.

11. INTERPRETATION OF THE RULES

The R.Y.A. shall judge, bearing in mind the present rules, all cases not foreseen or seemingly inaccurately defined.

Any driver who infringes any of the rules of the U.I.M. or of the R.Y.A. is liable to be penalized.

12. RACE PROTESTS

A driver shall only protest facts pertaining to the race in which he takes part.

Any protest lodged by one driver against another, or by the race committee against a driver, shall be made in writing and signed by the protester. Protests lodged by a driver against another shall be accompanied by a protest fee of £1. This fee shall be refunded if the protest is upheld. Protests shall be handed to the jury within the time stipulated in the programme. A written protest shall not be withdrawn.

All protests shall be as complete as possible and include all documents pertaining to the case. These documents are, as the case may be:

(a) race instructions;
(b) plan showing position of drivers;
(c) explanation of the case (stating rule infringed);
(d) protest fee;
(e) all other relevant documents.

A protest regarding the qualification of a boat, an engine, the owner, the driver, or against the validity of an entry or of the rules must be made before the start. Starting in the race is considered acceptance of the conditions. Such a protest lodged after the race shall not be considered unless the driver can prove that the relevant facts were unknown to him before the start.

The protester shall be liable to pay such fees as may be incurred for the inspection of an engine, and the race committee shall require a deposit to be made by the protester before dealing with the protest. The protester shall not be liable for this fee if his protest is upheld, and in which case his deposit, if any, shall be refunded.

13. PROTESTS AGAINST THE RESULTS

Protests concerning the results shall be lodged within an hour from the official results being posted. They shall be judged at once by the jury.

Paragraphs (*d*) and (*e*) of rule 12 apply.

14. APPEALS

The R.Y.A. requires that:

(*a*) the appeal, the grounds for the appeal and a deposit of £5 shall be lodged with the race committee of the club within ten days of receiving the race committee's decision; and

(*b*) shall be forwarded by the race committee to the secretary of the R.Y.A. within two months of receipt by the race committee. The deposit shall be returned if the appeal is upheld.

15. NON-APPROVED RACES

Any driver who competes in a race which is not approved by the R.Y.A. shall automatically forego the third party insurance provided with his licence for that event.

In the case of an international meeting being organized by a club which is not recognized by the R.Y.A. and which has not asked for permission to organize such a meeting, the R.Y.A. shall:

(*a*) notify the organizing club that the drivers may be suspended:

(*b*) notify the drivers that they may be suspended in their country, if they take part in international races not approved by the R.Y.A.

The R.Y.A. may request the U.I.M. to extend this suspension to other countries.

16. FOREIGN ENTRIES

The R.Y.A. shall sanction in writing any entries for foreign competitive events.

The organizers will not accept any non-sanctioned entry.

Direct correspondence between the organizing club and R.Y.A. drivers shall be permitted, but no entry shall be accepted unless approved by the R.Y.A.

For World or European Championships, only the R.Y.A. shall correspond with the national authority concerned.

17. RESCUE CRAFT FOR CIRCUIT RACING

(a) *Sportsboat. Rescue craft shall be standing by during a race.* Each shall carry two good swimmers, a signal flag, an efficient fire-extinguisher for fuel fires, ropes and a boathook. Adequate first aid equipment shall be provided. An ambulance must be in attendance at all race meetings.

(b) *Hydroplane.* At least one rescue boat shall be capable of planing at 20 m.p.h.

A rescue boat shall be manned by a minimum of two experienced crew.

A rescue boat shall attend drivers' meetings.

A rescue boat shall carry first aid equipment.

A rescue boat shall carry a boarding ladder.

A rescue boat shall carry at least one fire-extinguisher, minimum capacity 1 kilogram, and approved by the British Standards Institute or the Fire Offices Committee.

A rescue boat crew shall understand the racing flag code:

Yellow flag held stationary means caution.

Yellow flag waved vigorously means extreme danger.

Red flag means race stopped.

Chequered flag means race ended.

Black flag with number applies to boat with that number and requires the boat's withdrawal from the race.

Tinted goggle lenses and visors are not recommended.

271

18. ENTRY FORMS

Entry forms for international, national, open or invitation events shall· be circulated to the secretaries of interested clubs at least twenty-one (21) days before the event.

19. WORLD AND NATIONAL RECORDS

The establishment of world and national records is subject to the U.I.M. Record Rules and the following requirements. The U.I.M. and/or the R.Y.A. recognizes no other records other than those established under these rules.

(*a*) *Eligibility:* Members of recognized clubs are permitted to compete for the following recognized records:

    (i) National records, i.e. for Great Britain for all classes recognized by the R.Y.A.

    (ii) World records, i.e. international records for all classes recognized by the U.I.M.

(*b*) *Notice of Record Attempt or Trial:* Any person proposing to attempt a record in Great Britain under the U.I.M. and/or the R.Y.A. rules must give at least four weeks' notice in writing to the Secretariat of the R.Y.A. The applicant will then be sent the appropriate application form which must be correctly completed and returned to the R.Y.A. together with the appropriate payment laid down by the R.Y.A. (£100 for international/national record, £50 for national record.) The applicant shall also meet any expenses incurred by the R.Y.A., and the expenses of the required officials.

20. SCRUTINEERING

Pre-race scrutineering shall be carried out by clubs for all races.

For international and national Sportsboat events an appointed R.Y.A. measurer shall be incharge of all scrutineering arrangements.

For international and national offshore events an appointed R.Y.A. scrutineer shall be in charge of all scrutineering arrangements. (There is a list of scrutineers in the Handbook.)

21. POWERBOAT DECLARATION FORM

For Offshore Races only, it must be clearly understood that the implementation of this scheme is a club prerogative and *not* a right of the competitor. Competitors who wish to ascertain whether the scheme is in operation at a particular meeting must seek guidance from the organizing club.

The declaration form may only be signed if

(a) you have applied for the renewal of a powerboat licence valid for the type and status of the event you intend to enter,
or

(b) you have mislaid your licence, and it is valid for the type and status of the event you intend to enter,
or

(c) you have had your boat measured, and can produce the completed and signed measurement form. (Not applicable to offshore races.)
or

(d) you have mislaid a valid measurement certificate for the boat you intend to enter.

The declaration will be sent by the club to the R.Y.A., together with the deposit. For LICENCE declarations the fee is £20. For MEASUREMENT declarations the fee is £5.

If the declaration is not honoured, or the appropriate documents not received by the R.Y.A. within seven days, the declaration fee may be forfeit. Failure to honour the declaration may also incur suspension of the licence for a considerable period.

The signing of the declaration form and payment of the fee does not constitute any insurance premium or indemnity. In the case of any doubt over licences or insurance, do not race.

22. PUBLICATION OF RESULTS

In any international, national, open invitation or inter club meeting which consists of more than one heat the results shall be prominently displayed before the commencement of the following heat. At least fifteen minutes shall be allowed between publication of the final results and the prize giving, to allow a competitor sufficient time to lodge protests against the results.

23. GAS TURBINE ENGINES

(a) Circuit racing. The use of gas turbine engines shall be permitted in all inboard sportsboat classes, but they shall be entered in a special division of that class.

They shall be classified in accordance with the formula adopted by the F.I.A. for motor racing, modified as follows:

formula's numerator multiplied by $\dfrac{75}{96\cdot25}$

reducing the formula to the following:

$$A = \frac{\text{Capacity} = 0\cdot075}{(3\cdot10 = \text{Pressure Ratio}) - 7\cdot63}$$

(b) Offshore Racing. For details of the national offshore Gas Turbine class, see separate rules available from the R.Y.A.

24. ADVERTISING

Unlimited advertising is permitted on all racing boats, with the following exception:

For Offshore Racing: No advertising (or sign writing of any kind, including the name of the boat) is permitted within 24 ins. (18 ins. for Class III and IV) of the racing number in the same plane.

25. MEASUREMENT AND REGISTRATION

All boats participating in international and national races shall conform to the appropriate class rules issued by the U.I.M. or R.Y.A.

All craft complying with these classes shall, where required, be measured and registered with the R.Y.A.

In club and basic events, craft may be admitted which do not comply with U.I.M. or R.Y.A. class rules, at the discretion of the organizing club.

26. OBSERVERS, JUDGES AND JURY

(a) *Sportsboat Racing:* For international and national races there shall be an R.Y.A. observer, who shall be independent of the race committee and shall perform no other function or office. The observer shall ensure that the results are sent to the R.Y.A. immediately following the race.

For international events only, one extra observer may be appointed to the jury by each national authority participating in the meeting. The Race Protest Committee will be nominated before the start of a National meeting and will consist, as far as possible, of representatives from each competing club.

(b) *Offshore Racing*

(i) The R.Y.A. Observer is Chairman of the Jury, and conducts and directs the meeting, but he does not have a vote, nor may he take part in arriving at a final decision.

(ii) For National races members of the jury may perform another function or office in connection with the race. For international races, jury members shall N O T be permitted to perform such other functions or office.

(iii) For National races, the remaining members of the Jury shall be appointed by the organizing Club, and must comprise an odd number, and not less than 3. For International races the number shall be not less than 5.

(iv) A protestee has the right to object to a member of the jury, on the grounds that such member is an 'interested party'.

(v) The reasonable out of pocket expenses of the R.Y.A. Observer and members of the jury shall be met by the organizing Club.

(vi) At International events one extra member may be appointed to the jury by each National Authority participating in the meeting.

(vii) The protest must be heard at the race meeting.

27. HANDICAPPING FOR SPORTSBOAT RACING

(a) International and national races shall not be run on an individual handicap system.

(b) No class shall be handicapped behind another class of greater capacity in its series.

(c) A percentage disqualification clause can only be introduced to classes with three or less starters and then only in the second and subsequent heats.

(d) For international and national events where group handicapping is used, clubs shall set handicap times on the fastest known boat starting in each class.

(e) The new classes may be handicapped separately or together with existing classes, depending on the entries at each race.

(*f*) Classes O I and O N shall be handicapped separately from existing sportsboat classes.

(*g*) Mercury B P and Johnson and Evinrude G T engines in the I and N classes shall be handicapped separately, regardless of the hull design to which the engine is fitted. This shall not, however, apply to the 'o' series.

(*h*) Where the racing is run in several heats, the same number of points must be allocated for each heat of the race.

In all cases, the 10% reduction system for points must be used.

28. R.Y.A. MEASURERS

Measurers shall not measure any boat which they have designed or built or in which they have any financial interest.

29. PENALTIES

(*a*) All infringements of general racing and safety rules, or any attempt by owner or driver to gain an unfair advantage over other competitors should be penalized.

(*b*) Clubs shall be penalized if they improperly cancel a national event (i.e., at short notice).

(*c*) In the case of a club permitting a gross infringement of the licensing and insurance rules, the club may be fined up to a maximum of £500.

30. OFFICER OF THE DAY

Officers of the Day should not participate in any event at which they are officiating.

The Officer of the Day for an Offshore Powerboat Race should be situated in the startboat, unless there is an alternative foolproof method of controlling the start.

31. AMBULANCES

It is mandatory for an ambulance to be in attendance at all sportsboat race meetings, and neither practice nor racing can start before an ambulance is in attendance. Should the ambulance have to leave during a meeting for any reason, racing must cease until either it returns or a substitute is provided, N.B. – An ambulance conforming to the above must be approved by one of the following bodies:

(i) The local authority.

(ii) A central Government department.

(iii) An organization that has been approved by Customs & Excise and given permission to operate an ambulance service (item (iii) covers such organizations as St John Ambulance and and the British Red Cross).

Alternatively, if an ambulance fails to honour its commitment, racing may only commence if the club complies with the following requirements:

A qualified doctor is present throughout practice and racing, who shall inspect and approve the following equipment:

(i) a suitable vehicle, immediately available, and capable of carrying a B S I approved stretcher;

(ii) a B S I approved stretcher which is immediately available;

(iii) suitable blood transfusion equipment together with the necessary dry plasma;

(iv) any other medical equipment the doctor may require, including an airway.

32. DOCTOR

It is mandatory for a doctor to be present at every International Sportboat meeting.

33. FLAG SIGNALS

The following flags must be carried by all Rescue boats, and all drivers must obey their signal.

(i) *Red Flag*	*Stop*
(ii) *Yellow Flag (stationary)*	*Caution*
(iii) *Yellow Flag (waved)*	*Immediate caution*
(iv) *White Background with Red Cross*	*Injured person on board*

NATIONAL SAFETY REGULATIONS

'This section has been drawn up to assist clubs, competitors and scrutineers. It does not replace the U.I.M. or the R.Y.A. class rules'. (Notice that this section is for the information and benefit of competitors as well as the organizers).

Whilst these are national rules, clubs shall ensure that advice is given to overseas competitors of those requirements in the advance programme in the case of international events.

Please note that for the purposes of licensing and the implementation of these rules, sportsboat and hydroplane racing shall be divided by the following classes:

Sportsboat racing: Classes S J to S Z; S1 to S00; National Stock Outboard Series; Junior Sportsboats, Classes O F, O I, O N and O Z. Hydroplane racing: Classes O J to O D and Racing inboards.

Scrutineers may advise the race organizers of the time and/or number of staff required to carry out inspection, bearing in mind the number of entries and type of racing envisaged.

Whilst the scrutineer will try to ensure the fitness of the boat at the time of scrutineering and under the conditions prevailing, it shall be the driver's ultimate responsibility to ensure the fitness of his boat and to decide whether or not to start in the race once he has passed scrutineering.

Scrutineers shall check the rules for the category of boat in the particular event together with the advance programme and strike out all non-applicable items on the check sheet prior to inspection.

A scrutineer shall reject a boat if it does not comply with any of the items covered on the official check sheet supplied by the R.Y.A. or for any other item not covered by the check sheet, and he shall then refer the matter to the race committee to make its decision. Such a decision shall be made by the race committee in good time before the start of the race.

In all cases of complete rejection by the race committee or scrutineer a full report shall be made to the R.Y.A. technical committee to assist in the modification of the rules if necessary.

The check sheet may not necessarily cover every item that a scrutineer may wish to check on a particular boat; nor does every item refer to every class of boat.

Competitors are recommended to accept scrutineers' advice.

The check sheet items normally shall be taken in order, and it is the competitor's responsibility to have his boat complete and ready to race at the time required. Any incomplete entry may, at the scrutineer's discretion, be put back to be re-examined later if time permits. The Race Instructions shall contain detailed scrutineering arrangements.

In interpreting these requirements it shall be understood that the word 'shall' is mandatory, whereas the word 'should' is directive but not mandatory. Items are marked as follows to indicate to which type of racing they are applicable:

H = Hydroplane, O = Offshore and S = Sportsboat.

ALL BOATS MUST BE RE-SCRUTINEERED AFTER AN INCIDENT, BEFORE GOING BACK INTO THE RACE. IT IS THE DRIVER'S RESPONSIBILITY TO SEE THAT THIS IS CARRIED OUT.

1. MEASUREMENT CERTIFICATE

OS This will confirm the boat meets the measurement requirements of the rules and a further measurement check should not therefore be necessary at scrutineering. The certificate shall, however, be produced. For international events, the U.I.M. Homologation form must be produced.

2. TOWING CLEAT OR EYE, OR SAMPSON POST

HOS (a) Shall be adequate in itself and shall be adequate for towing the boat when waterlogged.

HOS (b) Shall be strongly fixed to the structure, not merely to the decking. It should be remembered that this item may have to carry the whole weight of a partly waterlogged boat.

3. PAINTER/MOORING LINES

HOS (a) Shall be strong enough for the purpose in (2) above, and shall be long enough for mooring.

HOS (b) Shall not be worn, and all ends shall be whipped or welded.

OS (c) The painter shall be attached to a bow eye or sampson post where available and shall be secured in the cockpit preferably by a jamming cleat to avoid the crew having to clamber out on to the bow to accept a tow.

HS (d) It shall not be long enough to reach the propeller.

4. SHARP EDGES

HOS   All mascots, lights, bow fittings and other sharp edges, shall be adequately protected or removed.

5. WINDSHIELD

OS   (a) Shall be well secured.

HOS   (b) Shall not be of plate or ordinary glass.

HOS   (c) Shall be masked by rubber or plastic on any bare edges.

HOS   (d) Shall not be so designed that it would restrict the driver from being ejected. For Class I/II windshields shall not present a hazard if the crew is thrown forward.

H   (e) For hydroplanes windscreens shall not be permanently fixed in position and shall be fixed to the hull by suitable rubber bands at front and side and shall be capable of being knocked off in the event of an accident.

HOS   (f) Scrutineers may order the removal of any windshield that appears dangerous.

6. STEERING GEAR

HOS   (a) Steering wheel and drum shall be secured and locked on to the shaft.

HOS   (b) Steering wheel unit shall be fixed, to, or through the dash panel, or a steering mounting bar, and shall be through-bolted and locked.

HOS   (c) Steering wheel strength shall be checked; if the wheel is split or cracked, the wheel shall be rejected.

Wheels of the laminated-rim type shall be checked for weakness caused by the breakdown of the laminations.

Plastic composition wheels shall be checked for early fatigue where the spokes join the boss to ensure the wheel cannot be forced to spin on the internal boss without undue minimum amount of pressure.

HOS   (d) Where shackles or such devices are used to attach the steering to outboard engines, they shall NOT be of a non-ferrous metal. Scrutineers shall satisfy themselves that this is so even if the shackles are painted.

HOS   (e) Pulleys shall operate freely and shall be through-bolted with positive locking.

HOS   (f) Steering wires shall be in good condition and shall have free running throughout their path, with adequate tension throughout their travel.

HOS   (g) Wires shall be secure and where doubled to form an eye shall be around a thimble and shall be secured with two bull-dog clips or equivalent.

HOS   (h) Lock wiring on all shackles, stretching screws, etc. in the system shall be secure.

HOS   (i) There shall be no undue degree of play in the steering system but steering wires shall not be over-tightened in a 'piano wire' fashion.

HOS   (j) For outboards – attachments to the engine, for inboards – attachments to tillers and/or quadrants and their fitting to the stock shall be in good condition and secure.

HOS   (k) Engine or tiller and rudder shall operate with full and free movements in the correct sense.

HOS   (l) Rudder assemblies, glands, keys, etc. shall be in good condition and secure with locked nuts and/or tight split pins.

HOS   (m) Rack and pinion steering shall be in a good mechanical condition with no excessive backlash. Casings should also be checked.

HOS   (n) All pulleys with riveted pins of non-ferrous material shall be rejected or the pins shall be replaced by a positively locked steel bolt. Pulleys should also, if possible, incorporate a bush.

HOS   (o) All pulleys with any tension shall not cause the yoke to clamp down on the pulley wheel.

 HS   (p) All pulleys which use an attachment hook of non-ferrous material shall be rejected.

HOS   (q) All attachment hooks shall be closed.

HOS   (r) Sheathed steering cables shall not be permitted.

  O   (s) Wires to the steering wheel running across the front of the dashboard shall be effectively shielded.

HOS   (t) It is also recommended that wires running fore and aft inside the cockpit be similarly shielded.

HOS   (u) Tiller steering is not permitted, except in Junior Inflatable Club racing.

7. CONTROL CABLES

HOS   All control cables shall be taped or screwed down securely.

8. FUEL TANKS

HOS   (*a*) Shall be secure in all directions.

HOS   (*b*) Shall not leak.

HOS   (*c*) Shall have sensible filling and venting arrangements where applicable that are not close to any hot parts such as exhaust manifolds.

HOS   (*d*) Should be insulated or isolated from the engine, etc., preferably by bulkheads.

HOS   (*e*) It is recommended that there should be an easily accessible means of shutting the fuel supply off from the tank(s).

9. FUEL LINES

HOS   Shall be leak-resistant and run in a manner to avoid damage. Lines shall be in good condition with proper connectors. Flexible hoses and pipe runs should be clipped up at suitable intervals with fair runs to the engine (at all points of travel in the case of outboards). Lines shall be so run that they do not become trapped. Fuel lines should be fire-resistant, non-collapsing.

10. THROTTLE CONTROL

HOS   (*a*) Fly-off throttles shall only operate in an open position when held by foot or hand and shall return when released to idling speed, or to stop in the case of hydroplanes.

HOS   (*b*) Lever unit shall be securely attached.

HOS   (*c*) Control unit, especially foot control, shall be properly connected, work freely and shall not be in a position where it can be fouled.

HOS   (*d*) Control unit shall be within easy reach of the driver in his normal position.

o   (*e*) For offshore boats with separate compartments for driver and co-driver, both positions shall be provided with an engine or throttle cut-out.

11. GEAR CONTROL

OS   Where the rules require neutral or reverse gear position, the gear shift control shall be within easy reach of the driver in his normal seated position.

12. JACK PLUG

HS (*a*) Path and length of the cord shall ensure disconnection of the plug whatever direction of ejection.

HS (*b*) Plug cord and attachments shall be adequate.

HS (*c*) Shall actually cut the engine completely when operated.

HS (*d*) No device shall be fitted to render the jack plug inoperative.

HS (*e*) The plug cord shall be securely attached to the jack plug and driver.

13. SEATS

HOS (*a*) Seats shall be of adequate strength and firmly secured.

HOS (*b*) All seats required by the particular class rules or the rules of the event shall be in position.

14. ENGINE MOUNTINGS AND TRANSMISSIONS

for outboards:

HOS (*a*) Mounting brackets and clamps shall be secure and in a satisfactory condition.

HOS (*b*) Engine mountings shall be attached to the transom with at least two clamps and two bolts, or four bolts.

HOS (*c*) All clamps shall be adequately tightened.

for inboards:

HOS (*d*) Engine mountings shall be sound, and the mounting bolts securing to the hull shall be pinned or lock-nutted.

HOS (*e*) Where an outdrive is fitted, the outdrive ring connection to the transom and the unit to the ring shall be secure.

HS (*f*) Transmission and all parts motivated by the engine shall be efficiently shielded so as to prevent damage to persons or structure in the event of breakage. For shafts in excess of one foot in length the shielding shall not allow more than $\frac{1}{2}$-inch clearance at either end.

HOS (*g*) Bearers shall not be saturated with oil.

15. ENGINE CONDITION

HOS (*a*) The engine shall be free of dangerous corrosion, oil or fuel leaks or excessive heating and shall not be a danger to any adjacent structure. Oil leaks are a particular source of fire danger.

(*b*) For inboard engines flame traps are recommended.

16. ELECTRICAL HARNESS

o Properly protected terminal boards shall be used with flexible (not solid core) cabling supported well up to the terminals and at suitable intervals throughout their run. Where relative movement or vibration occurs across a gap, cables shall be sheathed in plastic or metal tube anchored at both ends. Reinforced cable suitable for marine duty should be used. Electrical equipment in engine compartment shall be a minimum and away from heat or fuel.

17. EXHAUST SYSTEM FOR INBOARDS

HOS Exhaust systems for offshore boats shall be water-injected or water-jacketed. There shall be adequate insulation where required, and runs sited to avoid fire.

18. PROPELLER SECURITY

HOS (*a*) Propeller shall be sound, particularly at the blade roots.
HOS (*b*) It should be ascertained that the propeller nut can be securely locked.

19. CAVITATION PLATE

o Offshore Class IV only, see Class IV Rules.

20. BATTERY STOWAGE

HOS (*a*) Batteries where carried shall be easily accessible and prevented from movement in any direction.
HOS (*b*) Shock cords shall not be accepted for batteries in excess of 10 lb. weight. Remember that a 35 lb. battery weighs over one-sixth of a ton at 10 g. See that there is adequate support below the battery.
HOS (*c*) Batteries shall not be placed in a sealed compartment.

21. ENGINE ELIGIBILITY

HOS Whilst the boat's registration certificate will state the class and type of engine, scrutineers shall check to ensure that an engine has not been changed from that recorded. Scrutineers are not expected to remember specifications of each and every engine, but they should inspect for any fairly obvious modifications and/or non-standard or specialist fitting which is not permitted by the class rules.

Scrutineers are entitled to request any post-race strip or examination of leading boats, or those influencing Championship points, which they consider necessary (e.g. port modification, bore/stroke, pistons in production engines, crankshafts, injection pump settings, etc.).

22. STRUCTURAL STATE

Scrutineers are not expected to undertake a 'condition survey' of the boat but general appraisal shall be made of the structure. The following points should however be checked.

HOS *(a)* Split planks, fractured frames and beams and transom knees or their equivalent in reinforced plastic or alloy hulls.

HOS *(b)* Steering mounting (structure).

HOS *(c)* Shaft brackets and mechanical items other than those already covered.

HOS *(d)* Fins – to ensure they are of adequate structure and are attached securely.

HOS *(e)* Bilge shall be free of oil, fuel or debris. Remember oil causes structural deterioration, fuel is dangerous and debris chokes pumps, etc.

23. PADDLES

HOS *(a)* The number required shall be stowed for immediate use but not loose.

HOS *(b)* They shall be of a practical form related to the size of the boat and in usable condition.

24. LIFEJACKETS GENERAL

HOS *(a)* Lacing ties and/or straps shall be adequate and in good condition.

HOS *(b)* Zips where used shall be in working order.

HOS *(c)* Tears or rents or bad repairs whereby buoyancy will leak out shall not be permitted.

HOS *(d)* Jackets shall be dry and not oil or waterlogged.

Offshore Racing:

(*e*) Lifejackets shall be worn by all persons on board throughout a race.

The efficiency of a lifejacket is a matter of exclusive responsibility of the wearer, but the following conditions must be complied with.

(i) Jackets must have an inherent buoyancy of at least 20 lb. for international racing and at least $13\frac{1}{2}$ lb. for national racing.

(ii) Lacing ties and/or straps shall be adequate and in good condition.

(iii) Zips are not permitted as the sole means of fastening a lifejacket, where zips are used as an ancillary means of closure they shall be in working order.

(iv) Tears or rents or bad repairs through which buoyancy material may leak out shall not be permitted.

(v) Jackets shall not be oil saturated or waterlogged.

(vi) Jackets must have a lifting eye or becket attached to the main harness.

(vii) Jackets must not be able to wash up over the wearer's head, but be secure to his body.

N.B. Jackets to BS 3595 are still completely acceptable, provided they meet all the above requirements.

Hydroplane Racing:

(*f*) For circuit racing, the type of jacket where air is trapped in special panels, even though these jackets are equipped with foam plastic in isolated envelopes, shall not be permitted.

Whilst kapok filled jackets would comply with the following requirements, as would some with plastic foam sealed in compartments, the latter should have unicellular foam filling.

The jacket shall have at least 12 lb. buoyancy with any two compartments torn open. For testing purposes, the jacket thus prepared shall support an iron or steel weight of 14 lb. The jacket and weight should be thrown into the water with the weight securely attached and the jacket shall break surface.

It shall be possible to lift a 10 st. man clear of the ground by the shoulder straps or by that part of the jacket covering the shoulders. It is recommended that jackets should have a collar and groin strap and reinforcement in the area of the small of the back.

Sportsboat Racing:

(*g*) (i) Lifejackets must be worn by all persons on board through-out the race.

(ii) Lifejackets must have at least 18 lb. of inherent (solid) buoyancy.

(iii) The disposition of the inherent (solid) buoyancy [rule (ii)] must be such as to ensure that an unconscious person shall float face up in the water.

(iv) All jackets shall have an adequate harness and fastenings, including leg or crutch straps.

(v) The type of jacket where air is trapped in special panels (even though the jackets are equipped with foam plastic in isolated envelopes) are not permitted.

(vi) If a jacket uses plastic foam buoyancy, it must have a unicellular foam filling.

(vii) It shall be possible to lift a 10 st. man clear of the ground by the shoulder-straps or by that part of the jacket covering the shoulders.

(viii) For testing purposes, the jacket shall support a metal weight of 20 lb. The jacket and weight should be thrown into the water with the weight securely attached, and the jacket shall break surface.

N.B. – It is also recommended that all jackets should have a protective back or reinforced waistcoat, incorporated in their design.

Junior Sportsboat Racing

(*h*) the jacket must have 18 lb. solid buoyancy, a collar, and it is recommended that these jackets have an adjustable crutch strap fitted.

Inflatable Racing

(*i*) For inflatible racing the jacket shall have the British Standard No. 3595 stamped indelibly on the jacket together with the date of manufacture and kite mark. The life jacket shall have an inherent buoyancy of at least $13\frac{1}{2}$ lb.

25. CRASH HELMETS

HOS (*a*) Crash helmets shall be worn by all persons on board throughout the race, except in cabin category of Class I/I I.

HOS (*b*) All helmets shall be to B.S.S. 1869 or 2495 (with temple protection), Snell Standard, Snell 70, or ASA Z90 and shall be coloured 'fluorescent fire orange'. Hydroplane drivers should have a matt black stripe over the helmet, from front to back.

HOS (*c*) Modifications shall not infringe on the standard and bolts used for the fitting and attachment of a visor shall be small and on no account shall they protrude from the inner surface of the helmet.

HOS (*d*) Chin straps shall be in good condition and operative.

HOS (*e*) Helmet shall be devoid of dents or splits.

HOS (*f*) Helmet visors shall be in good condition and devoid of cracks, and easily detachable (i.e. not bolted).

S (*g*) Visors must not be secured in any way which prevents them lifting up (i.e. by taping).

S (*h*) Advertising will be allowed on driver's helmets up to eye level only.

26. ANCHOR

O (*a*) Shall be of a weight and type adequate to hold the boat.

O (*b*) Shall be properly stowed to prevent damage but shall still be accessible.

27. ANCHOR LINE

O (*a*) Shall be of a size and strength appropriate to the boat.

O (*b*) Shall be in good condition.

O (*c*) Shall be at least 30 fathoms (180 ft) in length.

O (*d*) Shall be attached at the time of scrutineering, to the boat and the anchor. It shall perform no other function.

28. FIRE EXTINGUISHER

HOS Where required by the rules of the class shall be in satisfactory condition and easily accessible.

Only fully charged extinguishers shall be permitted and they shall not contain carbon tetrachloride. It is recommended that the extinguisher be capable of putting out a petrol fire of at least 4 sq. ft.

29. FACE NUMBERS

HOS (a) Shall conform to the class rules of U.I.M. rules and the numbering must be clear and firm.

HS (b) For hydroplanes or sportsboats using number boards, these shall be non-metallic and of adequate thickness. The board shall be securely fitted (clamps are permissible) and shall be sited so that movements under way by the driver or crew shall not obscure the board.

O (c) Where deck-top numbers are required by rules, they shall be underlined by a black bar, equal in thickness to the digits themselves, and shall read from the helmsman's position.

H (d) Hydroplanes shall have displayed on both sides of the fore-front of the hull, black numbers to the following minimum dimensions: Height 11 ins.–12 ins.; Stroke width 2 ins. Numbers to be displayed on a white background extending at least 2 ins. beyond any numeral. In the case of single numerals, the white background shall cover a minimum of 15 ins. × 9 ins.

30. REVERSE GEAR

OS Reverse gear, where required by class rules, shall be demonstrably operative.

31. BUOYANCY

HOS It is recommended that all boats shall have sufficient buoyancy to keep afloat in all conditions. Buoyancy materials shall be adequately fixed to the hull and so disposed as to keep the bow clear of the water.

S For Sportsboat racing all boats shall have sufficient buoyancy to keep afloat in all conditions. Buoyancy aids or material shall be adequately fixed and so disposed as to keep the bow above water and induce the hull to remain the right way up. Because of possible hull damage, sealed compartments forming an integral part of the boat do not satisfy this rule.

Scrutineers shall not be responsible for determining the adequacy of the buoyancy in any boat, but may suspend clearance if in doubt and refer the matter immediately to the race committee.

32. BOAT NUMBER ON TRAILER

o   To assist recovery, boat numbers should be painted clearly on the trailer on the starboard side at the hitch.

HS   For sportsboats and hydroplanes the name of the boat should be painted clearly on the trailer at the starboard side of the hitch.

33. COMPASSES

o   (a) Main compass shall be securely mounted and should be able to be read by pilot and navigator.

o   (b) There shall be no large metal objects in the near vicinity of the compass.

o   (c) Deviation cards shall be required as evidence that the compass has been swung.

The secondary compass may be of a hand-bearing type. It is recommended that the compass is not swung with the boat on the trailer.

34, 35, 36, 37, 38, FIRST AID KIT, FOGHORN, TORCHES, ORANGE FLAG, DINGHY

o   (a) First aid kit shall be proprietary made-up set and shall be in a self-contained box.

o   (b) All these items shall be stowed securely but within easy sight and reach and shall not be stowed in a bag or box with other equipment.

o   (c) Foghorn shall be in proper working order and shall be tested.

o   (d) Torches shall be of the signalling type in working order and suitable for use at sea.

o   (e) Smoke signals are recommended for daylight use and flares after dusk. Flares, etc., normally have a stamped expiry date, and if they have expired, or the date is illegible, or the condition poor, they shall not be accepted.

o   (f) The dinghy where required for Class I/II shall be on deck or in the cockpit ready for immediate use. It shall be inflated or automatically inflatable. For automatic inflatable dinghies a correct manufacturer's guarantee or test certificate shall be required.

o   (g) Orange flag shall be at least 2 ft 6 ins. sq.

39. CHARTS

o Chart or charts shall be produced for the particular course. The normal procedure is for charts to be deposited at race control on signing in and have them returned at a specific time after scrutineering.

40. BILGE PUMP

o (a) Shall be in proper working order and properly secured to the boat.

o (b) Shall be reasonably accessible for operation.

o (c) Shall have a suction pipe to the lowest suction point of the bilges, and a discharge pipe overboard.

o (d) It must be possible to pump out all sections of the boat, even if separated by water-tight bulkheads.

o (e) Competitors are advised to carry buckets as well.

41. ENGINE WELL

o For boats with engine wells, any non-sealed openings, other than self-draining holes in the transom, shall be above a horizontal line through the lowest point of the top of the transom.

42. ACCESS TO THE FOREDECK

o All walkways where applicable shall be non-slip and shall enable practical and safe access in a seaway from the cockpit by means of foot rails, treads and handholds or the equivalent of adequate strength. A rope fastened to the stem head only and temporarily secured in the cockpit will not suffice.

43. FITTED EXTINGUISHER SYSTEM

o This system shall be fitted to all inboard-engined boats and shall be properly installed and engineered. Sensors and injectors shall be in the danger regions of the engine compartment. Maintenance at manufacturer's recommended intervals is required, and evidence that this has been carried out shall be available.

44. DOMESTIC ACCOMMODATION AND EQUIPMENT

o As required by the rules of the cabin category.

45. HATCH ACCESS

o There should always be an alternative escape route from a cabin.

46. RADIO

o This shall be in operative condition and should be checked.

47. NAVIGATION LIGHTS

o The correct number shall be carried operating over the correct arcs.

There are also sections dealing with stock outboard engine series and inflatable powerboat rules; which, like all British powerboat racing, is controlled and administered through the R.Y.A.

BRITISH NATIONAL STOCK OUTBOARD SERIES

1. INTENTION

(*a*) The whole aim and intent of this series is to limit racing to Standard Stock Engines, and to exclude all engines and attachments manufactured for purely racing purposes.

Similarly, the intention is to limit the hulls admitted to a simple mono-hull, easily constructed by the amateur, or readily available from boat manufacturers.

(*b*) All boats racing in this series must comply with the R.Y.A. General Safety Regulations. Additionally it is mandatory to carry a suitable paddle.

In the event of any doubts of interpretation of these rules the decision of the R.Y.A. shall be final.

2. DURATION

The R.Y.A. reserves the right to change any rule affecting safety without notice.

3. ENGINES

Only single engine installations are permitted. Only motors which conform to the following rules are admitted to this series.

Definition: An outboard motor is defined as the complete unit of powerhead, transmission, underwater unit, covers and fittings, exactly as sold in accordance with the maker's published catalogue, and specification, and available through all sales channels.

A list of engines meeting the requirements of the rules is published annually by the R.Y.A.

It shall be possible to lift the unit from the hull whilst afloat. The fuel tank is not included in the motor unit.

The unit so lifted and set up on shore shall be able to work fed by its tank. The motor mounting fixed on the boat, the control levers, the tachometer and its drive, the battery and wires, fuel tank and pipes, are not included in the motor unit.

Engine Types: The series motor shall be catalogued by an industrial firm as being manufactured in standard production series, that is to say, with all parts interchangeable and with identical dimensions to makers' tolerances, weight and materials.

Modifications: (i) The complete motor unit, as supplied by the manufacturers, shall not be subjected to any modifications except those specified below.

(ii) Reboring is allowed up to the limits intended by the manufacturer and within the limits of the class. The manufacturer's standard parts shall be used.

(iii) Sparking plugs are unrestricted.

(iv) For safety reasons, it is permitted to install a spring to the carburettor butterfly valve, provided no part of the motor is modified.

Adjusting the controls of the carburettor and the ignition advance and retard mechanisms is allowed, but only with the original system provided by the manufacturer and without any modifications.

Thermostats and overspeed switches may be removed.

Revolution counters or tachometers may be fitted to the motor.

Any alterations or modifications made by the manufacturers on more recent motors of the same type may be applied to earlier motors after such alterations and/or modifications have been accepted by the R.Y.A.

The angle of attachment of the motor and/or its height shall not be altered whilst the boat is under way.

Reverse gear is compulsory and shall be operative with engine running.

Motors with exhaust systems whose noise level, in the opinion of the race organization committee, is too high may be disqualified.

The race organization committee's decision shall be final.

4. PROPELLER

The propeller is unrestricted.

5. STEERING

Steering attachments are unrestricted.

As a safety measure it is permitted to reinforce the engine steering bar attachments, saddle bracket and the rubber mounts of the motor and motor mounting.

The employment of self-locking nuts or the addition of lock nuts, drilling and wiring, split pinning or keying is permitted.

6. CLASSIFICATION

The British National Stock Outboard Series are divided into the following classes:

N.B. Up to 365 cc inclusive
N.E. Over 365 cc and up to 750 cc inclusive
N.F. Over 750 cc and up to 850 cc inclusive
N.G. Over 850 cc and up to 1,050 cc inclusive
N.I. Over 1,050 cc and up to 1,500 cc inclusive
N.N. Over 1,500 cc and up to 2,000 cc inclusive

7. HULL

Only mono-hull form is permitted. The hull and deck shall not present in any of its longitudinal or transverse sections any configuration which could create aerodynamic lift.

Transverse steps, tunnels, hydrofoils or devices which could produce aerodynamic lift are prohibited.

The following exceptions are permitted however: clinker construction, lapstrakes and spray-rails. If stopped short of the transom, they must be tapered off over a minimum length of 6 ins.

The small tunnels or air-traps which are unavoidable, are permitted, but they must not exceed at any lateral section a total length of 6 ins., measured on a horizontal line, with the boat on an even keel.

A single underwater fixed vertical fin for directional stability is allowed. Fixed or adjustable trim-tabs fitted to the transom are permitted, provided they do not extend beyond the rear of the motor or laterally beyond the extended line of the hull.

8. DIMENSIONS

Classes	Length	Beam	Depth
N.B.	12 ft 3 ins.	4 ft 3 ins.	15 ins.
N.E., F. & G.	13 ft 11 ins.	4 ft 7 ins.	17 ins.
N.I. & N.	14 ft 9 ins.	4 ft 11 ins.	19 ins.

(All classes must have a minimum transom depth of 15 ins. measured in the centre.)

9. MEASUREMENT

The length of the hull is measured between perpendiculars overall, fore and aft. The beam is measured at the widest point of the hull. The depth is taken at the centre line on the mid length and is measured from a lateral line joining the upper edges of the cockpit opening. Such lines being produced parallel to the fore and aft centre line if the cockpit does not coincide with the mid length position.

Minimum dimensions for cockpit opening, applicable to all classes. Fore and aft 27 ins. Thwartships 35 ins. Only seats for the number of persons aboard need be fitted.

The carrying of crew is optional, provided the crewman is an R.Y.A. licence holder.

N.B. – THE LIST OF ACCEPTED ENGINES WILL BE REVIEWED ANNUALLY, NO ENGINES WILL BE ADMITTED TO THE SERIES AFTER 31 JANUARY OF THE YEAR CONCERNED.

NATIONAL INFLATABLE POWERBOAT RACING RULES

1. GENERAL

The following rules and definitions are for standard production inflatable boats used for circuit racing, which is defined as racing on a circuit not exceeding five miles.

2. CLASS SUB-DIVISIONS:

The classes shall be sub-divided as follows:

Junior	up to 250 cc
Class A	up to 41 h.p. (catalogued engines only)
Class B	up to 750 cc

Holders of the junior basic licence are restricted to National Class Junior (up to 250 cc), P1 (up to 399 cc) and P2 (up to 599 cc).

3. HULLS

(a) A list of acceptable models is available from the R.Y.A. All manufacturers' changes and specifications must be submitted to the R.Y.A. for approval before they can be considered eligible.

(b) At least 50 boats to the same hull design shall have been built before the type is eligible to race. Types considered by the R.Y.A. to be specifically or primarily designed for racing are prohibited.

(c) Hulls may not be modified except in regard to the following:
Type, number and position of seats;
Steering, throttle and gear controls;
Engine mountings;
Removable engine shims
Stringers, runners and keel sections, provided they do not contravene rule (d).

(d) The hull must be inflated with atmospheric air. There shall be sufficient compartments to ensure that the boat shall float when half is destroyed. No assembled device shall exceed one-third of the total length of the boat, excluding the manufacturers' specified floor stretchers.

(e) Whilst the underwater hull form is free, no rigid attachments shall be fitted to the underside of the hull.

(f) Toe bindings, in the form of straps, shall be permitted, provided that the strap is formed of a single strap the maximum length of which does not exceed 4 ins. The strap must be of an elastic neoprene/rubber material (no fibre materials are permitted). It is recommended that water ski type bindings are used.

4. STEERING

Steering by means of a steering wheel is compulsory.

5. ENGINES

(a) Shall be Production Marine Outboard Engines.

(b) Only one engine shall be fitted.

(c) Engines shall only be used if 1,000 units to the exact same specifications have been produced in any twelve consecutive months.

(d) 100 per cent of the propulsive effort shall be transmitted into the water whilst proceeding at racing trim in calm water.

(e) Engines shall be designed for a minimum transom depth of 15 ins.

(f) Engines shall not be modified in any particular whatsoever from the maker's specifications, except as listed below.

(i) Reboring within the maker's limits, provided the maker's standard over-size pistons are used. Crankshaft regrinding within the maker's standard limits, and using the maker's standard over-size bearings.

(ii) Valve timing (within standard limitations).

(iii) Ignition timing (within standard limitations).

(iv) Sparking plugs.

(v) Engine mountings.

(vi) Throttle and steering gear connections.

N.B. – Whilst the fuel system, i.e. pump, filters, etc., on the engine itself may not be altered, the fuel tank and supply system to the engine, as installed aboard, need not be standard production items.

(g) Marine engines shall be fully described and included in the maker's catalogue and advertisements of his engine range advised to all dealers as part of the normal sales procedure.

(h) Any alterations or modifications made by the manufacturer on more recent engines of the same type may be applied to earlier engines. Any motors up-dated in this way shall comply with the subsequent specifications in full. It is not, however, permissible to modify a current engine to comply with obsolete specification.

(i) (i) All boats shall be able to go astern by reverse gears in the primary transmission.

(ii) Only underwater units and transmission as sold and originally specified with the engines shall be used.

(iii) Only those propellers listed by an engine or propeller manufacturer, and available for general sale, will be acceptable. It is permitted to use any of the listed propellers whether or not it is specified for that particular unit in use. The competitor will be responsible for the production of proof of acceptability of any propeller in question.

(iv) The engine shall be through-bolted to the transom.

N.B. Konig underwater units are not allowed.

6. FUEL

Only commercial fuel as available to all competitors for marine or automotive purposes in the United Kingdom shall be permitted. Any additive is prohibited, except lubricating oil. Fuel tanks shall be firmly secured and it must not be necessary to move a tank for switching over from one to the other.

7. SAFETY

The National Safety rules for sportsboats (S) which generally define the fitness of a boat and scrutineering requirements shall apply. (These rules apply to circuit type racing whether on the sea or inland. For offshore inflatable racing the safety rules as applicable to offshore (o) class III will apply.)

The following equipment is obligatory and shall be satisfactorily stowed.

A mooring line attached forward, which shall not reach the propeller.

A paddle.

An operative jack plug.

A crash helmet to BS 1869 or 2495, Snell Standard, Snell 70 or ASA Z90, and coloured fluorescent orange.

A life jacket conforming to rule 24 of the National Safety rules.

8. RACE NUMBERS

(a) A driver shall obtain a race/registration number from the R.Y.A.

(b) The race number shall be painted on both sides of the forward third of the hull, in a vertical, or near vertical position.

(c) Numbers shall be displayed on a white background which shall extend at least 2 ins. beyond any numeral. The numbers shall be black on white backgrounds, 12 ins. high, with a stroke width of 2 ins. In the case of single numerals the white background shall cover a minimum of 15 ins. by 9 ins.

In the case of there being insufficient space for the above rule to be fully complied with, the dimensions should be reduced proportionally.

9. INFLATABLE RACING VENUES

The following venues have been approved for national inflatable racing with the limitation of starters shown:

Venue	Limitation
Fairford	30
Frodsham	30
Grangewater	20
Martinpool	25
Ringwood	40
South Cerney	30
Turnford Quarry (Lea Valley)	20
Welsh Harp	40
Welwyn Garden	20

We read in Powerboat Racing General Rule 25 (see page 275) how all boats taking part in international or national races shall 'where required' be measured and registered with the R.Y.A. In the *R.Y.A. Handbook* is a most useful list of measurers appointed by the Association, which gives their names and addresses and the classes for which they measure, i.e. U.I.M. Measurer, Class III Offshore Measurer or Classes I/II Offshore Measurer.

REGISTRATION FEES

The charge of £5.00 is made by the R.Y.A. for the issue of any powerboat measurement certificate unless the owner is a life or full member of the R.Y.A. when the certificate is issued gratis.

MEASUREMENT FEES

The following maximum measurement fees are laid down by the R.Y.A. and may be charged by the measurers concerned. If, however, you present your boat for measurement at a club which has an R.Y.A. appointed measurer and which has allocated a special day when the measurement of boats will take place, measurement fees will probably not be charged by the club concerned.

Class I and II: £7 for the measurement of the boat and 5p per mile travelling expenses.

Class III, U.I.M. and National Tourist: £5 for measurement of the boat and 5p per mile travelling expenses.

Measurers are also entitled to charge £1 for the weighing of U.I.M. boats.

The Powerboat Racing Handbook (PB1) contains the procedure and regulations governing boats and engines for classes I and II; also the Racing Rules for Marathon classes (minimum distance 750 nautical miles); however, since the two most popular (largely by reason of expense) are Classes III and IV let us now have a look at extracts from these two. First, the Class III Rules.

OFFSHORE POWERBOAT RACING RULES
FOR CLASS III

1. GENERAL

The following basic rules and definitions are for powerboats which have been designed and are suitable for extended sea passages.

All races shall be run in accordance with the General Rules of the R.Y.A.

Organizers shall not be permitted to make any additions to these rules which by their nature would affect the eligibility of any boat *except* in circumstances specifically affecting safety or in respect of special laws which may apply to the particular locality of the race. Organizers shall seek the approval of their national authority to make such additions.

Organizers shall have the right to refuse any boat which they deem to be unsuitable and/or which does not conform to the requirements of these rules.

The international regulations for preventing collisions at sea shall apply at all times.

2. DURATION

If it is desired to change these rules at the end of two years or at any subsequent date at least one year's notice of such changes shall be given.

Notwithstanding the above, the R.Y.A. reserve the right (1) to make adjustments which they may from time to time consider necessary for the continued well-being of the sport and which, by their nature, would not exclude any boat or engine which would have been permitted to race under these rules had such adjustment not been made, and (2) to change any rule affecting safety without notice.

3. GENERAL CLASSIFICATION

In all races for the purpose of defining an overall finishing order all competing boats, irrespective of sub-division, shall be grouped under one general classification.

Boats may, however, be sub-divided into categories other than those provided for in these rules, for the purpose of awarding subsidiary prizes.

Races may be organized for any sub-division but all boats in those sub-divisions shall be eligible provided they conform to the requirements of these rules irrespective of their means of propulsion.

4. HULL AND CLASS SUB-DIVISIONS

Class sub-divisions shall be divided in accordance with the following:

(a) Engine Capacity

3A 30 cu. ins. (491·6 cc) up to and including 55 cu. ins. (901·3 cc).

3B over 55 cu. ins. (901·3 cc) up to and including 80 cu. ins. (1,311·0 cc).

3C over 80 cu. ins. (1,311·0 cc) up to and including 125 cu. ins. (2,048·4 cc).

3D over 125 cu. ins. (2,048 cc) up to and including 250 cu. ins. (4,096·7 cc).

The figures given as cubic centimetre equivalents are approximations. The cubic inch measurement shall always take precedence.

(b) *Overall Length:* The overall length shall be taken between perpendiculars at the extremities of the structure including the skin or shell, which constitutes the floating vessel excluding any extensions as illustrated on the measurement diagram.

Class	Minimum Length
3A	14 ft
3B	14 ft
3C	15 ft
3D	17 ft

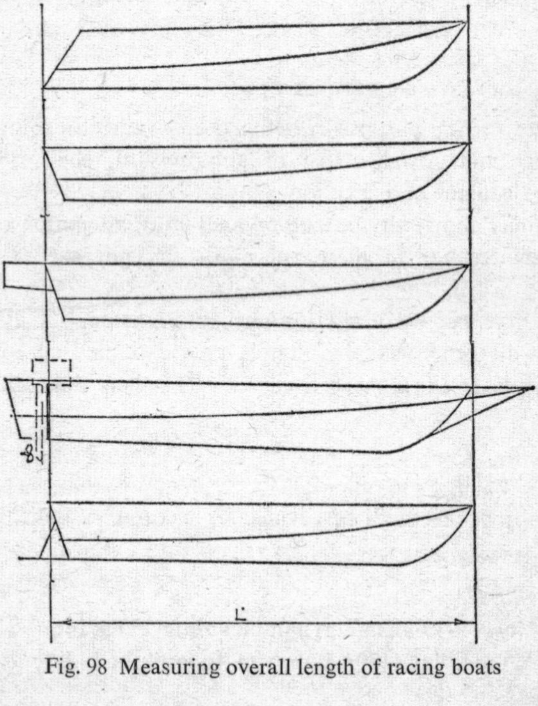

Fig. 98 Measuring overall length of racing boats

(c) *Cockpit Openings:* There shall be seating positions for two drivers with a clear minimum cockpit opening of 2 ft 6 ins. fore and aft by 1 ft 9 ins. athwartships per driver with permitted radii of 9 ins. within that opening.

There shall be a minimum clear depth of 15 ins. at these openings with the exceptions of seats, steering wheel and controls, which shall be measured from the top of the opening or from the top of the cockpit coaming if it is substantial.

All members of the crew shall whilst underway and racing be contained within the structure of the boat as defined under 'overall length'.

(d) *Hull Dimensions:* The outer surface of the hull excluding any protuberances such as chine rubbers and spray rails shall contain a 'cube' of the following dimensions.

Class	Height ('X')	Width ('Y')	Length ('Z')
Class A and B	1 ft 6 ins.	4 ft	6 ft 9 ins.
Class C	1 ft 6 ins.	4 ft	7 ft 6 ins.
Class D	1 ft 6 ins.	4 ft	9 ft 0 ins.

The cube may be split in the longitudinal direction in the vertical plane provided the two halves so obtained are set side by side.

(e) *Engine Well:* All outboard engined boats shall have watertight engine wells except where the engine is mounted on a separate structure abaft the stern.

Any holes cut into the engine well for the purpose of control cables, etc., shall be watertight and should be as high as possible and shall be above the level of the lowest point of the transom cut out.

(f) *Windshield:* Windshields if fitted, shall be strong and well-supported. All edges of glass, plastic and framing shall be effectively padded.

Transparent windscreens shall be made of non-splintering glass or plastic material.

(g) *Guard Rails or Wire Lifelines and Handholds:* A pulpit *with* stanchions and guard wires or adequate handholds shall be fitted to enable members of the crew to work on the foredeck or aftdeck.

The guard wires or handholds shall extend sufficiently far aft to enable members of the crew to proceed from the cockpit onto the foredeck in safety.

A rope fastened to the stemhead and temporarily secured in the cockpit will not suffice.

(h) *Mooring/Anchoring Cleat:* All boats shall be fitted with a well secured cleat or sampson post on the foredeck adequate for anchoring in a seaway and for towing at sea over a prolonged period.

5. ENGINES

(a) *Propulsive Effort:* One hundred per cent of the propulsive effort shall be derived from the water whilst proceeding at racing trim in calm water. Pure airjets and airscrews shall be excluded. Water jets shall be permitted.

(b) *Engine Eligibility:* Standard Marine Production touring engines, sub-divided into:

(i) The outboard type, whereby the complete propulsion unit comprising power head, bracket, drive mechanism, underwater unit can be detached from the boat and could start and run as a self-contained entity. Fuel tank and battery (if applicable) are not included.

(ii) Inboard type whereby the power unit, i.e. engine is mounted inside the boat on mounting(s) secured to the structure. The propulsion may be either by an outdrive unit, a water jet propulsion unit or conventional shafts whether direct or via return, e.g. V-drive, transfer gear-boxes, etc.

A standard Marine Production engine is defined as the standard product of a marine engine manufacturer established as such for at least six months prior to the application for homologation of an engine. The engine being already marketed to the general public through the normal retail procedures of advertising, distributors and agents. There must be a catalogue which specifies what is included in the retail price, the latter being stated on an official price list.

In the case of the outboard type official price shall be for the total entity as described in (a) (i) above.

(c) Industrial or automobile engines being the standard product of a manufacturer. Defined as basic engines composed of crankcase, crankshaft, cylinder block and cylinder head, these components being considered as forming the basic engine in the state whereby they are machined and prepared in accordance with the normal manufacture process at the assembly stage e.g. not at casting or forging stage.

(*d*) *Production Quantities:*

   (i) OUTBOARD PRODUCTION ENGINES, 5,000 PER ANNUM OF EACH MODEL. Where the same model is made in alternatives of shaft length, changed rotation, and electric starting at varying prices per alternative, the sum of the total outputs per alternative is accepted to meet the rule total, provided alternatives and prices are described in the catalogue and price lists.

N.B. This can vary according to the R.Y.A.'s information on file.

EACH MODEL. They may be sold without gear-box, with gear-box, in unit with V-drives or Z (out-drives). The sum of alternatives as above if equal to or in excess of, the rule total can be accepted provided they are catalogued and priced as such.

   (iii) INDUSTRIAL AND/OR AUTOMOBILE BASIC ENGINES, ANNUAL PRODUCTION RATE 5,000. It is not necessary for such engines to be catalogued as such nor a price quoted, always provided homologation can establish the origins and production, e.g. motor car production.

6. HOMOLOGATION AND MODIFICATIONS

N.B. These are NATIONAL rules: all engines of all types will be homologated by the R.Y.A.

It is the competitor's (owner's, entrant's, partner's) responsibility to ensure his engine is homologated irrespective of whether he instructs the engine maker, boat builder, agent, etc.

Intending competitors should write to the R.Y.A. stating the class sub-division and desired engine – described in identifiable detail – the R.Y.A. will then advise the information required for homologation.

N.B. This can vary according to the R.Y.A.'s information on file.

All descriptive material must be the official printed literature of the makers. Odd duplicated sheets, letters of declaration, etc., will NOT be accepted.

Modifications:

   (*a*) *Outboard Type:* Following modifications permitted:

   (i) Crankshafts may be reground and cylinder blocks rebored within the maker's standard limits, but only to a maximum of

60,000th of an inch and provided the capacity limits shall not be exceeded.

(ii) Valve timing (within standard limitations).

(iii) Ignition timing (within standard limitations).

(iv) Where the fuel supply pump and/or fuel filters are part of the Engine Unit as defined (5(*a*)(i)) no alterations allowed. It is permitted to install filters and pumps, whether additional or not, in the fuel lines between the tank(s) and engine unit(s).

(v) Sparking plugs.

(vi) Steering attachments.

(vii) Any type of propeller may be used.

Makers listed optional extras:

(viii) Adjustable trim whilst under way is allowed utilizing a properly engineered system.

(ix) Changed Rotation. If an engine of the outboard or inboard type, utilizing an outdrive transmission (homologated in accordance with article 7 (*c*)) is sold with only one direction of propeller rotation, it is permitted to change the rotation by using the manufacturer's standard parts. Such parts and/or kits of parts must be available at the same rate of annual production defined for outboards or outdrives under rules 5 (*c*) (i) and 7 (*c*). All specifications of such parts and/or kits of parts must be submitted to the R.Y.A. prior to the unit being converted, together with all supporting documents and evidence for homologation. No converted units will be accepted for racing – unless parts are accepted by the R.Y.A. as eligible.

N.B. In all cases, competitors are advised to consult the R.Y.A. if doubts exist over eligibility.

(*b*) Inboard Type: Following modifications permitted:

(i) Crankshafts may be reground and cylinder blocks rebored within the maker's standard limits, but only up to a maximum of 60,000th of an inch and provided the capacity limits shall not be exceeded.

(ii) Ignition – the ignition system is free.

(iii) Fuel supply pump.

(iv) Fuel filters.

(v) Sparking plugs.

(vi) Engine mountings.

(vii) Fuel, oil and cooling water pipes and hose connections, hose clips.

(viii) Throttle connections may be modified; in the case of Z or similar drive, transmission steering attachments may be changed.

(ix) Fuel injection pump adjustment (within standard limitations).

(x) Power trim as described under 6 (*a*) above is permitted.

(*c*) *Automobile and/or Industrial Engines:* The basic engine as defined may not be modified or altered in any particular whatsoever *except* for possible attachment of engine mounting feet, a gear-box and/or clutch, thrust bearing mounting and other attachments for marinization only. Marinization of the engine is free. Exclusive of the *basic engine* as defined 5 (*b*), tuning is free. Reboring and grinding of blocks and crankshafts is permitted, provided manufacturers' standard limits are not exceeded.

(*d*) *Forced Induction* ('Super' or 'Turbo' charging): For all engine types if forced induction is used then for the purpose of compliance with the sub-division capacity limits, the engine will be deemed to have a capacity of 1·25 times its swept volume.

In the case of Standard Marine Engine types 5 (*a*) (i) and (ii), forced induction is only permitted whereby the Supercharger (or Turbocharger) is part of the Standard Specification homologated as such and which as a type on its own meets the minimum annual production quantities.

7. TRANSMISSION AND INSTALLATION

(*a*) Propulsive effort: one hundred per cent of the propulsive effort shall be derived from the water whilst proceeding at racing trim in calm water. Pure airjets and airscrews shall be excluded. Water jets shall be permitted.

(*b*) Each driving shaft and/or jet unit as installed must have a neutral capability between the propeller or jet and engine unit. The neutral capability must be easily operable from the helmsman's position.

(*c*) Where transmission for Inboards is by means of Z drive (outdrive) units, the latter must be a standard production unit, available as for Standard Engines and produced at an annual rate of 150. Units to be homologated as engines.

(*d*) Boats with more than one shaft shall be capable of maintaining a course in a set direction on any one propeller.

(*e*) A protective cage or hoops or similar protective structure shall be fitted over all connecting shafts and couplings. In the event of a failure this protection shall be capable of containing the shafts and other couplings from causing damage to the hull skin, fuel tanks, any other installation and/or component and from causing any danger to the crew.

(*f*) Engine Compartments: inboard engines shall be enclosed in their own compartment(s) with the exception of normal ventilation. Each and every engine need not be contained in its own compartment. Holes in bulkheads and casings for ventilation shall not be in close proximity to the driver(s) unless some form of flame trap is fitted.

(*g*) Exhaust: exhaust pipes shall pass out through the structure of the vessel at an angle depressed below the horizontal at the point of exit. All exhaust shall be water injected, or water-jacketed, over the full length of the pipe(s) with the exception of the necessary connections and attachments.

8. FUEL

Only commercial gasoline up to 103 octane or diesel fuel as available to all competitors for marine or automotive purposes in the country where the race is organized, shall be permitted.

All fuel shall be carried in built-in tanks which do not obstruct working or living spaces or access to them. However, standard arrangements for outboard engine tanks are permitted provided they are firmly secured and it is not necessary to move a tank in order to switch over from one tank to the other.

9. SAFETY

(*a*) *Extinguisher System:* For all inboard engine installations a properly engineered extinguisher system shall be installed over the engine(s). Strategically placed fire detection equipment shall be fitted which shall operate the extinguisher(s) automatically or if a manual system is fitted give early warning of fire at the helmsman's position. This rule does not apply to outboards.

(b) *Equipment:* The following equipment shall be carried and stowed to the satisfaction of the race committee. Equipment that is starred for use in emergency shall be readily accessible.

*One hand fire extinguisher.

*Six currently valid parachute-type distress flares, and six orange smoke signals.

*A first aid kit.

An efficient fog-horn.

A waterproof torch or signalling lamp.

Two paddles.

A radar reflector and a means of hoisting it clear of the superstructure.

A permanently fitted manual bilge-pump.

Suitable gear for anchoring and berthing including one anchor, not less than 30 fathoms of suitable warp or chain.

An orange flag measuring at least 24 ins. by 15 ins., and the means of hoisting it to indicate retirement.

A fitted steering compass, properly swung, with deviation card displayed.

A second auxiliary compass which may be of the hand bearing type.

White forward top light, red and green side-lights (or combined lantern) and white stern light, in accordance with sections 7(a), 7(c) and 10 of the international regulations for preventing collision at sea.

Up-to-date charts covering the course of the race.

Sea anchor.

(c) *Lifejackets:* See Lifejackets general, p. 285.

(d) *Crash Helmets:* Crash helmets shall be coloured orange and shall be worn by all persons on board throughout the race. Such crash helmets shall conform to British Standards 1869 or 2495 or shall have been confirmed as being at least equal to one of these standards by a foreign organization or institution of equivalent standing to the British Standards Institute.

Visors shall be easily detachable (e.g. not bolted).

10. RACE NUMBERS

All boats shall be allocated a race number by the national authority which shall be painted in waterproof black enamel on a yellow or white background.

These numbers shall be so exhibited that they are clearly visible on either beam and from above. Those on the beam shall be placed in the forward half of the boat.

Those numbers displayed on the foredeck shall read correctly from the helmsman's position and shall be underlined by a black bar.

The individual numbers shall conform to the following minimum dimensions, the only exception being where the size of the boat does not allow the minimum size to be carried.

Height	Width	Thickness	Spacing
12 ins.	9 ins.	2 ins.	5 ins.

11. NATIONAL FLAG

All boats are to fly the Red (or, if entitled, the Blue or White) Ensign throughout the race.

Alternatively, the Union Flag or appropriate ensign shall be painted on a panel not less than 18 ins. by 12 ins. on both sides of the hull.

12. MEASUREMENT AND REGISTRATION

All boats shall be measured by an official measurer appointed by the national authority.

The national authority shall issue a certificate of measurement and registration to the owner confirming the boat's compliance with these rules at the time of measurement.

The certificate shall become invalidated on change of ownership, or when any change is made to the boat which is covered by these rules or in the case of a rule change.

Such changes shall necessitate re-measurement of the affected part(s).

13. CREW

The minimum age of the crew shall be sixteen years of age.

All members of the crew under the age of eighteen on the day of the race shall be required to submit the written consent of their parent or guardian to their taking part in the race and their acceptance of the rules governing the race.

There shall be at least two persons in each boat holding current licences issued by their national authority.

Only the licensed drivers shall be permitted to drive.

Any infringement of this rule shall entail at least immediate disqualification.

14. CONTROL

All boats entered for racing shall be subject to the direction and control of the race committee.

It shall be the sole responsibility of each boat's driver(s) to decide whether or not to start or to continue in the race.

It must be emphasized that these are all extracts from *The Powerboat Racing Handbook*, and not the complete rules. To include them all would defeat my purpose which is to give sufficient information, and to give those readers who are prospective powerboat racers an idea of the thoroughness with which the regulations that govern their sport have been drafted and also a better idea of this 'framework' within which the sport operates.

I apologize if these quotes however seem a little lengthy, but it has been my experience that nothing is tedious to the enthusiast and if you are reading this section you are probably an enthusiast. If not – may you swiftly become one! The next lot of Rules are those which govern the coastal water outboard powerboats – those ranging from 15 ft down to 12 ft in length.

OFFSHORE POWERBOAT RULES FOR CLASS IV

1. AUTHORITY

The following basic rules and definitions are for outboard powerboats only which have been designed for use in coastal waters. These rules are issued by the Royal Yachting Association and apply to all national offshore powerboat races held under the auspices of clubs in the United Kingdom. They may be supplemented or amended with the approval of the R.Y.A.

'Basic' Races shall be run within an area extending not more than
All races shall be held on courses as defined for *Basic Races*, i.e.
2 miles offshore and not more than 8 miles from end to end. The
course may not exceed 40 miles in overall length.

2. DURATION

Changes or modifications to these rules, which the R.Y.A. may
consider to be in the best interests of the sport, may be introduced
at any time without advance warning. The exception to this rule is
that no change may be made to the class engine limits (either overall or between sub-divisions) without giving competitors a minimum
of six months' notice.

3. CLASS SUB-DIVISIONS

Class IV shall be sub-divided into five categories according to the
manufacturers' catalogued h.p. rating, as follows:

> I V A up to 45 h.p.
> I V B over 45 h.p. and up to and including 55 h.p.
> I V C over 55 h.p. and up to and including 65 h.p.
> I V D over 65 h.p. and up to and including 85 h.p.
> I V E over 85 h.p. and up to and including 100 h.p.

4. OVERALL LENGTH

The minimum overall length for the four sub-divisions shall be
taken between perpendiculars at the extremities of the structure
(including the skin or shell) which constitutes the floating vessel,
excluding any extensions and shall be as follows:

> I V A Minimum overall length 12 ft 0 ins.
> I V B Minimum overall length 12 ft 6 in.
> I V C Minimum overall length 13 ft 0 ins.
> I V D Minimum overall length 14 ft 0 ins.
> I V E Minimum overall length 15 ft 0 ins.

5. UNDERWATER HULL

Any underwater form shall be permitted (subject to rule 6), provided that the lowest part of the hull shall include at least 60 per

cent of the overall length measured along the fore and aft centre line. At this part the hull shall have a minimum width of 10 per cent of the maximum beam of the craft (measured over the structure outside and ignoring rubbing strakes, overlapping decks, etc.), measured not more than 6 ins. above this lowest part over the defined length.

6. GENERAL ELIGIBILITY

Hulls: Boats shall be standard production craft of the family run-about, ski boat or small cruiser type, of which a minimum of twenty craft to the same hull design shall have already been built and fully completed (ready, apart from engine and engine controls, to put to sea) at the time of application for homologation with the R.Y.A. In the form in which it is normally sold to the general public the craft shall be capable of seating at least four people, either in the cockpit or (if applicable) the cabin.

Boats may be modified internally (with regard to strengthening, alterations to type or numbers of seats, etc.) but *no modifications* shall be permitted to the external shape or external geometry of the hull or deck with the sole exception of fitting an engine thrust block and/or normal deck fittings. No part of a thrust block shall extend below the bottom of the transom. The steering position may not be modified from that which is standard.

If the seating has been changed from that which was fitted as standard by the boatbuilder, then the boat must be fitted with a minimum of two identical seats. The positioning of these seats is free, subject to the standard steering positions not being changed. In order to abide by the spirit of the rules, if the floor is removed, it must be replaced by another capable of supporting the weight of the crew at any point.

Engines:

It is the competitor's (owner's, entrant's, partner's) responsibility to ensure his engine is homologated irrespective of whether he instructs the engine maker, boat builder, agent, etc.

Intending competitors should write to the R.Y.A. stating the class sub-division and desired engine – described in identifiable details – the R.Y.A. will then advise the information required for homologation.

All descriptive material must be the official printed literature of the makers. Odd duplicated sheets, letters of declaration, etc., will N O T be accepted.

Production Quantities:

(i) O U T B O A R D P R O D U C T I O N E N G I N E S, 5000 p.a. O F E A C H M O D E L. Where the same model is made in alternatives of shaft length, changed rotation, and electric starting at varying prices per alternative, the sum of the total outputs per alternative is accepted to meet the rule total, provided alternatives and prices are described in the catalogue and price lists.

(ii) Engines shall not be modified in any particular whatsoever from the maker's specification except as listed below:

(a) Reboring within the maker's limits, provided the maker's standard over-size pistons are used. Crankshaft regrinding within maker's standard limits, and using the maker's standard over-size bearings.

(b) Valve timing (within standard limitations).

(c) Ignition timing (within standard limitations).

(d) Fuel pumps and filters which are part of the engine specification as homologated may not be altered.

Additional lift pumps and filters may be fitted on the boat in the fuel lines between the tank and the engine.

(e) Sparking plugs.

(f) Mounting securing brackets may not be altered from standard except if necessary to enable the engine to be through-bolted to the transom.

(g) Throttle and steering gear connections.

(iii) Any alterations or modifications made by the manufacturer on more recent engines of the same type may be applied to earlier engines. Any motors updated in this way shall comply with the subsequent specification in full. It is not however permissible to modify a current engine to comply with an obsolete specification.

(iv) The choice of propellers is free.

(v) Engines fitted with power trim are prohibited, unless the Race Organizers can be satisfied that the power trim has been rendered inoperative for the race in question.

Price Limits: The recommended retail price of the boat in its unaltered production form (complete with seats, steering and usual standard fittings) *plus* the recommended retail price of the engine(s) and transmission *shall not exceed:*

For Class I V A £1,200
For Class I V B £1,350
For Class I V C £1,500
For Class I V D £1,800
For Class I V E £2,040

Registration and Homologation: For Class IV Championship races all competing boats shall be 'registered' with the R.Y.A. The competitor shall obtain from the R.Y.A. a Class IV Owner's Declaration form, which he shall complete, supplying all the information requested. The completed form, signed by the competitor, and accompanied by a fee of £5 shall be sent to the R.Y.A. a clear seven days before the boat is to be raced in a Class IV Championship race. The R.Y.A. will then issue an Owner's Declaration Certificate, incorporating a racing number, which will carry the prefix 'X' to distinguish it as a Class IV number.

The Owner's Declaration Certificate must be available for examination at all Championship races. The racing number allocated by the R.Y.A. shall be used at Championship races, and shall take precedence over conflicting numbers at non-Championship races.

Note: The Owner's Declaration Certificate is not in itself a guarantee of eligibility and it is the responsibility of race organizers to satisfy themselves of the complete eligibility of all craft entered in their races.

Infringements: Spot checks will be carried out, unannounced, at Championship races, to verify that boats comply with the above Eligibility Rules. Proved infringements of any part of the Eligibility Rules printed above must be reported to the R.Y.A., when any or all of the following penalties only may be applied:

(i) Withdrawal of any Championship points accrued during the race when the infringement took place.

(ii) A maximum fine of £50.

(iii) Suspension of the driver's licence.

7. WINDSHIELDS OR WIND DEFLECTORS

Windshields shall be well-supported and if the scrutineer is dissatisfied with the safety of any windshield he is entitled to request its removal. All edges of glass, perspex or metal frames shall be shrouded in rubber or soft plastic material.

8. ENGINE WELL

All boats shall have watertight engine wells, except for inflatable boats.

9. FUEL

Only commercial fuel (maximum 101.7 octane) as available to all competitors for marine or automotive purposes in the United Kingdom shall be permitted. Any additive is prohibited, except lubricating oil.

10. STOWAGE

Fuel tanks shall be firmly secured and it must not be necessary to move a tank for switching over from one to the other.

All equipment shall be securely stowed to the satisfaction of the race committee. Equipment listed in para. 11 shall be so stowed as to be readily available in emergency.

11. SAFETY

The following equipment is obligatory:
Two daylight distress signals and three hand flares, all currently valid.
A fire extinguisher, which must be fully charged and shall not contain carbon tetrachloride.
A compass.
A hand bilge pump or other suitable bailing arrangement.
A mooring line attached forward.
Two paddles.
A suitable anchor with sufficient warp attached.
A first aid kit.
A fog horn, or other suitable noise-maker.
A yellow flag, and the means of holding it aloft.
Crash helmets shall be worn by all persons on board throughout

the race. They shall conform to BS 1869 or BS 2495 or shall have been confirmed as being equal to one of these standards by a foreign institution of equivalent standing to the British Standards Institute. Crash helmets should preferably be orange coloured.

Lifejackets shall be worn by all persons on board throughout the race and shall conform to BS 3595 or the 1970 Board of Trade Standard, or shall have been approved by a foreign institution of equivalent standing to the British Standards Institute. *All* jackets shall have at least 13½ lb. solid buoyancy.

12. RACE NUMBERS

The National Authority will allocate, to all boats, a race number, which shall be painted in waterproof black enamel on a yellow or white background.

These numbers shall be so exhibited that they are clearly visible on either beam and from above. Those on the beam shall be placed in the forward half of the boat.

Those numbers displayed on the foredeck shall read correctly from the helmsman's position and shall be underlined by a black bar.

The individual numbers shall conform to the following minimum dimensions, the only exception being where the size of the boat does not allow the minimum size to be carried.

Height	Width	Thickness	Spacing
12 ins.	9 ins.	2 ins.	5 ins.

The Class IV 'X' prefix need only be half the height, width and thickness of the actual numbers. The yellow or white background must extend at least 2 ins. either side of the number and at least 1 in. above and below the number.

13. CREW

The minimum age of crew other than the licensed drivers is sixteen. All competitors who are under eighteen on the day of the race shall be required to submit the written consent of their parent or guardian to their taking part in the race and confirming their acceptance of the rules governing the race. In each boat there shall be at least two persons embarked throughout the race who (a) belong to a recognized yacht club, and (b) hold current drivers' licences issued by the R.Y.A.

(Note: For *non*-Championship races only the driver need hold an R.Y.A. driver's licence.)

All crew must remain *seated* within the confines of the cockpit, whilst actually racing, except when moving from one seat to another within the cockpit.

The Royal Yachting Association administers a wide range of National Championships.

Full details of the various Championships are available from the R.Y.A. Secretariat. As I have already said, the best thing is to join a club. They are not expensive, the subscriptions vary but if you can afford to pay for petrol you can certainly afford the very modest fee for the average club. The newcomer must make himself sufficiently competent in club races before the club will recommend him to the R.Y.A. for a national licence. Once he has this he can enter open events held at other clubs. This opens up the possibilities enormously because the different club courses each have their own special characteristics and hazards. And obviously the competition is more strenuous. Your new club will have books or at least a set of rules; study them and learn them and do not be afraid of taking advice.

If it is offshore powerboat racing which takes your fancy you will have seen from the R.Y.A. list that this is run in three classes under the authorization of the U.I.M. through the R.Y.A. The most popular class is Class III. This is because of the relatively low cost both of the boat and also of maintenance. Each year sees the promotion of new long distance offshore powerboat races as for example the race in 1972 from Britain to Monte Carlo. Three classic international events for Classes I and II are the Via Reggio race in Italy, the Miami to Nassau race in the United States and the Cowes to Torquay race in the English Channel. The last race is sponsored by the *Daily Express* for the Beaverbrook Challenge Trophy and for £1,000. It is run in September.

The photographs in plates 20 and 21 show the following:

Plate 20 – The start of the Paris 'Six Heures' race in the Seine.

Plate 21 – 'Woodmariner' and James Beard.

And if after looking at these, you want to go straight off and buy a racing powerboat, who could possibly blame you!

CHAPTER 9

Care and Maintenance of Hull and Engine

IN the business of laying-up a boat at an end of a season and the fitting-out of her at the beginning of a new one, there is scope for a good deal of 'do-it-yourself'. The two governing factors here are the size of your boat and the amount of time that you can spare to work on her. For those who have gardens, a runabout or a small cruiser capable of being trailed can be housed for the winter period under some sort of cover, provided of course that you have the room. For those with larger boats, or alternatively for those without gardens, a winter store will have to be found. This generally means spending the winter under cover in a ship-builder's yard. Ship-builders expect to house boats. Not only that, they expect to have the work of fitting them out in the spring as well. For example not many yards today welcome you for the winter period and then allow you to do the entire job of fitting-out the boat yourself. It is often possible, however, to reach some compromise whereby you, the owner, do a proportion of the work.

Boats may be laid-up under cover in a shed; they may be laid-up in the open but under covers or they can be laid-up in a mud berth where the vessel is afloat part of the time as the tide ebbs and floods. Fourthly they may be laid-up afloat; this naturally depends on the climate of the country in which the boat is laid-up.

If a boat has been laid-up afloat she will have to be slipped or docked in order to have her bottom painted etc. If she is already hauled out then this work can be done prior to launching her for the season. But whether the reader has the kind of boat which necessitates being laid-up ashore and a lot of the fitting work being done by the yard or whether he has ample room in the garage for the winter storage of his boat, it is important that he should know in general principles what fitting-out involves even if he is not doing the work himself since if he knows what should be done, he can that much more easily tell if it has been done, and done properly.

When does fitting-out take place? Well, the keener the owner the earlier, but I suppose, about March. Broadly speaking there are three principal things which are going to involve us in this fitting-out. There is the hull. This must be in a sound watertight condition, it must have protective paint and it must, on launching, look smart. There is the engine and this must be properly serviced before the season begins and with the engine comes the stern gear, the shaft and propeller. If there is an electrical system, as for example with a petrol engine, this must be carefully serviced as well. Also, there is the steering mechanism. This must be overhauled to make certain that it is functioning correctly and will not break down under strain.

There are of course a hundred-and-one other jobs but these are the main items. So let us have a look first at the hull.

Care of the hull

This, as we know, can be built of a variety of materials: wood, aluminium, steel, glass reinforced plastics, reinforced concrete, etc. First of all we must clean the hull, whatever it is made of, thoroughly and let it dry. If the existing paint is not in good condition and the hull is wooden we will probably have to get right down to bare wood and build it up again. If the hull is of G.R.P. we may not have to paint it if the hull is new but after one season, and certainly after two, we will, since we must cover up the marks and scratches which inevitably are collected. G.R.P. hulls get scratched and marked by other yachts, quaysides, posts, dinghies etc. just like wooden hulls. The only difference is the method of stripping off the paint. With a G.R.P. hull it is advisable to use a paint stripper, like for example, the International Paint Company's 'Pintoff'. With a wooden hull you can also use a stripper or you can use a blow-lamp and scraper to burn off the paint. This is largely a matter of personal taste. There are many who hold that stripping is better than burning and vice-versa. You can't use the two together, however, because strippers are inflammable. If the boat is aluminium you can again use a stripper but if she is a steel vessel then you will have to chip off the paint. As any one who has tried to do this will know, it is a tedious business at best, and one if possible, much best left to the yacht-yard.

In the case of a wooden hull, if there are any hollows or dents or perhaps round holes on the tops of counter-sunk screws where the dowels have come away, these must be stopped up and any bare patches must be spot painted. Then you rub down using water sandpaper and dry the hull thoroughly. The number of undercoats depends largely upon the condition of the paint. If the paint is in bad shape certainly give two undercoats. If the paint was so bad that you have gone down to bare wood or, for example, if you wanted to change the colour (and once again for this you want to get down to bare wood) then you will certainly need two undercoats. After each undercoat has been applied, you should rub it down lightly to give an adhesive surface to take the next coat.

Nowadays many people use polyurethane paints and varnishes. The main difference between conventional paint and polyurethane is that with the former, once you have primed and made the surface good, you build up with undercoats until you put the top coat on of enamel for a glossy finish. In the case of polyurethane paints, there is no basic difference between the enamel and the undercoat except that the enamel is glossier. But there are plenty of people who prefer and still use conventional paints; it is a question again of personal taste. If your boat is a runabout, for example, which has frequent rough launchings and has been dragged up and down beaches and in consequence needs certainly a yearly repaint, an owner might (taking into account the extra cost and extra time needed in rubbing-down) well prefer conventional paints to polyurethane, in spite of the fact that they dry more quickly and are much harder wearing. Another owner, however, knowing that the boat was going to have much rough usage, might go for the hard-wearing quality of the polyurethane paint. It is always a good idea to take advice about painting and there are, it must be admitted, always plenty of people prepared to give it to you! Personally, I have always found people who sell paint very helpful and also have had much good advice from yacht-yards.

Today, with the average small cruiser, there is very much less varnishing to be done than even a few years ago. This is because so many boats now are built in G.R.P. However, most of them have a certain amount of wood trimming and this, if the boat is to look really nice, will have to be attended to regularly. With varnishes the modern synthetics, the polyurethane varnishes, have pretty well completely superseded the old copal varnishes. The modern varnishes are much quicker drying and far, far tougher. If your boat has a certain amount of varnish work and it is in good condition, all you will need to do is to rub-down well and revarnish. If your varnish is in very bad condition then you must use a stripper, working a small area at a time. You can use an electric power sander to help you but do remember to use it with extreme caution. If parts of the varnish work are stained you can remedy this by applying bleach to the dark marks. A bleaching solution can be made from oxalic acid crystals. You apply the bleach with a clean small brush and when you have finished, brush off the small crystals that remain but whatever you do, don't breathe them.

Once the surface is clean and clear of dark spots examine it for any holes, indentations etc. If there are any, you can use grain filler which can be obtained in a number of shades. If necessary you can thin it with white spirit or varnish. There should now be a perfectly smooth surface to varnish. Never apply varnish too quickly. Plenty of coats and thin coats is the secret; six coats is not necessarily too much. Each time roughen the surface a little with sandpaper to get proper adhesion of the next coat. But remember with varnish, as indeed with painting, the secret is preparation. Varnish does not disguise marks that you have failed to get out of the wood, indeed it tends to exaggerate them.

Care of deck fittings

We now want to have a look at deck fittings and other metal parts and the steering gear, rudder fittings etc. All deck fittings must be carefully examined and any rusted rivets, screws, bolts etc. replaced. All metal parts must be cleaned. Steering gear, rudder fittings, wire steering cable etc. must be checked and oiled carefully. The stern gear must be examined and its fittings tested for tightness. Water and fuel tanks must be examined, the former swilled out with fresh water before refilling; all inlets and outlets cleaned out and the circulation checked. The bilge pump or pumps must be greased and if necessary their washers must be renewed.

We must examine carefully the interior of the hull making sure that the bilges are clean and sweet. If the vessel is a cruiser and has a water-closet, this must be checked to make sure that it is working efficiently.

Just as with a house the inside needs painting very much less frequently than the outside, so it is with cruising boats. Nevertheless the time will come when the inside will have to be painted and varnished, or whatever. This is a good job to do in the winter when the boat is laid-up and is a good way to help pass the long boatless winter months! It perhaps goes without saying that all general gear must be examined and overhauled; anchors, cable, ropes, fenders etc. and so we come to the engine.

Care of the engine

Here a very good parallel can be drawn between motor boating and motoring. It concerns the extent of knowledge of, and perhaps pre-occupation with, the engine. While nowadays almost all motorists have at least a rudimentary knowledge of the function of the engine of their car, the degree of this knowledge varies greatly and may be said to run from that of a motorist whose only use for a car is to get from 'A' to 'B' quickly and in comfort, to the man or woman for whom the use of a car is competitive – be it formula racing, rally driving, or any other one of the many forms of truly competitive motoring. To such a person the engine is the car.

So it is with boating. Between the simplest form of low-powered sportsboat or motor-cruiser and the small or large racing sisters, we have already seen in the earlier chapters of this book there are many varieties of types; and so there are varieties of boat owners.

It quite often happens that a person who takes up powerboating may already have had considerable experience of motor car or motor bicycle engines. Such a person, particularly those who have been engaged in the racing game, needs no teaching.

To the boat owner with little experience of engines, the situation is not unlike that of a new car owner. But there is one difference. Most of us have sufficient knowledge of the workings of a petrol engine, and in some cases a diesel engine, to be able to make a reasonably competent diagnosis when our car engine for some reason or other fails us. But if we are unable to take it further than that and effect a cure there is always the garage. Our car may have to be towed there it is true, but at least in normal circumstances there is, with obvious exceptions like deserts, a garage within reasonable reach. In the case of motor boats, particularly those boats which are single engined, if that engine should break down when we are well away from the land, then there is no one to repair it but ourselves; and here lies the difference. This chapter will contain, therefore, a section dealing with simple remedies and diagnostic techniques for the use of the relatively inexperienced (engine-wise) boat owner.

Before however, we come to our 'diagnostic' section, let us in this chapter on general maintenance, which includes winter storage, make a list if only to refresh our memories, of the basic things which must be done when we lay-up our boat at the end of a season, if that engine is to give us satisfactory service the following year.

The first thing to do after the last run of the season is to clean the entire engine unit externally. In the case of petrol engines the carburettor should be removed. Wash out the float chamber and gauze strainers and make sure that jets are clear. Reassemble carefully, checking for air leaks. Pump out the sump and fill to the low mark with inhibiting oil. The gearbox should be pumped out too and then refilled. If it is separately lubricated, refill with the right grade oil to the normal level. Then the engine should be run for a minute or two in neutral gear so that the oil is properly circulated.

Now the tappet cover may be removed and the tappet clearances checked. The same inhibiting oil as used in the sump should now be used to swab all valve gear. When replacing the tappet cover, use a new joint since a second-hand joint will frequently leak. Take out sparking plugs and pour enough inhibiting oil into each cylinder to cover the tops of the pistons. Give the engine a turn or two to circulate this oil and replace plugs.

With diesel engines it is necessary, when laying-up, to remove the ordinary fuel, which of course is diesel, in this case by replacing it with a fuel which is left in for the winter. To get the ordinary fuel out of the fuel pump and injectors the engine then may be run for a short spell.

Speaking of diesel engines, the injectors must be removed at the end of season lay-up and carefully checked. The best way to do this is as follows. The injectors must be fitted to their pipes but angled so that the spray from each squirts well clear of the engine. Now turn the engine looking carefully at each injector. You will soon notice if the spray from any of the injectors dribbles after the injection period has finished or if there are signs of droplets of fuel showing that the injector is defective. Any trouble here will be a job for professional servicing. When the injectors are replaced the pipe union at each must be left slack. Turn the engine until fuel appears from each injector. Now tighten union nuts. This is to make sure that pressure lost between pump and injectors when the injectors were being examined is replaced. Before the injectors are replaced, it is a good idea to look carefully at the nipples at each end of the pipe for signs of wear. If in doubt, the pipe must certainly be replaced. Once again, this is a job you might prefer a service station to do especially since without special tools you will not be able to remove properly the defective nipples at the ends of the pipe.

In the case of electrics the main thing is to take the battery or batteries ashore and keep it or them charged and properly stored. The cooling system must be drained. Make quite certain that the circulating pump has no trapped water. Assuming that the boat is going to be laid-up on shore, open the sea cock and make sure that all water gets away. It is a very good idea to break one or two pipe unions in the cooling system to make quite certain that the entire system has been drained. It is often not sufficient merely to open the drain cock on the engine.

A word now about outboard engines. Because of their relative portability, outboard engines present little difficulty as a winter storage problem. You can store them in the yacht-yard, in a service station or you can store them at home depending on your own facilities and how much work you want to do yourself on the engine. If you are going to lay-up the engine yourself you should first run the engine in clean fresh water. This will clear it of salt and dirt. Obviously you run the engine in neutral gear and at a slow speed.

One method of winterizing an outboard engine is to spray inhibiting oil into the carburettor air inlet. The engine now being stopped, disconnect controls and fuel pipe. Take off the cooling water strainer and clean it. Now having got all water out of the motor, hang the latter up where you can work at it. Sparking plugs may now be removed. Remove the propeller, clean and grease the shaft. Take out the upper and lower plugs in the gear case to drain it. Unless there is water in the oil which indicates a leak, refill the gear case with new oil. If there is water in the old oil it is probably a good idea to seek professional advice.

Take off the engine cover and examine the head. Using degreasing fluid now clean it thoroughly. The carburettor float chamber, fuel filter and sediment bowl must be removed, washed-out and replaced. With electric starting, the battery must be taken ashore and stored just as with an inboard engine. While also on the subject of electrics examine the contact-breaker points and check for gap. Now replace the engine cover having oiled exposed working parts, but before storing the engine, replace sparking plugs having first put a small quantity of oil into each cylinder and worked the starter to spread the oil around. The engine may now be stored. Never stand it so that the weight comes on the skeg but hang the engine up by the clamps which attach it to the vessel's transom. The fuel tank should be emptied and washed out with a little petrol and the fuel line flushed by working the pump.

Diagnosing and curing engine troubles

If we lay-up our engine carefully along the lines I have indicated or with a proper yard or service station we should have little or no trouble at sea. But in an imperfect world one must always be ready to deal with imperfections and so I intend as I had promised to close this chapter with a short section on diagnosing and curing the simpler engine troubles. The first and alas rather common trouble is that of failure to start at all. In Chapter Two we saw how engines may be two-stroke or four-stroke, so I propose to take two-stroke engines first, then four-stroke and finally diesel engines, in that order.

With the two-stroke engine a failure to start may result from a number of causes but it is fair to say that whatever type of petrol engine you have, the cause of trouble will most frequently be either electrics or fuel; so let us look at electrics first. A very common cause is an oiled-up sparking plug. The cure is to remove the plug, take it to pieces, clean, dry it thoroughly and put back. Another cause is dirty contact points in the magneto. Remove the cover of the magneto and clean the points thoroughly; you can use a knife to do this or a small file. If it is a fuel cause, it may be that the carburettor is choked and the cure is to remove the jet and clean it thoroughly. In this connection you may also find that the carburettor will not flood; this is possibly because the petrol system is blocked – almost certainly, in fact. The cure is to clean the filters, unscrew the union at the carburettor and if no petrol comes through, blow hard up the pipe.

Just as frustrating as non-starting, is the tendency of an engine to run for a few minutes and then stop. The probable causes of this are either a blockage in the petrol system or overheating; the cure of the former is to clean the system as already outlined, and the cure for the latter is to clean the filters and valves on the water pump.

Finally, you may find that the engine runs but loses power. There are three possible causes for this: too much oil, a partial blockage of the exhaust system, or firing erratically. If it is too much oil then you have the oil–petrol mixture wrong and you should add more petrol to the mixture in the tank. If the exhaust system is partially blocked, it will be necessary to clean it and to do this you must take it down. If you have erratic firing, the simplest cure is to adjust the air valve on the carburettor.

Let us now turn to four-stroke engines and begin, as before, with starting difficulties. Once again, we may have dirty sparking plugs, in which case the cure is to remove them, take them to pieces, clean, dry and replace. It may be that the jet is choked; if so, it must be removed and thoroughly cleaned. Another cause is weak magneto. Here the cure is to strip the magneto and for many people this is something which is best left to those with expert knowledge. However, another cause of difficult starting is too small a valve clearance, and this, which can be cured by adjusting the tappets, is not beyond the reach of the ordinary boat owner.

All too common a fault in many people's experience, is that the engine starts and runs and then suddenly stops. There may be all sorts of reasons for this: if the engine spits before stopping, it is possibly dirty jets and we have already seen that the cure for this is to remove and clean thoroughly. It may on the other hand be water in the carburettor in which case the carburettor must be removed and thoroughly cleaned. It may be that petrol pipes or filters are blocked, in which case you must unscrew the union at the carburettor and if no petrol is coming through, blow hard up the pipe. If blocked filter seems to be the cause, then clean the filters. On the other hand, you may have been unfortunate enough to have a cylinder head gasket broken, in which case you must remove the cylinder head and fit a spare gasket (a reminder to carry a spare gasket!).

However, if the engine suddenly stops without spitting and has coil ignition, there is a good chance that the earth wire may have broken in which case you must inspect the earth wire and if necessary replace it. A more serious cause of sudden stopping is the breaking of a timing chain. This means that a spare chain must be fitted. The chances are that you will not have a spare chain with you and even if you do it is something of an expert's job.

If the engine is firing erratically this is very likely caused by a dirty distributor. Remove the cover and clean and, if necessary, file the points smooth. A fault which is serious enough to necessitate stopping the engine immediately, is loss of oil pressure which can be seen easily in the oil pressure gauge. There are a number of causes for this. It may be choked oil filters, in which case the cure is simple; remove filters and clean them. It may be sludge in the sump. This necessitates draining out the oil, cleaning the sump and refilling with new oil. It may be diluted oil. Once again, oil must be drained and the sump refilled. This is only a temporary measure because the cause of dilution must be found. However loss of oil pressure can come from a worn bearing and this means relining and once again is certainly a job for the expert. The cause of diluted oil may be simple, or may be complicated. It may, for example, simply be too rich a mixture, in which case you adjust the air valve on the carburettor as before. It may be a broken cylinder head gasket and we have already noted the remedy for that. On the other hand, it may come from worn cylinders, in which case the latter will need reboring and once again, a job for the expert.

Now let's have a look at diesel. If a diesel engine will not start the chances are extremely likely that it is an air lock in the fuel lines. To cure this test the pump, clean the filter and drain out the air. If a diesel stops suddenly, the chances are that the fuel lines are blocked but it may be that the timing chain is broken, in which case a spare chain must be fitted and I would recommend that this is an expert's job. If you find that a diesel is missing on one or more cylinders, this may simply mean that the valves require adjustment; on the other hand, it could mean choked sprayers, in which case an expert must remove the latter for cleaning. Dirty sprayers which, as we have seen, is an illness demanding expert treatment, can also cause a diesel engine to knock, particularly when the throttle is opened.

It goes without saying, or at least it should, that a proper and adequate selection of tools should be carried on board. For example; spanners to suit each size of nut. In addition to this a ratchet, extension bar and sockets to suit all principal nuts on the engine should be carried. A good selection of small tools should be carried; pliers, a tool for setting sparking plug gaps. There is a good tool made by Champion Spark Plug Ltd; it has blades for cleaning, adjusting and checking. Carry also a screwdriver and a file; an adequate supply of the right engine and gear oils, also light general purpose oil and plenty of water-resistant grease. And finally, don't forget to carry a good supply of cotton waste.

CHAPTER 10

Inland Waterways Cruising

Inland cruising in Great Britain

ALTHOUGH the purpose of this section is to indicate the pleasure and opportunities which exist for inland waterway motor yachting, at the same time it is important that we should realize the work which is being done by the Inland Waterways Association Limited of 114 Regent's Park Road, London N.W.1. This body, founded as recently as 1946, is a national organization which exists to promote the restoration, maintenance and development of our British navigable rivers and canals. It is well worth supporting and joining. You do not have to own a boat to become a member of it. The network extends to approximately 3,000 miles of navigable rivers and canals in Britain, including a number of waterways not connected to the main system. About 2,000 miles of this network is the responsibility of the British Waterways Board and the remainder are administered by independent river and navigation authorities like, for example, the Thames Conservancy or the Great Ouse River Authority. The system extends to most parts of the country.

The Inland Waterways Association is continually lobbying successive governments to implement a positive plan for the retention and improvement of our rivers and canals based on multi-functional use. Among other things the Association encourages the development of pleasure cruising on canals and there is little doubt that the rapid growth of this, both in hired and privately owned craft, has helped considerably in securing the future of many previously little used rivers and canals.

It has taken many years to convince national and local authorities that our rivers and canals have an important future as recreational and amenity waterways and it is true to say that but for the work of the Association's voluntary members, many inland waterways would

330

have been closed long ago. Thanks mainly to the Association's campaign, pleasure cruising, canoeing, angling, etc., have supplemented the waterways' commercial carrying role and have so helped to guarantee their future as a system. But indeed, although the Association first promoted canal cruising holidays as part of the campaign for increased waterways use, there is little doubt that the greatly increasing number of privately owned and hire pleasure craft has contributed considerably to the improvement of the system itself. It is possible to travel by boat from Godalming in the south almost to Ripon in the north and from the mountains of Wales in the west to the lowlands of the Fens in the east. Contrary to popular belief, Britain's canals are not prosaic waterways bordered by satanic mills and factories. Although canals do sometimes pass through industrial areas there are hundreds of miles of rural waterway which can be explored by boat. Almost all of England's historic towns and cities are situated on a navigable waterway and some of the loveliest countryside in the land can be visited by river and canal.

It is a great misconception to think that the canals are dirty. It is true that they frequently join industrial centres but they were built in such a way that they are usually well off the road routes, many of them exploring open countryside a long way from towns and traffic. Indeed they provide a way of seeing England that the motorist does not know. The inland waterway traveller sees sights and hears sounds unseen and unheard by any other. In short, the inland waterways offer a marvellous family holiday.

As pretty well everyone knows, variations in level are navigated by means of 'locks'. If you work a lock yourself it takes about fifteen minutes; with experience you can shorten this time. They are not difficult to work at all. All that is needed is common sense. British Waterways Board booklets set out the working details in a readily understandable way. The lock gates are balanced and open quite easily when the water levels are equal on both sides. They are sufficiently light for women to work. Maximum speed on a canal is 4 m.p.h.

In 1954, the Association of Pleasure Craft Operators was formed. Its members were the leading firms in this rapidly expanding field. This Association is recognized by the British Waterways Board as the official negotiating body for the Inland Waterway Holiday

Industry. A.P.C.O. is a trade association linking together in friendly cooperation reputable firms offering inland waterway holidays and facilities, enabling them to exchange information and advice, coordinate and improve their activities and thus offer a better service to the customer. Details of A.P.C.O. may be had from the Secretary, 26 Chaseview Road, Alrewas, Burton-on-Trent, Staffordshire, England.

Inland cruising in Europe

But if the inland waterway system of England is far more fascinating than many people perhaps would suspect, that of Europe is even more so. It is possible to cover hundreds and hundreds of miles in Europe by means of river and canal. The Belgians, Dutch, Germans and French, have long used inland waterways for commercial purposes on a big scale. European holiday makers must have seen often the rows of great diesel-engined barges as they line up to wait to 'lock through' or perhaps lying alongside a quay at Chalon-sur-Saöne in France or stemming the current of the Rhine, great bluff bows disdainfully shoving the water away on either side.

The route from say, Calais down to the Mediterranean, has long been known to yachting folk. It is a route, partly canal, party river, by means of which a boat can reach the Mediterranean without having to sail all round down through the Bay of Biscay, down the Spanish coast, and through the Straits of Gibraltar and so forth. But for many other people the waterways of France and other European countries provide not so much a convenient short cut from one sea to another, as a source of cruising delight in themselves.

There is no difficulty involved in continental inland waterway cruising. You will of course require the usual passport both for yourself and your ship: in the case of ship, you need the ship's papers and certificate of registration if she is registered. If she is not registered, I have personally found that the bill of sale has been quite acceptable. But what you will require is a 'permit' ('Permit de Circulation' in France, for example); also, the requisite 'carnet' or customs documents. Rules and regulations differ slightly in each country. In order to make certain that you have the proper papers

332

it is advisable to consult the appropriate tourist office of which ever country or countries you intend to visit. If you belong to any association or cruising club, they too will be able to supply you with the information you need. I cannot do better than recommend you to read any or all of the excellent books by John Marriner who, in his yacht, has had extensive experience of this form of cruising.

Lock system

Some people are undoubtedly put off cruising on the inland waterways by reason of the number of locks on canals and because, in many cases, these must be worked by the crew. I am now referring to the British Inland Waterway system. There is no need to have this fear. Locks vary it is true, but the principle is the same. Consequently once you have mastered the technique, passing through the average canal lock is perfectly simple.

Let us assume that you are entering an empty lock. The lower gates are standing open and ready. A member of your crew should now jump ashore at the steps provided for the purpose at the tail of the lock. He closes the lower gate behind the boat making sure that they come together properly and are not fouled in any way. Make sure that the lower paddles are closed. If your boat is much smaller than the lock, you should put lines ashore. This will keep her against the lock wall and prevent her from being washed about as the lock fills. You will have to take in the slack of these lines as the boat rises with the water. You will find that the upper end of the lock will be fitted frequently with ground and gate paddles. Where this is so, the ground paddles must be drawn first. They should be drawn slowly, one at a time. The gate paddles admit water through the upper gate and should only be fully drawn when the water has risen to their aperture level. The object of this is not to swamp the boat if it is near the gate. When the lock is full the upper gate or gates can be opened. The boat now moves out into the upper pound. In general the lower gates of the lock are not so well adapted to hold up the water as the upper ones owing to their larger size.

When going up a flight of locks, the simplest procedure is as follows. A member of the crew walks ahead of the boat drawing off the locks in readiness. The same person can also keep a good look-out for any boat approaching from the opposite direction. If this does prove to be the case, he should wait and signal to his own boat that another craft is approaching, because it is bad manners to delay oncoming traffic by sneaking in ahead of them, unless it is perfectly obvious that there is time for your own boat to pass through the lock before the other boat arrives on the scene. Should a lock not be drawn off, the approaching (that is to say the ascending boat) should keep well away from the lower gates until the lock is empty. When a lock is being filled for a boat however, her bows may rest against the upper gate. A boat should never be allowed to drift back to the upper gates when a lock is being emptied. Watch out always that your boat is not caught or jammed by obstructions in the lock walls.

Never try and take the road from a working-boat by passing and overtaking. The yachtsman should always consider working boatmen and canal officials. To the working-boatman time is money and this should never be forgotten. For example, when working through a flight of locks, if you find yourself being overtaken by a working-boat, let it pass. For one thing the boatman will work the locks very much faster than you will and, as I said before, for him time is money. Loaded boats must keep to deep water but the general rule on the canals is, keep right, or 'port to port'. The rule is not rigid and it is a good idea to ask the rule when passing on to a strange canal.

Moorings

The cruiser in inland waterways should always choose his moorings with care. For example, in a part where there is much commercial traffic, watch out that you do not moor in shallow water where the boat cannot approach the bank, because the passing traffic will either wash you aground or cause you to heel over at an angle a great deal too steep for comfort. If you moor on a towpath side, make sure that mooring lines are kept clear of the towpath; indeed it is a good idea to avoid a towpath side where practicable. Never moor near a lock. Unless you are moored on recognized moorings, exhibit a riding light on those canals where there is much traffic after dark. On many canals there is a speed limit but whether there is or not, never drive your boat at such a speed as to cause a breaking wave which follows behind the stern of the boat. This is the chief cause of bank erosion. It is also good manners to reduce speed when passing moored craft.

The Broads

That part of the inland waterways of East Anglia known as the Broads presents a somewhat unique situation. It is almost too well known to need description. It has been a holiday centre for many years and the training ground of many a future yachtsman. There are numerous books on the subject and many organizations devoted to the business of hiring craft of all shapes and sizes but designed basically for Broads navigation. The three rivers which make up the Norfolk Broads, the Bure, Yare and Waveney, were once a great centre of trading. Such trading was carried on by the sailing wherry since there are no horse towpaths on these rivers. If mention of horse-drawn canal barges reminds some readers of Toad's adventures in such a craft in *The Wind in the Willows*, let it also remind them (and for those who do not know that delightful book, let me inform them) that there is still much of England as delightful as it was in Toad's day to be glimpsed by those who travel by river and canal through the countryside. But probably the real charm of inland waterway cruising consists in the *variety* of the scenery, whether it is semi-industrial or completely pastoral. You are always getting somewhere new at a pleasant pace; and there is adventure too. Round the next bend, anything may happen! It is a great way to see a country.

CHAPTER 11

Knotmanship

JUST as there would appear to be a wide difference between the 16 ft outboard-powered sportsboat and the 45 ft sea-going motor-cruiser, carrying with it a difference of approach to such matters as whether to say port and starboard when to the sportsboat owner left and right would seem perfectly adequate; so it can be argued that for the latter the need to know how to tie more than a couple of the time-honoured seaman's knots is questionable. But as I pointed out in the introduction to this book, the rules of seamanship and boat-handling have been evolved over many years and with them the seaman's language and the seaman's code, a code of behaviour whose ultimate purpose is efficiency.

To put this business of knotmanship in its simplest terms, the essence of a seaman's knot is that it should be tied easily, that it should tighten under strain but that it should be undone easily. Over many years various knots have been evolved for various uses and this is why I think it is worth devoting a short section on how to tie them.

These knots fall into easily identifiable groups. There are knots for joining one rope to another. There are knots for joining a rope to a metal ring, such as the ring of an anchor or a ring-bolt in a quay. There are knots for joining rope to a wooden spar or to a stanchion or to a bollard. Finally, there are knots for making a loop in a rope. I have taken one or more examples of these principal knots.

Let us start off with the knots that join two ropes' ends together. The two best known are the reef knot and the carrick bend; these are illustrated in figures 99 and 100. There is an essential difference between these two. They are both good safe knots but if the ropes are of unequal size you *must* use the carrick bend whereas if the ropes are more or less the same size you may use the reef knot. To tie the latter you cross the ends over in opposite ways, left over right, then right over left as in the figure. For the carrick bend you make the cross in one end of the rope, then bring the other rope's end up through the bight, (that is to say the loop of the first) over the cross, down between the standing part and the end and back up through the loop on the opposite side to the first end.

Fig. 99 Reef knot   Fig. 100 Carrick bend

Now let us look at the breed of knot known as a hitch. For making a rope fast to a spar and many other purposes we use a clove hitch (see figure 101). The method of making it can be seen clearly from the illustration. Look now at figure 102. This shows a development of the hitch known as the rolling hitch. If you make a clove hitch and pull it to one side or the other it may slip but by making

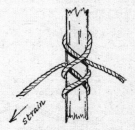

Fig. 101 Clove hitch   Fig. 102 Rolling hitch

a clove hitch, by passing the end twice round the spar each turn over the standing part of the rope and then completing the hitch with a half hitch on the opposite side we have a knot which will not slip down that spar. Remember always to pass two turns on the side from which you expect the pull to come, as indicated by the arrow in the illustration.

When we want to join our rope to a ring bolt or the ring of an anchor we make use of one or other of the two knots illustrated in figures 103 and 104. Figure 103 shows the round turn and two half hitches and I think the method of tying is self-evident from the drawing. Figure 104, illustrating the fisherman's bend, shows

Fig. 103 Round turn
and two half hitches

Fig. 104 Fisherman's bend

clearly the difference between these two knots. The round turn and two half hitches is slightly easier to cast off than the fisherman's bend.

Finally we come to this question of making a loop and the best

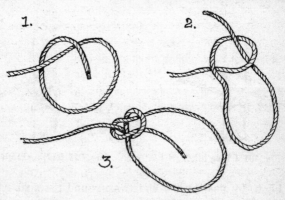

Fig. 105 Bowline

knot for that is certainly a bowline. Look at figure 105. Take the end of the rope in one hand and the standing part of the rope in the other. Place the end over the standing part to make a cross. Hold this cross between the index finger and the thumb with the thumb

338

underneath. You have now formed your loop. Turn your wrist to the right, away from your body and bring the end up through the loop you have formed. Hold the cross of this loop in your hand, leaving your free hand to manipulate the end. You complete the tying of the knot by dipping the end under the standing part, bringing it up again and passing it down through the loop. In figure 106, which is a running bowline, the method may be followed from the drawing. It is simply a slip knot which, like the bowline itself, can be immensely useful at times.

It was in 1948 that man-made fibre rope became available com-

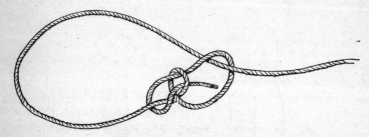

Fig. 106 Running bowline

mercially. Such ropes as nylon, terylene and other varieties, are found everywhere. They have virtually superseded the vegetable fibre ropes. They have characteristics all of their own. They are slightly more expensive than the natural fibre but they last longer and in the end are probably more economical. Both nylon and terylene are stronger than vegetable fibre rope; nylon being three times and terylene nearly twice as strong. They have considerable shock resistance; for example, nylon can stretch 30 per cent of its length and after being stretched has great powers of recovery. Man-made fibre rope is light. It is immune to temperature change and barely affected by water and furthermore is immune to rot. If it has any disadvantages at all it is that it may lose strength when exposed for long periods to sunlight. There is also a slight disadvantage in connection with friction, since a man-made fibre rope under strain can, on occasion, develop a glazed area where it is working against metal and if much heat is generated, the rope fibres may become fused and its strength impaired. These by comparison, however, are small disadvantages and it is little wonder that man-made fibre rope has taken over the scene.

Having said all this, it must certainly be admitted that natural vegetable fibre rope can still be found in yacht chandlers and is certainly still much in use. This is largely a question of cost. Probably the most common vegetable fibre rope is manila which comes from the fibre of *Musa textilis* that grows in the Philippine Islands and is shipped from Manila, hence its name. From the leaves of the *Agave rigida* comes another rope known as sisal. Sisal is by no means as reliable as manila but it is cheaper. Then there is hemp. This is made from the fibres of the stems of the hemp plant

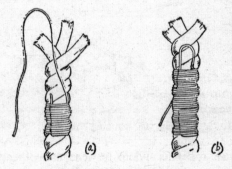

Fig. 107 Common whipping

(*Cannabis sativa*), grown world-wide. The best comes from Italy. It is softer than manila and sisal but heavier. It wears as well as manila and it is more flexible. There is also coir which is made from fibres of the husks of coconuts, mostly from Ceylon. Its main advantage is that it is light and floats on water and until the advent of the water-resistant man-made fibre rope it was ideal rope for, for example, a kedge warp. In conclusion, although it is more expensive, nylon rope is popular since it can be said to be three times as strong as manila of the same size, is lighter in weight and has the other advantages already mentioned.

Rope is made, as most people know, by laying up strands. The ends of rope will tend to become unravelled with use as the strands unwind. It is therefore necessary to fuse these together in the case of small man-made fibre rope by the simple procedure of applying a lighted match; with medium and large man-made fibre rope and with all vegetable fibre rope, by a method known as whipping.

There are various methods of whipping but that known as the common whipping is perfectly adequate for our purposes and is illustrated in figure 107. We take our whipping twine or thin nylon twine and place one end along the rope, as in the illustration. We pass turns of the twine over the rope, against the lay of the rope. This means that we pass the twine against the direction in which the strands of the rope are laid. We pass our turns of twine, working towards the end of the rope, hauling each turn tightly. We now lay the other end of the twine along the rope as shown in the drawing. We pass the remaining turns over it and take the loop over the end of the rope with each turn as we do so. When the loop becomes too small to go over the end of the rope we pull this second end through the turns we have passed over until taut; then we cut off the end and we have our whipping.

Nowadays, much use is made of 'plaited' rope. This can be either 8-plait or 16-plait. The former is softer in character, the latter is more suitable for heavier loads. As a rough guide: use nylon when both strength and stretch are wanted, terylene for minimum stretch and use plaited nylon ropes for anchor warps and ropes which are frequently handled. Multi-plait rope is also good for mooring ropes.

This section on rope and knots is merely an introduction to a subject which well repays further study.

Index